30$^{\underline{00}}$

ARTISTS IN WOOD

American Carvers of

Cigar-Store Indians, Show Figures,

and Circus Wagons

by FREDERICK FRIED

Bramhall House • New York

BY FREDERICK FRIED

Artists in Wood

A Pictorial History of the Carousel

Fragmentary Landmarks

DESIGN BY MARGERY KRONENGOLD

To Charlie Z.

ACKNOWLEDGMENTS

THE realization of this book is largely due to the assistance of Elizabeth Wilson Robb, whose cooperation increased with the knowledge of her impending death. Her recollections, photographs, papers, and other substantive material have been invaluable. Charles Robb, grandson of the carver, supplied the photographs from Robb's files, pages from his and Demuth's catalogue, letters, trade card, and other business data, as well as some of the sample carvings owned by his father, Clarence Robb.

I am indebted to Miss I. Myrtle Guethlein for the photographs, drawings, letters, and biographical material on John Philip Yaeger; to Mrs. Edward A. Furst, great-great-granddaughter of William Rush, for the use of the Rush scrapbook; to Richard E. Conover for his assistance with the identification of obscure circus wagons; to my wife, Mary Hill Fried, for her translations and assistance; and to the institutions and individuals listed below for their measure of generous assistance.

Abby Aldrich Rockefeller Folk Art Collection
Richard E. Ahlborn
Albany Institute of Art
Arents Collections, New York Public Library
Roy F. Arnold
Robert Bahssin
Katherine Bauerschmidt
J. W. Beggs
George O. Bird
Mrs. Roberta Braecklein
Peter A. G. Brown
Chicago Historical Society
Circus World Museum
Alexander P. Clark
Cooper Union
Copyright Office, Library of Congress
Louis Corti
Charles Deitsch
Wm. Demuth & Company

Dr. Edwin L. Demuth
Richard L. Doyle
Sterling D. Emerson
Warren R. Fiske
Henry Ford Museum and Greenfield Village
Charles P. Fox
Anne Castrodale Golovin
Carl W. Haffenreffer
L. C. Hegerty
Herbert W. Hemphill, Jr.
Mrs. Faith Henning
The Home Insurance Company
Paul Horsman
Index of American Design, National Gallery of Art
Romana Javitz
Mary Ann Jensen
Louis C. Jones
André Juneau
Gerald Kornblau
Mrs. Walter Liebling
Père C. E. Marquis
Edna Martin
Maryland Historical Society
Musée du Quebéc
National Academy of Design
New York Historical Association
New-York Historical Society
Lyman Pendergast
Mlle. Charlotte Perron
Fred D. Pfening III
Père Laurent Proulx
Bernard Quint
Rhode Island Historical Society
Norman S. Rice
Shelburne Museum
H. R. Bradley Smith
Mrs. Robert I. Smith
Smithsonian Institution
Edward Stoddard
John William Stroh
Gordon E. Teubner
Theatre Collection, McCaddon Archives, Princeton University
The Tobacco Institute, Inc.
Virginia Museum of Fine Arts
Betty J. Walters
William L. Warren
I. Warshaw

Contents

Introduction   xi

1 · Shipcarvers at the End of the Wooden Ship Era   *3*

2 · Tobacco and the Image Makers   *9*

3 · Shipfronts to Shopfronts—Indians to the Rescue   *29*

4 · The Art of Show-Figure Carving   *77*

5 · Circus Wagons—Builders and Carvers   *85*

6 · Artists in Wood   *115*

       Philadelphia   *115*

       Baltimore   *125*

       Washington, D.C.   *135*

       Detroit   *137*

       Ashland, Wisconsin   *153*

       Providence   *154*

       Gloucester   *156*

       Canada   *157*

       New York   *171*

Appendixes

       Notes   *249*

       List of American Show-Figure Carvers   *263*

       American Auctions of Show Figures and Their Prices   *270*

       Collections of Show Figures   *278*

       Bibliography   *279*

Index   *289*

This artist in wood, unrecognized, misunderstood;
His gallery—the riverways, harbors, the sidewalks of cities.
Storefronts framed his chiseled art that beckoned for trade;
The cities' signs at his bench were made.
His creations on circus wagon wheels rolled
Through each hamlet, metropolis and town,
Like so many Santos worshipped at the shrine,
Yet no one knew these works were his that were shown.
He's now long dead—his work labeled, "Artist Unknown."

Introduction

UNTIL recently, a great mystery surrounded that part of American folk sculpture commonly known as cigar-store Indians, show figures, and circus-wagon carvings. In nearly all instances, when exhibited these were labeled "artist unknown." This category of American folk sculpture for a long period of time was unexplored. But with the rapidly growing interest in folk art during the last twenty years, with the building of private collections, and with the formation of several museums—most notably the Museum of American Folk Art in New York City and the Shelburne Museum in Vermont—the interest in accreditation increased. The void offered a challenge to the researcher who did not foresee that it would take four years of following clues and leads to reveal the personae in his whodunit.

At a much earlier date, other people had shown an interest in the subject. Perhaps one of the first to take note of the carver's creations was a young reporter for *The New York Times* who later became Curator of Prints at the New York Public Library, Frank W. Weitenkampf. An excellent report on the art of the show-figure carver appeared in *The New York Times* on August 3, 1890, under the title, "Lo, the Wooden Indian: The Art of Making Cigar-shop Signs." In 1911, Kate Sanborn, a writer and one of the earliest collectors of tobacconists' figures, wrote a small volume *Hunting Indians in a Taxi-Cab* using photographs taken by the author. While the book did not identify the carvers of the various figures, it did serve partially as a graphic record of the more outstanding examples found on the sidewalks of several cities. In the 1920s, the Whitney Studio Club of New York City, later to become the Whitney Museum of American Art, and the Dudensing Gallery in New York held shows devoted mainly to "Early American Art."

In 1931, the Newark Museum held an exhibition of American folk sculpture showing figureheads, cigar-store figures, portraits, eagles, inn signs, and decoys. In the introduction to the catalogue of this exhibition, Holger Cahill, the earliest known art historian to deal with the subject wrote:

The work of these men, as here exhibited, is folk art in its truest sense—it is an expression of the common people and not an expression of a small cultured class. Folk art usually has not much to do with the fashionable art of the period. It is never the product of the art movements, but comes out of craft traditions, plus that personal something of the rare craftsman who is an artist by nature if not by training. This art is based not on measurements or calculations but on feeling, and it rarely fits in with the standards of realism. It goes straight to the fundamentals of art—rhythm, design, balance, proportion, which the folk artist feels instinctively.

The sculpture in this exhibition has significance for us as a genuine expression of the art spirit of the American people, and as a demonstration of the fact that talent has never been lacking in America even when opportunities for the study of art techniques have been very limited. . . . It is among objects such as these that we must look for the earliest American sculpture, and among their makers we may discover talent of a high order. . .

From November 30 until January 15, 1933, the Museum of Modern Art repeated the Newark show along with folk paintings exhibited earlier in 1931 at the Newark Museum. The show was entitled "American Folk Art: The Art of the Common Man in America." It made an immediate impact on the viewers and the press, and its success guaranteed its repeated showings in other cities.

Among the first to recognize folk sculpture as an important American art was the sculptor Elie Nadelman, whose home and studio in Riverdale, New York, had many examples which he had collected. Another was Edith Gregor Halpert, who established, in her Downtown Gallery in New York, a section devoted to American folk sculpture, called the American Folk Art Gallery. Mrs. Halpert was advisor to Abby Aldrich Rockefeller in her collection of American folk sculpture, now in Colonial Williamsburg in Virginia.

Henri Marceau's research of the life and works of William Rush resulted in a fine biography and an exhibtion of America's finest wood sculpture in Philadelphia in 1937. Another collector, Anthony W. Pendergast of Terre Haute, Indiana, concentrated on adding all the tobacconists' Indians and show figures he could find to his already immense collection and, in 1953, he wrote a thin volume in collaboration with W. Porter Ware called, *Cigar Store Figures in American Folk Art*. Pendergast found his collection unmanageable and sold off all but a few figures, most of which are now in the major folk art museums and collections in the United States.

In 1940, Pauline Pinckney, a former researcher with the Index of American Design, had written a book, *American Figureheads and Their Carvers,* which was followed some years later by M. V. Brewington's book, *Shipcarvers of North America*. Jean Lipman's excellent book, *American Folk Art in Wood, Metal and Stone,* published in 1948, added new information on American folk sculpture and illustrated many kinds of wood sculpture long neglected as American art. In 1950, *The Index of American Design* by Erwin O. Christensen appeared and, in 1952, *Early American Wood Carving* by the same author was added. All these indicated a growing interest in American folk sculpture and the desire to learn the identities of the hitherto anonymous carvers. However, few, if any, were positively identified and accreditation was mostly general and vague.

In the search for "artists in wood," the researcher's clues seemed to be nonexistent; rarely was a work signed, and it is the instance of the one carver who incised his or his firm's name on the pedestals of his figures that set the search in motion. This was Samuel A. Robb. The search led to immigration files, census reports, wills, tax records, real estate records, trade journals, city directories, marriage and death certificates, church and baptismal records, school files, and studies of cemetery files and tombstones for clues of relatives. Hundreds of letters were written to persons of similar names, and telephone calls were made to whomever it was thought might supply even the smallest lead. An undertaker's records supplied the name and address of Elizabeth Wilson Robb as the payee for the burial of her mother, Agnes Robb. Although twenty-one years had passed since then, a visit to the address provided the thrill of discovering that Robb's daughter was still alive. However, it took three months to convince Miss Robb to open the door, and another month before the first papers and photographs were produced. What a reward in seeing a photograph of Robb and his shop! However, a near fatal accident hospitalized Miss Robb, and the realization that she would have to give up her apartment to enter a nursing home (probably to the end of her days), brought her closer to the researcher who, at her request, visited her almost daily, with his notebook and prepared questions. Her last days were brightened by the knowledge that she was making an important contribution to the history of American folk sculpture, and to her father's memory.

Another important discovery at this time was locating Robb's grandson, Charles Robb, whose father, Clarence, was Robb's son by his first marriage. This good fortune produced many photographs of Robb's association with the circus-wagon builders, the William Demuth catalogue of show figures, some Robb records, family papers, the trade card, and other important items from the Robb business, including some small carvings used as samples by the firm. During the course of research on Robb, his associates, and his competitors, more and more of the workings of, and workers in, the art and industry of ships, show figures, and circus-wagon figures came into focus. Further research was rewarded by locating living relatives of other carvers, and more records and photographs were uncovered. The search led to other parts of the country and further probing uncovered more carvers, carvings, and descendents who, for the most part, were most cooperative, many never having attached any importance to the work of their ancestors. Another year of research in remote areas of the United States and Canada uncovered additional facts, and by 1968 the book that started out with the title *Artist in Wood* became *Artists in Wood*, and a single biography that had multiplied to include thirty-seven additional carvers was finished.

However, this is only a beginning. The researcher hopes that the publication of this work will stimulate others to undertake the search and open up other areas of investigation. With the recognition that folk art sculpture is an important, exciting, and vital part of American art history, efforts must be exerted to have the subject included in the curriculum of our major universities and colleges. With the development of more folk art historians, it is hoped that more and more "artist unknown" labels will be replaced with names of the men and women who have added a chapter to American art history.

F. F.

ARTISTS IN WOOD

Fig. 1a. View of South Street, New York, 1876. Ships' figureheads, nautical instrument makers' signs, and other shop signs show the carvers' art. In the distance are the first cables being strung from the Brooklyn Bridge's New York tower.

1 · Shipcarvers at the End of the Wooden Ship Era

IN 1849, along the docks of New York's East River, the great sailing vessels lay side by side from the Battery to Corlears Hook, their spars jutting out over the traffic of South Street like a great forest. Below their bowsprits, in most cases, were carved figureheads by which the ships were usually recognized. Sometimes, a billet or decorative scroll was used. On the stern was often some symbolic carving representing the interests of the shipowner, a custom followed in the past: a nameboard of carved raised letters with an acanthus leaf scroll, perhaps a sunburst with an American eagle in low relief, usually influenced by the engravings of the period, or, as with the rounded stern of the newer clippers, little or no decoration or carved work of any kind.

On South Street, New York, within a two block area, from Market Slip past Rutgers Slip, where the Manhattan Bridge now arches overhead, was a string of five carving shops busily at work producing figures, scrolls, billets, and other carvings for the shipyards around and above Corlears Hook up the river. The shipbuilding yards extended in a solid line from

Grand Street to Twelfth Street, and from morning until evening the sound of the broadaxe could be heard up and down the East River.[1]

The Mechanic's Bell, erected on city property on September 19, 1831, at Rivington and Stanton Streets between Isaac Webb's shipyard and Plantation Market, was recognized as a signal to the mechanics to start and stop work and for the meal periods, and as a reminder of the growing force of organized labor. The bell was rung at 6:00 A.M. to begin work; 8:00 A.M. for breakfast; 9:00 A.M. to resume work; 12:00 noon to 1:00 P.M. for lunch, and at 6:00 P.M. to cease work for the day. The bell could be heard clearly across the East River to the yards at Wallabout and Williamsburgh.[2]

Up to and during the 1840s the shipcarvers in Baltimore, Philadelphia, Boston, Bath, and other ports, even those on the Detroit and St. Lawrence Rivers, had enough work supplying decorative carvings for the ships under construction in their shipyards. But with the discovery of gold in California in 1848, the rush to build fast clipper ships to take men and supplies to the gold fields kept the shipcarvers, their journeymen, and apprentices working full time to meet the demand.[3] In fact, by 1850, there was a scarcity of experienced hands, and wages reached the astonishing level of $2.50 to $3.00 a day. The shipwrights, carpenters, and caulkers—all classified as mechanics—had eighteen years earlier negotiated a ten-hour day instead of the prevailing fifteen after a showdown between the New York Journeymen Shipwrights' and Caulkers' Benevolent Society and the shipbuilders of New York.

In the British Isles, on the other hand, mechanics were having their difficulties. In 1845, a strike by journeymen carpenters resulted in a wage increase from 15 shillings and 17 shillings a day to 17 shillings and 20 shillings, but in 1847, reductions followed and many journeymen were dismissed. With these difficulties and the knowledge of high wages and steady employment in America, many shipbuilding mechanics set sail for America on the packets plying the British and American ports, which were already crowded because of the failure of the potato crop in Ireland. Younger men also came as the period of apprenticeship in Britain was long and the rewards doubtful.[4]

By the middle of the nineteenth century, the merchant marine of the United States showed on its register a total of 3,535,454 gross tons of vessels, an amount second only to that of the United Kingdom, excluding their colonies, which then totaled 3,565,133 net tons or about 3,850,000 gross tons.[5]

The shipbuilding industry was active in coastal regions from Maine to Baltimore. While the south was a rich storehouse of excellent ship timber, it failed to develop a shipbuilding industry, although Charleston and Norfolk had been active during the period before and shortly after the revolution. In New York, however, the famous Black Ball line was adding many new ships to its fleet, most of which were built by New York's foremost shipbuilder William H. Webb. There was also intense activity in the whaling industry and the coastwise carrying trade. All this activity added to the work of the carvers. Many shipcarvers were supplying decorative work not only to their local shipbuilders but also to their clients as distant as Wiscasset, Maine; Portsmouth, New Hampshire; and Mystic, Connecticut. Some carvers specialized in certain types of figure carving.[6]

During the 1840s in New York, among the experienced and talented carvers working on ships' figures were Thomas Millard, Jr., with a shop at 191 Cherry Street; John L. Cromwell, who was first at 179 Cherry Street and later at 419 Water Street; and Jacob S. Anderson, also on Cherry Street. Anderson and Cromwell were once apprentices of Jeremiah Dodge, whose son Charles J. Dodge was at 75 Columbia Street.

In 1847, Cromwell had moved his home across the river to Williamsburgh, an area that had attracted many of the prospering merchants by its farmland, pastures, hills, and easy access by boat and ferry. Twenty-five years earlier, the passenger traffic to Brooklyn had been conducted in double scull rowboats, while carriages and cattle were ferried over in lighters under sail. These eventually gave way to boats propelled by horsepower, and they in turn yielded to the irresistible power of steam. Real estate agents were promoting this new area as an attractive suburb near but away from the city. South Second, Third, and Fourth streets attracted several shipcarvers, some of whom had been apprenticed to Cromwell, and others whose shops were near each other and who had maintained an afterwork friendship that lasted during their lifetimes.

While shipbuilding was going ahead at a rapid pace, signs of eventual trouble were beginning to manifest themselves, not only in New York, but to all the builders of wooden sailing vessels. Use of steam and the iron hull was increasing rapidly and great improvements had been made in the new steamboats under contract. In 1847, Westervelt & Mackay were under contract to build the first American oceangoing mail steamships. William H. Brown built the *Arctic* in the same year; William H. Webb built the *United States* for Charles H. Marshall & Co. of the Black Ball line of packets; the *Falcon* was built in 1848 for the California trade as was the *Georgia* by Smith & Dimon and the *Ohio* by Jeremiah Simonson. In 1849, Westervelt & Mackay built two steamships for the Havre line.[7]

During this transitional period, despite the wider use of steam and the iron hull, designers of wooden sailing vessels produced the sleekest and swiftest sailing ships ever to be launched. New York's shipyards were noted for the excellent design, materials, workmanship, and quality of their ships, their remarkable speed under sail. These vessels had no equal anywhere and the fame of the East River shipyards and builders spread throughout the world. Here was the greatest concentration of shipbuilding activity in the United States, as John McLeod Murphy stated:

With the boundless resources of our country, the art of shipbuilding never can retrograde; with pine from Maine, live oak from Florida, copper from Michigan, iron from Pennsylvania, pitch from Carolina, cotton from Mississippi, hemp from

Kentucky, and timber for spars from Vermont, the New York mechanic can build you a ship which, in the union of all its intricate parts, will symbolize the binding elements of the American confederation.[8]

It was this very confederation which also was to contribute to the decline of wooden shipbuilding.

The business of wooden shipbuilding in New York had been operating under high pressure and late in 1854 the first effects began to assert themselves. Competition from the more experienced and long-established shipbuilders, and limited capital, forced new builders to suspend business; and the effects of a few were sold by the sheriff. The result was to bring on a letdown in local business, the first in many years. With wages for experienced labor from $2 to $3 per day, timber prices that rose by nearly a third, and refined iron prices that more than doubled, many contracts could not be fulfilled. The same conditions prevailed during the following year, and a lack of harmony between labor and employers led to much hard feeling. Labor, in an excellent bargaining position, demanded higher wages and was able to force employers to yield to its demands.[9] The 1852 steamboat law went into effect in 1853. Its regulations made shipbuilding operations unbearable as well as unprofitable and forced capital to invest in other than marine property. Besides, steam railroads offered a greater advantage in many areas. By 1856, the excitement of the California gold rush had worn off and California trade had virtually collapsed, its market glutted. Ships upon arrival in California found their cargoes unsalable, and many of the vessels either were allowed to rot at the docks in San Francisco or were ordered back to New York or the Far East without opening their hatches.[10]

While America was still building fleets of large wooden-hull steamships and sailing vessels, Great Britain and other foreign countries were switching to steam-propelled, iron-hulled ships. In 1850, Great Britain's experimentation with iron-hull vessels culminated in the transatlantic run of the *City of Glasgow*. In the latter part of 1856, the United States found itself in an economic depression and by 1857, it had reached such serious proportions that its effect was felt all over the country.[11]

In New York, once famous for its packet and clipper-ship construction, production of vessels of all types was at its lowest point in almost half a century. Another depressing influence was the pressure upon Congress to withdraw the mail subsidy from the Collins line of steamers, which was shortly done. Production of wooden ships and barks fell from forty in 1855 to twenty-four in 1856, twenty-eight in 1857, seven in 1858, two in 1859, and none in 1862. In 1866, Jeremiah Simonson built four side-wheel steamboats, and Webb & Bell built the ferryboat *Winona* for the Union Ferry Company of Brooklyn. In 1869, William H. Webb built the ship *Charles H. Marshall* of 1,600 tons, the last of its kind, and several other vessels were built by a few shipbuilders. The last square riggers built in New York and its vicinity were two half-brigs by C. & R. Poillon in Brooklyn—the *Ruby* which was completed in December of 1873, and the *Garnet* in 1877. With the completion of these two boats, New York City as a shipbuilding center was nearing its end.[12] However, South Street was still the street of ships (Fig. 1a).

The depression of 1857 affected not only New York's shipcarvers but many other ports as well. Baltimore and Philadelphia lost contracts to yards where timber was abundant, labor unorganized, and hence considerably cheaper. The shipyards along the Kennebec River and the Maine coast, as well as some yards in Boston, offered such advantages. Although the Civil War brought back nearly full employment for its duration, the building of wooden ships was near an end except for the coastwise schooners that were to be built for some time—mostly in the shipyards of Maine—and few of which carried any kind of carved work on bow or stern (Fig. 1b).

During the Civil War, the ironclad, *Monitor,* designed by Ericsson and built in the shipyard of A. J. Rowland at Greenpoint, was launched on January 30, 1862, just 100 days after the keel was laid, and was put in commission on February 25. On March 9 she had concluded her maiden voyage to Hampton Roads and at once engaged the Confederate ironclad, *Merrimac,* which had been playing havoc with the wooden ships of the United States government. The success of the *Monitor* was so immediate and complete that the government ordered a large fleet of similar ironclads, of which seven were constructed at the Rowland shipyard in Greenpoint. This engagement illustrated most convincingly the obsolescence of the wooden hull.[13]

At the close of the Civil War, many of the wooden-hull steam vessels were put up at public auction by the United States government. These were placed on coastwise lines and some inland waters. By 1873, these vessels were no longer in service because, in many instances, they had been constructed of unseasoned timber and were not given the proper care during their military service. As wooden vessels gave way to those of iron, which eventually gave way to those of steel, the need for wood carvings at the prow or stern became minimal. Some United States warships had scrolls at the bow but usually they were bronze castings. The shipcarver had to seek work from other sources to supplement the carving of steamboat eagles, scroll heads, block letters, architectural work, and church carvings.[14]

Fig. 1b. Heroes Out of Fashion. *Figureheads and stern carving from South Street shipcarving shop, 1883.* Harper's Weekly, *January 6, 1883.*

Fig. 17. Thomas Dartmouth Rice as Jim Crow. *Larger than life-size carving, probably made by Charles J. Dodge, Courtesy Shelburne Museum.*

2 · Tobacco and
the Image Makers

Great Britain to Great Raleigh owes
This plant and country where it grows.

SUCH WAS the legend on a tobacconist's sign in Ludgate Street, London, in 1760. After the American Revolution, a critic wrote suggesting the sign read:

To Rubicon and North, Old England owes
The loss of country where tobacco grows.[1]

The first instance was a tribute to Sir Walter Raleigh for his introduction of tobacco into England and the second, a barb directed against King George and Lord North, his prime minister at the time of the American Revolution. While Sir Walter Raleigh has been generally credited with the introduction of tobacco into England, history reveals that the first Europeans to discover tobacco were the sailors of Christopher Columbus's expedition to the New World. In the admiral's journal, which was published some years after his voyage, Columbus refers to "certain dried leaves" that the natives brought, which emitted a distinct aroma. The leaves were discarded. A few days later, Columbus noted a native in a canoe carrying the same kind of dried leaves, which he offered to the explorer. Columbus did not understand this strange offering but was to learn of its nature several weeks later when an Indian wrapped the dried leaves in a palm leaf, lit one end, and put the other in his mouth, drawing in and exhaling the smoke. De Jerez, a scout on one of the expeditions, was probably the first European to become a smoker.[2] Tobacco or *tobaco* was the pipe or tube in which the Indians smoked the plant. The name was transferred by the Spaniards to the plant itself. The first plant was taken to Spain about 1558 when Sir Walter Raleigh was but six years of age. Jean Nicot, French Ambassador to Lisbon, sent seeds of the tobacco plant to Catherine de' Medici, the queen of Henry II of France, and this and his other services in diffusing the knowledge of tobacco, resulted in the scientific name of the plant—*Nicotiana*.[3]

Sir Walter Raleigh made his first voyage to America in 1576 at the age of twenty-four when he joined his half brother, Sir Humphrey Gilbert. He returned to England two years later. After being knighted by Queen

Fig. 2. Black Boy *or* Virginian. *Height 30 inches. Used as a tobacconist's sign in England from the seventeenth to the mid-nineteenth centuries. Courtesy Smithsonian Institution.*

Elizabeth, he attempted to establish colonies in America, sending two expeditions. From the first expedition:

> They returned homewards, passing by Virginia, a colony which Sir Walter Raleigh had there planted, from whence Drake brings home with him Ralph Lane, who was the first that brought tobacco into England. . .[4]

Actually, Sir John Hawkins (1532–1595), British admiral and slave-trader, is assumed to have begun the tobacco vogue in Britain about 1564. Among those returning to Britain with Ralph Lane, Roanoke's first governor, was the historian and mathematician, Thomas Harriot (1560–1621), who reported in his "briefe and true report of the new found land of Virginia" that tobacco was among the commodities found there to be raised and merchandisable. Thus, tobacco became America's first industry. In England, tobacco was pounced upon as a miraculous panacea. Scholars toasted it as a cure for almost every known disease, but tracts were also written calling it the cause of all diseases.

In England, King James I called smoking "a custom loathsome to the eye, hateful to the nose, harmful to the brain, and dangerous to the lungs, resembling the Stygian smoke of the pit that is bottomless." In Austria, its use was forbidden for nearly twenty-five years. In Russia, the Czar commanded all smokers to be flogged for their first offense and executed for their second, while users of snuff were threatened with having their noses cut off. Pope Urban VIII proclaimed, "We interdict and forbid all persons of either sex to take tobacco in the porches or interiors of Churches, whether by chewing, smoking, or inhaling in the form of powder."[5]

Nevertheless, tobacco became very popular and tobacconists' shops were set up throughout the British Isles. The carving of signs for these shops followed naturally, and since tobacco was connected to Indians in the popular imagination, these signs were usually Indian figures. They appeared in front of tobacco shops, usually over doorways, and were called Black Boys or Virginians (Fig. 2).

During the sixteenth and seventeenth centuries when reports of the Indians were brought back to England, the illustrations used depicted them more as Negroes than redmen. Negro boys were popular in England throughout the seventeenth century, some coming as slaves from the West Indian plantations. It was fashionable for the ladies of the court to employ young boys as pages, dressing them in silks, feathered turbans, an occasional wig, and, in extraordinary cases, a jeweled staff. Using the familiar Negro boy as a model, the carvers of tobacconists' Indian figures gave them a headdress of tobacco leaves instead of feathers, as well as a kilt of the same. The right hand extended and usually held a long clay pipe, while under the left arm was the roll of tobacco. A necklace of large beads finished the meager costume, and the figure was placed on or was part of the carved block. The height of the figure was from eighteen to thirty inches.

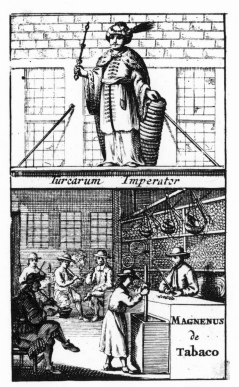

Turcarum Imperator

MAGNENUS
de
Tabaco

FIG. 3b

The figure was usually carved from a single log of oak or elm, and all extending parts such as the arm were carved separately.[6] For protection against the elements, the figure was painted and frequently given a coat of tar or asphaltum. The crown and kilt were usually painted in vivid colors and the necklace in gold or metallic paint. Sometimes, a medal hung from the necklace on which was incised the brand of tobacco. The first illustration of a tobacconist's sign appeared in Brathwait's *Smoking Age*, published in England in 1617 (Fig. 3a), showing a small figure mounted on a stand, depicting the then current conception of an American Indian smoking a rolled tobacco leaf and holding a tobacco roll under the left arm. An entry in Machyn's Diary reports, "The day of Desember 1562, was slayne in John Street, Gylbard Goldsmith, dwellyng at the sene of the *Blake Boy*, in the Cheap, by ys wyff's sun." Another instance of its early use is documented in Ben Jonson's play, "Bartholomew Fair," Act I, Scene I, 1614: "I thought he would run mad o' the Black Boy in Bucklersbury, that takes the scurvy roguy tobacco there."[7] These figures also appeared on the continent (Fig. 3b) and in the seventeenth century there was one in Amsterdam with the following inscription:

> *Joshua prayed to the Lord from the bottom of his heart,*
> *that the sun and moon might stand still.*
> *The best Varinas and good tobacco in the leaf*
> *are sold here at the Indian.*[8]

FIG. 3a

Fig. 3a. The first known illustration of an Indian as a sign for a tobacconist's shop at the time of James I in England. From Brathwait's Smoking Age, *1617.*

Fig. 3b. Dutch Tobacco Shop, 1669.

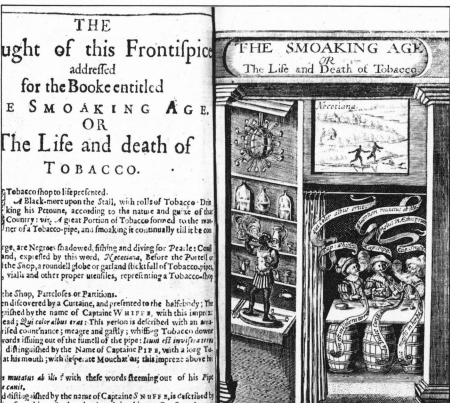

Another sign used over tobacconists' shops in England was the tobacco roll, which represented a "twist" or "pigtail" also known as "carottes," measuring over a foot in length. Sometimes they hung in pairs and threes. The Roll Trinidado, leaf, and pudding tobacco were popular. An interlocutor said in Ben Jonson's "Cinthia's Revels," "I have three sorts of tobacco in my pocket."[9] Still another type of tobacco sign was represented by three hands, all stemming from one arm. The first held snuff, the second hand held a pipe, and the third a plug of tobacco. Below was painted the doggerel, "We three are engaged in one cause; I snuffs, I smokes, I chaws."[10]

With the introduction of snuff into England and Scotland in the late seventeenth and early eighteenth centuries, the Highland Laddie made his appearance, carved with plumed bonnet, tartan across his chest, and knee-length kilt (Fig. 4). He stood in the doorways of the tobacco shops, his right hand extended, holding a pinch or a mull of snuff. He also was used as a sign for public houses. These figures came in varying sizes from twenty-four inches to life size. After the rebellion of 1745, when everything was done by the British government to extinguish the nationality of the Scots, when Scotch ballads were forbidden, and the kilts were banned by the legislature, this item appeared in the newspapers:

We hear that the dapper wooden Highlanders, who guard so heroically the doors of snuff-shops, intend to petition the legislature, in order that they be excused from complying with the act of Parliament with regard to their change of dress; alledging that they have ever been faithful subjects to his Majesty, having constantly supplied his Guards with a pinch out of their Mulls when they marched by them, and so far from engaging in any rebellion, that they have never entertained a rebellious thought; when they humbly hope that they shall not be put to the Expense of buying new cloaths.[11]

Many of these figures were destroyed during the reaction to the rebellion and today are scarcer than the rare Black Boy.

Carved wooden signs had been in use in America since the eighteenth century and perhaps earlier although none is known to exist from the earlier period. As cities expanded more shops opened to handle the various needs of the communities. Illiteracy was common and many could not read or write but signs were easily recognizable by the symbol of the service or product offered.

The carving of shop signs, especially for inns and taverns, was part of the work of the shipcarver, who usually relegated it to a journeyman or an advanced apprentice. They were either painted in the shop by one of the carvers who—besides being skilled in gilding, striping, lettering, and

Fig. 4. Highland Laddie. *Carved and painted wood. Height 33½ inches, base 2¾ inches. English, c. mid-eighteenth century. Courtesy Arents Collection, New York Public Library.*

Fig. 5. A small figure, perhaps used as a New England inn sign. Courtesy Index of American Design.

figure drawing—made sketches for the client's approval; or by a limner specializing in signs.

Some of the most outstanding signs of Philadelphia during the latter part of the eighteenth and early nineteenth centuries were made by some of America's most distinguished artists. Matthew Pratt, who was born in Philadelphia in 1734, was a schoolmate of Charles Willson Peale and of Benjamin West, at "Videl's school up the alley, back of Holland's hatter's shop." Pratt was as famous for his signs as he was for his works of art. William S. Mount, born in Setauket, Long Island in 1807, was a hard-working farmer's boy who at the age of seventeen entered his brother's shop as an apprentice sign painter. To earn a living, some of the artists painted portraits, glass tablets for mirrors and clocks, while in Philadelphia, John Quidor, whose shop was in Pearl Street between Elm and Centre, enjoyed the reputation as a painter of "backs" of fire engines.[12]

Of the earlier signs that appeared there was a small figure of a gentleman with one hand to his side and the other in a Napoleonic pose, hand in tunic, which may have been a New England inn sign (Fig. 5); the year, 1720, on his belt is probably an approximation added at a later date. The carver meant for the figure to endure the elements and made it a very solid and sturdy sign ignoring such details as muscles and modeling, which were perhaps beyond his ability, but nevertheless creating a recognizable bid for the patron, promising hospitality and cheer. In the collection of the Bostonian Society in the Old State House is a figure, forty-two inches high, known as the *Little Admiral* which stood in front of No. 1 Long Wharf, Boston, serving as a sign for a maker of mathematical instruments, William Williams (Fig. 6). The date 1770, painted on the base, may have been a later addition as the costume would indicate this figure to be of the same period as the inn sign. The right hand may have held a telescope, sextant, or even a standard, and it is not too difficult to conceive that he is offering a pinch of snuff. In Nathaniel Hawthorne's "Shem Drowne's Wooden Image," the *Little Admiral* is attributed to that versatile artisan and may actually have been Drowne's attempt at a portrait of Admiral Vernon for the Admiral Vernon Tavern on King Street in Boston.[13]

Another figure, twenty-six inches high, with the date 1770 on its base, is in the Demuth Tobacco Shop in Lancaster, Pennsylvania, and was carved for Christopher Demuth at the time he opened his shop. The figure is sensitively posed with the weight on one foot and the right hand extending a box of snuff. The carving shows an understanding of the human face and form, a feeling for drapery, and a fair sense of proportion. This sign represents a young man in colonial attire.[14]

Tobacco shops spread through towns and villages and were supplied by the manufacturers and jobbers in the large cities. An advertisement of John B. Moody, manufacturer at 56 Pratt Street, Baltimore, at the head of Spear's Wharf, offered "leaf or plugtail tobacco in rolls and kegs, tobacco, segars and snuff." At the top of the advertisement was a linecut of an Indian leaning against kegs and rolls of the product. His headdress was of tobacco leaves instead of feathers, his left hand extended held out leaves of dried tobacco. On the opposite page was the advertisement of J. F. Kerner, another manufacturer of:

Tobacco, Snuff, and Cigars of various kinds, which he offers to the public at Reduced Prices, at his OLD STAND, No. 43 E. Baltimore street, corner of High Street, and also at his new store, No. 184 Lexington Market, (South Side) Three doors west of Eutaw st. . . . where he keeps a general assortment of the above article; and would call attention of Country Merchants, Grocers, Tavern Keepers, and Consumers generally, to call and examine his present stock, previous to purchasing elsewhere.[15]

His advertisement also had a linecut of an Indian with a spreading headdress and a large necklace of tobacco leaves. In his right hand he held a bow, over his left shoulder was slung a quiver of arrows and in his left hand he held out a bundle of dried tobacco leaves. In New York, the tobacco warehouses along Gold and Water Streets were but a short distance from the waterfront and the shops of the shipcarvers. When the wind was upriver, the aromatic odor of tobacco was carried for a considerable distance.

By 1860, the usually accepted sign for tobacconists was the cigar-store Indian. Indians as tobacconists' signs were known to have been in service in America in the early nineteenth century and perhaps in the eighteenth century. The earliest documented use of the Indian as an American tobacconist's sign appears in a watercolor drawing by the Baroness Hyde de Neuville of a small Indian to the side of a doorway of a tobacconist's shop on Greenwich Street near the corner of Dey Street in New York's Greenwich Village. The drawing is dated "Janvier [January] 1810" (Fig. 7).[16] Another use of the Indian as a tobacconist's sign appeared in an advertisement by Caldwell & Solomons of Albany, New York, in The Albany *Gazette & Daily Advertiser* of November 10, 1817 (Fig. 8a). The Caldwell & Solomons's Indian sign (Fig. 8b) is in an excellent state of preservation and in the collection of the Albany Institute of History and Art. The figure, thirty-one and one-half inches high, is extremely well carved, with a great amount of attention paid to details. The position of the tobacco leaves in the right hand has been altered and leaves broken off. The left

Fig. 6. The Little Admiral. *Height 42 inches. Served as a sign for William Williams, a maker of mathematical instruments. Courtesy Bostonian Society, Old State House.*

Fig. 7. Corner of Greenwich and Dey Street, New York, January 1810. From a watercolor by the Baroness Hyde de Neuville. A small tobacconist's Indian appears at the left of the entrance of the second building to the right. Courtesy I. N. Phelps Stokes Collection, Prints Division, The New York Public Library.

hand held a bow, now replaced with a staff. The carver is unidentified. However, the painting or repainting of this and another tobacconist's figure is noted in the account books of Ezra Ames, artist and portraitist of Albany, New York. Ames also painted flat board tobacconists' signs, charging George Pearson $40 on February 13, 1817, for a Pocahontas, and Joseph Frey for the "Old Darby and Joan" sign for a sum which is undecipherable.[17] Another Albany tobacconist, John Gott, was a ". . . manufacturer of Tobacco & Snuff at the sign of the Indian CHIEF," in the year 1835.[18]

An Indian, possibly made in 1790 and used as a tobacconist's sign, was the work of William Rush who was, perhaps, the first of the shipcarvers to make tobacconists' figures. A fellow shipcarver who knew his son, John Rush, spoke of the father as ". . . a solid citizen. . . . He had the artist spirit—even if it was for the most part given to the making of ship and tobacconists' figures."[19] In fact, William Rush, America's first native sculptor, was a wood-carver of extraordinary talents and carved busts and full-length figures of historic personages, ideal figures, and many other types of carved work. However, he made his living by carving ship and

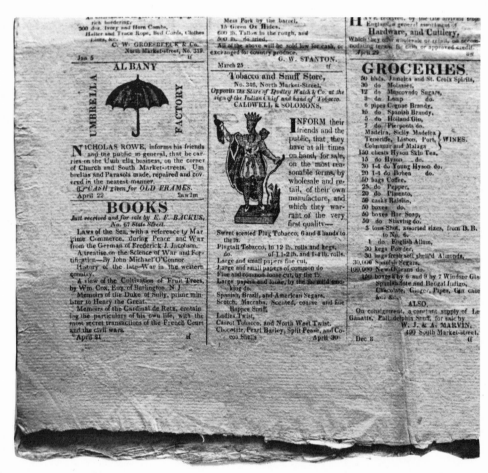

rich bordering.
300 doz. Ivory and Horn Combs,
Halter and Trace Rope, Bed Cords, Clothes Lines, &c.
C. W. GROESBEECK & Co.
North Market-street, No. 319.
Jan 5 tf

ALBANY
UMBRELLA FACTORY

NICHOLAS ROWE, informs his friends and the public in general, that he carries on the Umbrella business, on the corner of Church and South Market-streets. Umbrellas and Parasols made, repaired and covered in the neatest manner.

CASH given for OLD FRAMES.

April 22 2aw2m

BOOKS

Just received and for sale by E. F. BACKUS, No. 67 State Street.

Laws of the Sea, with a reference to Maritime Commerce, during Peace and War from the German of Frederick J. Jacobson.

A treatise on the Science of War and Fortification—By John Michael O'Connor.

History of the late War in the western country.

A view of the Cultivation of Fruit Trees, by Wm. Cox, Esq. of Burlington, N J.

Memoirs of the Duke of Sully, prime minister to Henry the Great.

Memoirs of the Cardinal de Retz, containing the particulars of his own life, with the most secret transactions of the French Court and the civil wars.

April 21 tf

Mess Pork by the barrel,
15 Green Ox Hides.
600 lb. Tallow in the rough, and
500 lb. do tried.
All of the above will be sold low for cash, or exchanged for country produce.
G. W. STANTON.
March 25 tf

Tobacco and Snuff Store,
No. 346, North Market-Street,
Opposite the Store of Dudley Walsh & Co. at the sign of the Indian Chief and hand of Tobacco.
CALDWELL & SOLOMONS,

INFORM their friends and the public, that they have at all times on hand, for sale, on the most reasonable terms, by wholesale and retail, of their own manufacture, and which they warrant of the very first quality—

Sweet scented Plug Tobacco, 6 and 8 hands to the lb.
Pigtail Tobacco, in 12 lb. rolls and kegs,
do. of 1 1-2 lb. and 1-4 lb. rolls.
Large and small papers fine cut,
Large and small papers of common do
Fine and common loose cut, by the lb.
Large papers and loose, by the lb. mild smoking do.
Spanish, Brazil, and American Segars,
Scotch, Maccaba, Scented, coarse and fine Rappee Snuff,
Ladies Twist,
Carrot Tobacco, and North West Twist.
Chocolate, Pearl Barley, Split Pease, and Cocoa Shells
April 30

Have received, by the late arrivals from England, a general assortment of
Hardware, and Cutlery,
Which they offer wholesale or retail, on accommodating terms, for cash or approved credit.
April 29

GROCERIES.

50 hhds. Jamaica and St. Croix Spirits,
30 do Molasses,
12 do Mascovado Sugars,
3 do Loaf do.
6 pipes Cognac Brandy,
15 do Spanish Brandy,
5 do Holland Gin,
7 do Pierponts do.
Madeira, Sicily Madeira, Teneriffe, Lisbon, Port, Colmanar and Malaga } WINES.
150 chests Hyson Skin Tea,
15 do Hyson do.
30 1-4 do Young Hyson do.
20 1-4 do Bohea do.
50 bags Coffee,
25 do Pepper,
20 do Pimento,
50 casks Raisins,
50 boxes do.
50 boxes Bar Soap,
50 do Shaving do.
3 tons Shot, assorted sizes, from B. B. to No. 6.
1 do English Allum,
30 kegs Powder,
30 bags fresh soft shell'd Almonds,
30,000 Spanish Segars,
100,000 New-Orleans do.
150 boxes 8 by 6 and 9 by 7 Windsor Gla[ss]
Spanish Bote and Bengal Indigo,
Chocolate, Ginger, Pipes, Gin case[s]
&c. &c.

ALSO,

On consignment, a constant supply of Le Gaux's, Philadelphia Snuff, for sale by
W. J. & A. MARVIN,
490 South Market-street.
Dec 8 tf

FIG. 8a

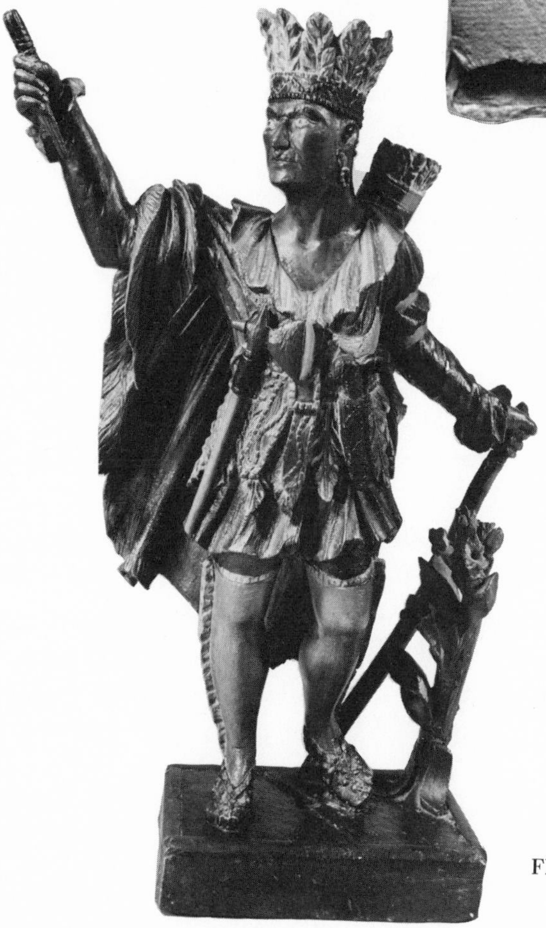

FIG. 8b

Fig. 8a. Advertisement of Caldwell & Solomons, November 17, 1817, from the Albany Gazette & Daily Advertiser. *Compare illustration with actual figure (Fig. 8b). A staff has replaced the bow, and part of the tobacco leaves in the right hand is missing. Courtesy New-York Historical Society.*

Fig. 8b. Tobacconist's Sign. *Probably carved by Ezra Ames of Albany. Height 31½ inches. This sign stood in front of the shop of Caldwell & Solomons at 346 Market Street, Albany. Courtesy Albany Institute of History and Art.*

shop figures, several of which were unknown until recently, and of which less than half a dozen survive. As a carver of Indian figures, Rush had no equal. The figurehead bust of Tamanend in the Naval Academy at Annapolis is attributed to William Rush—an honor even if it may not have been his work. A fellow shipcarver when asked,

"Are there any of his tobacconist's figures left?" replied, "I know of a few. There is a fine 'Mercury' in front of a store on Market Street near Twenty-first (in Philadelphia). It stood for years at the corner of Second and Dock. The figure in front of the cigar store on Third Street above Walnut is by Rush. I have known it as long as I have known anything, so to speak. If you look it up bear in mind it is not the standing figure on the street level, but the somewhat grotesque little Indian in an iron frame over the door. The outstretched arm is a restoration, the original member having been broken off years ago. The figure is a good specimen of Rush's early manner [Fig. 9].[20]

Another figure of Mercury in painted walnut of one-half life size was once used as a finial or decorative symbol on top of the circular Spring House or temple in Fairmount Park to the southwest of the Philadelphia Museum. Upon close examination one finds that the figure holds in its extended right hand what is most assuredly a snuff box (Fig. 10). As of this writing, another Mercury, most definitely by the chisel of William Rush, is languishing in the basement of the Maryland Historical Society in Baltimore under the mistaken belief that it was made in Italy! Its donor, A. J. Foble, of Cambridge, Maryland, upon presenting it to the Society in 1926, stated that his father purchased the figure in 1830 and that it had stood in front of his Cambridge tobacco shop for many years. The belief that it was made in Italy had stemmed from a newspaper article in the Baltimore *Evening Sun* of May 14, 1926: "It is dressed like one of Julius Caesar's legionnaires . . ."[21] Its resemblance to the Philadelphia Mercury is obvious and the carving of the hair, face, and robe leaves little doubt as to its carver. Mercury, the Roman god of commerce, or Hermes, the Greek god of science and medicine, was a common tobacconist's figure as tobacco was thought to have medicinal values which ". . . the Indians take against the crudities of the stomach."[22]

While Rush in Philadelphia, Jeremiah Dodge in New York, Isaac Fowle in Boston, and other shipcarvers along the Eastern seaboard were capable of carving excellent representational figures, there were other men at work who either were creating one-of-a-kind shop signs for their own purposes or were not trained in figure carving but were experienced carpenters supplying the needs of the local merchants. What remains of the work of the latter group is often referred to as "folk art." For the shops that were inland, away from the coast or the large cities where trained carvers were at work, the local wood craftsman was employed to create a likeness of a figure to represent the trade. When the abilities of the craftsman were too limited, a flat board cut in silhouette, painted on both sides, and put on a

Fig. 9. Tobacconist's Figure. *Carved by William Rush, probably before 1810. Once in an iron frame over the doorway of a tobacconist's shop on Third Street, above Walnut, in Philadelphia. The outstretched arm is a restoration. Photograph: courtesy Lyman Pendergast.*

stand sufficed. Occasionally, the board was embellished with carvings in low relief, creating a three-dimensional effect (Fig. 11). These boards were also used in the middle and third quarter of the nineteenth century. They had the advantage of being light and thus easily moved; they could fit into narrow doorways, were easily stored, and inexpensive. Sometimes they were elaborately carved, showing great skill and attention to details. One such board, the finest known, is in the collection of Edith Gregor Halpert at the American Folk Gallery in New York. The boards were usually of pine and, after painting, they were varnished on both sides. They had a tendency to warp, split, and get knocked over. Sometimes, they were carried off on Halloween, and even fed into Fourth of July bonfires.[23] Because of this, very few authentic examples survive.

Fig. 10. Mercury. *Carved by William Rush. Painted walnut, one-half life size, c. 1828. A tobacconist's figure holding out a snuff box. At one time this was used as a finial for the circular Spring House in Fairmount Park in Philadelphia. Courtesy Commissioners of Fairmount Park.*

FIG. 11

The local wood craftsman, when carving a three-dimensional figure, worked within his abilities, omitting details, yet creating a sign easily identified with the merchant's wares or services. A standard pose for tobacconists' Indians, copied or influenced by the tobacco advertisements and their illustrations, was a figure standing on a base of rolls, barrels, bundles, and packages of tobacco, snuff, and plug. An arm, usually the right, would be holding out some tobacco leaves. In the left hand were boxes and bundles of cigars, a mull of snuff; sometimes all of these piled on each other carved from the woodblock (Fig. 12). The pose was usually rigid and the proportions peculiar, revealing the carver's lack of training. When a local craftsman attained some reputation for the carving of such figures, he was called upon by other tradesmen and tobacconists to create similar signs. One such carver from the Baltimore–Wilmington area is known to have made at least three such figures, all quite similar, forty-two inches high on a four- to five-inch base (Fig. 13). All are carved close to the basic tree stump or mast, showing a minimal of cutting, yet the figures are endowed with a majestic stance and reveal a great dignity—as though to inspire confidence in the brand of tobacco sold inside.[24]

Another such figure with greater frontal detail is in the collection of the Historical Society of Berks County, Reading, Pennsylvania, and some similar figures of slightly smaller and larger sizes are in the Mercer Museum at Doylestown, Pennsylvania. All these figures may be by the same carver. Two others, thirty-five inches high, show some French influences—perhaps Canadian or New Orleans—and are in the Van Alstyne Collection at the Smithsonian. Two more figures (Fig. 14), by still a third carver, are in different costumes: one represents a French-Canadian trapper, and the other, an Indian from the southern regions of the United States. These show greater skill with more attention to the face, robes, and proportions. Both figures are bent forward, creating an illusion of movement, and both are very well preserved. They date from the middle of the nineteenth century.

Another small figure, forty-nine inches high, is of an Indian squaw (Col. Fig. 1). She stands on a bundle of oversized cigars, with one foot raised and her right hand extended offering cigars. She is dressed in a simple tunic with no decorations but with a revealing décolletage. The face is simple and extremely severe—not unlike the masks of the South Pacific Islanders, or of Africa. It is said to have been carved by an American slave named Job for a tobacconist in Freehold, New Jersey. The figure has been hollowed out to preserve it and to prevent the checking of the wood. This most unusual carving is in the collection of the New York Historical Association in Cooperstown, New York (see Col. Fig. 1a).

Sometimes a Negro was substituted for the Indian. One such figure (Fig. 15) represents a worker in the tobacco field gathering in a sheaf of tobacco leaves, one foot on a small roll of tobacco. Like the field hands, he is unshod and his rainment is simple. The carving shows sensitive

FIG. 12

Fig. 11. Flat board carved in high relief, and painted on two sides. Height 72½ inches, 14½ inches deep, and 8¼ inches wide. Courtesy Virginia Museum of Fine Arts.

Fig. 12. Indian. From the Baltimore-Wilmington area. Height 41 inches, base 5 inches. Found in an antiques store in New Orleans, present whereabouts of figure unknown. Almost identical to one in the author's collection.

Fig. 13. Indian. From the Baltimore-Wilmington area. Height 42 inches, base 4 inches. Courtesy Index of American Design.

FIG. 13

expression, fine detailing of the blouse, and good modeling of the arms and hands. Probably carved in the middle of the nineteenth century, this may be the work of Charles J. Hamilton, a Philadelphia carver, whose shop was at 423 North 11th Street in 1855. He moved twice between 1856 and 1859 finally establishing his shop at 1214 Girard Avenue where he was listed as a sculptor. Late in 1859 he moved to Washington, D.C., and took into partnership Elias W. Hadden, also a carver. There, at E Street North and about 13th Street West, they engaged in carving tobacconists'

Fig. 14. Indian. *From the middle of the nineteenth century. Overall size, 35¼ inches. Shows some French influences in the carving. Courtesy the Van Alstyne Collection, Smithsonian Institution.*

figures. Hamilton remained there until 1865. In 1881, he returned with his wife Leila A. Hamilton who found work as a clerk with the Treasury Department. Hamilton signed all his watercolors and oil paintings, but no figure is known to exist with his incised signature.[25]

David H. McAlpin, a tobacconist of New York who had his shop on Catherine Street after 1840 and moved to 77 Avenue D in 1866, had an Indian figure in front of his store for many years. During this time he was the treasurer of the Tobacconists' Association, a large influential group with its headquarters in New York City. McAlpin moved his tobacco works to his factory at Avenue D and East 10th Street and his Indian went along. The Indian, in a rather stiff pose, may have been the first of the "leaners" —that is, figures carved resting on a tree stump, or on an oversized cigar, or on a pileup of barrels, rolls, and boxes of tobacco and cigars. He wore a necklace of bear claws—a mark of bravery—a presidential medal that also hung from a necklace, a tunic belted by a knotted sash, sleeves banded around the biceps, elbow, and wrists, a draped feathered headdress, and long earbobs hanging to his collar. When the McAlpin Hotel opened in Herald Square in 1912, the Indian was placed in the lobby becoming part of the fixtures for many years until it was donated by Mrs. Charles McAlpin to the Museum of the City of New York.[26]

While the carving of the McAlpin Indian is not in the style or spirit of the work of any of the experienced New York shipcarvers, it could well be by one of John L. Cromwell's apprentices. Some of the leaning figures of Thomas V. Brooks, a Cromwell apprentice, are similar in design, costume, cutting, and attitude, and the McAlpin Indian may well have been one of his earliest carvings.

In 1830, a theatrical event took place that caught the imagination of the public, and immortalized a character in wood, song, and print as well as introducing a new word into the lexicon of American social issues.

> *Turn about an' wheel about an' do jis so,*
> *An' ebery time I turn about I jump Jim Crow,*

This refrain, sung in a broad Negro dialect on one of Cincinnati's main streets caught the attention of Thomas Dartmouth Rice, a former shipcarver's apprentice turned light comedian. Rice's personality was sometimes described as "slightly eccentric" but he had a talent for singing, for dancing a hornpipe after a style, and for stealing scenes from the leading actors. The historians of minstrelsy differ as to where Rice first heard the refrain, with Louisville, Pittsburgh, and Cincinnati each sharing the honors. The earliest account of Rice's first appearance as a Negro minstrel appeared in 1867:

As his engagement at Cincinnati had nearly expired, Rice postponed his public venture in the newly projected line until the opening of a fresh engagement would assure him the opportunity to share in the benefit expected to accrue by the experiment. This new engagement was made for Pittsburgh in the autumn of 1830. The old theatre of Pittsburgh was an unpretentious wooden structure of moderate seating capacity, but evidently good enough to satisfy the taste of the few who dared to face consequences and lend patronage to an establishment under the ban of the Irish and Scotch Calvinists. Entering upon duty at the local Old Drury, Rice prepared to take every advantage of his opportunity. There was a negro named Cuff in attendance at Griffiths' Hotel adjoining the theatre, who won a precarious existence by letting his open mouth serve as a mark for boys to pitch pennies into, at three paces, and by carrying the trunks of passengers from the steamboats to the hotels. This negro was the very man for Rice's purpose. Very little persuasion was required to induce him to accompany the actor to the theatre, where he was led through the stage door and quietly ensconced behind the scenes. After the play, Rice having blacked his face to the contraband hue ordered Cuff to disrobe and then proceeded to dress himself in the cast-off apparel. When the bell rang and the opening music for Rice's turn struck up, Rice, dressed in a fearfully dilapidated coat, a pair of shoes composed equally of patches and places for patches, and wearing an old straw hat which consisted of more rents than straw over a wild looking black wig, waddled into view. This extraordinary apparition produced a strange effect amongst the patrons of the pit and circle. Then Rice began his ditty, delivering the first line by the way of introductory recitative:

Oh, Jim Crow's come to town, as you all must know,
An' he wheel about, he turn about, he do jis so,
An' ebery time he wheel about, he jump Jim Crow.

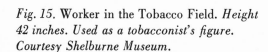

Fig. 15. Worker in the Tobacco Field. *Height 42 inches. Used as a tobacconist's figure. Courtesy Shelburne Museum.*

The effect was immediate. The novelty of the thing appealed to those present, and a big burst of applause greeted the introductory verse. The enthusiasm increased as Rice proceeded with succeeding couplets, and when gathering courage from the favorable temper of his audience the performer ventured to improvise matter for additional couplets from well-known local incidents, the applause was deafening. Such a demonstration had never been heard in the old theatre before. It seemed that Rice would be encouraged to continue his improvisations until the wee small hours, but a strange and unexpected thing happened.

It chanced that Cuff, the negro porter, who meanwhile had been crouching in deshabille under cover of a projecting flat behind the performer, by some means received intelligence at this point of the near approach of a passenger steamer to the local wharf. It appeared that Cuff had as a serious competitor in the luggage-carrying business, another negro of the name Ginger. In fact, there was great rivalry at the wharf between them. Directly Cuff heard the news of the approaching steamer, he had visions of his rival, Ginger, making an undisputed descent upon the luggage of the passengers. This was asking too much of a sacrifice of him. So after waiting several minutes for the performance to end his patience gave out entirely, and cautiously hazarding a glimpse of his profile beyond the edge of the flat, called out in a hurried whisper, "Massa Rice, must have ma close. Massa Griffiths wants me. Steamboat's comin'."

But the appeal was useless. Rice did not hear it, as at that moment he was making a happy hit at an unpopular city functionary which created roars of laughter. So once again poor Cuff protruded his face, this time still further on the stage, and called out more emphatically, "Massa Rice. Must have ma close. Steamboat's comin'." But the applause and laughter still continued and the poor baggage carrier was unheard and unheeded. At last, driven to desperation and forgetful in the emergency of every sense of propriety, Cuff in ludicrous undress darted on the stage, seized Rice by the shoulder and shouted excitedly, "Massa Rice, gimme nigger's close. Steamboat's comin'."

This incident, to use a theatrical phrase, fairly brought down the house, and the theatre lights had to be extinguished before the laughing audience could be persuaded to disperse.[27]

So it was that the art of Negro minstrelsy came into being. Following this performance, the song "Jim Crow" was being hummed, sung, and whistled by everyone.[28] Rice remained in Pittsburgh for two years, later performing in Philadelphia, Boston, and New York. He received an invitation to perform in England and made his first appearance at the Surrey Theatre, London, on July 9, 1836. "Jim Crow" proved even a greater success abroad and was the rage everywhere. Men wore "Jim Crow" hats and smoked "Jim Crow" pipes. Carved wooden figures of "Jim Crow" appeared in front of shops. The London papers, including the *Times* and *Morning Post,* agreed that Rice's engagement was the theatrical novelty of the year (Fig. 16).[29]

T. D. Rice, or "Daddy" Rice as he became known in his "Jim Crow" costume, appeared on playbills, songbooks, broadsides, tickets, and even as a tobacconists' figure. At least one carving was still serving its purpose past 1883.

Old Jim Crow, a famous figure cut forty years ago (1843) by "Charley" Dodge—now dead and gone—was in the Canal Street shop for repairs not long ago. A new foot was put on, a missing ear supplied, a piece chipped out of the cheek was replaced, the hat was reconstructed, and Old Jim Crow emerged as good as new. The figure is now doing service in an up-town hotel.[30]

T. D. Rice's career was brought to a close in 1858 after he was stricken with paralysis. He died in his native city of New York on September 19, 1860, at fifty-three.

A larger than life-size figure in the collection of the Shelburne Museum in Vermont is intended to be a portrait of T. D. Rice in costume (Fig. 17). Another figure represents the character "Jim Crow" as it appeared on playbills, songsheets, and the linecuts in advertisements.

Fig. 16. A song sheet of the period when Thomas Dartmouth Rice sang and danced to Jim Crow.

The carving of an occasional figure such as a "Jim Crow," a shop sign signifying some particular trade, or a tobacconist's figure was not considered on the same level of carving art as a ship's figurehead (and thus did not bring the same price) and certainly did not provide enough work to equal or replace the volume usually provided by the shipyards. But as the effects of the depression of 1857 on wooden shipbuilding began to be felt by the shipcarvers, they started looking for additional work within their craft in order to keep their shops open. The transition started in 1856. Carving tobacconists' figures was at first shunned by the shipcarvers but as the depression continued, when, a wholesale tobacconist supplier offered this work, the shipcarvers made their peace with the Indian.

WM. DEMUTH & CO.,
No. 403 BROADWAY, N. Y.,
IMPORTERS AND MANUFACTURERS OF
SEGARS AND SMOKERS' ARTICLES
WOODEN FIGURES.

WE would respectfully solicit from the Public generally an Inspection of our Large and Varied Assortment of

WOODEN SHOW FIGURES,

which we are constantly manufacturing for all classes of business, such as

SEGAR STORES, WINE & LIQUORS, DRUGGISTS, YANKEE NOTIONS, UMBRELLA, CLOTHING, TEA STORES, THEATRES, GARDENS, BANKS, INSURANCE COMPANIES, &c.

Before we commenced Manufacturing Show Figures, their use was almost entirely confined to Tobacconists, who displayed before their Stores a figure of what by a great stretch of imagination might have been recognised as an Indian—the workmanship of which, to say the least, was not very artistic.

Since then we claim not only to have Manufactured Figures which are both carved and painted in a manner which cannot be excelled, but also to have introduced a number of entirely new and original designs for same, to which we are constantly making additions to suit many other classes of trade (as stated above) besides the Tobacco.

But although our Figures invariably gave full satisfaction, still we wished to make a greater improvement in the line; and by the use of some more durable substance than Wood, thus prevent cracking, which will sometimes occur in Wooden Figures, especially when exposed to the climate of our Southern States.

For this purpose, after incurring a heavy outlay for Designs, Moulds, &c., we commenced the Manufacture of our New

METAL SHOW FIGURES,

(being the first parties in the country to introduce same), which have now been before the public for over two years, during which time we have sent large numbers to all sections of the country without ever having received the slightest word of complaint in regard to them.

We claim for these Figures the following qualities: that they are durable, and as light as wooden figures; are designed and executed in a highly artistic manner; and can be furnished at comparatively low prices.

We are constantly receiving orders for Statues and Emblematic Signs, and can furnish same, of any required design, to order, with promptness.

WILLIAM DEMUTH & CO.,
403 BROADWAY, New York.

M. THALMESSINGER & Co., Stationers, 308 Broadway, N. Y.

FIG. 19

3 · Shipfronts to Shopfronts–
Indians to the Rescue

Lo, the poor Indian! whose untutored mind
Sees God in clouds, or hears him in the wind.
His soul proud science never taught to stray
Far as the solar walk, or milky way;
Yet simple nature to his hope has given
Behind the cloud-topt hill, an humbler heaven.
Some safer world in depth of woods embraced,
Some happier Island in the watery waste,
Where slaves once more their native land behold,
No friends torment, no Christian thirst for gold;
To be, contents his natural desire,
He asks no angel's wing, no seraph's fire;
But thinks, admitted to that equal sky,
His faithful dog shall bear him company.

ESSAY ON MAN by Alexander Pope[1]

RETAILERS

IN 1839, James M. Chichester opened a tobacco shop at 704 Water Street, New York, specializing in cigars. In 1845, he moved his shop to 278½ Grand Street where he remained for three years before moving to a larger location at 51 Bowery. He lived over his shop which stood on the east side of the Bowery between Bogard and Canal Streets near Charlie White's Melodian and the Volks Garden, later the Atlantic Garden, opposite the Old Bowery Theatre. Chichester carried the "Cinnamon" cigar which was a favorite with theatre people. About 1852 or 1853, Chichester, who was jobbing, started to carry the fixtures of the trade, and the wooden Indian, or show figure, as it was properly called, was among them.[2] Chichester employed Thomas Millard, Jr., whose ship-carving shop was at 260 South Street, to supply him with a variety of figures in several sizes. Chichester's Bowery tobacco shop, with an array of wooden Indians and other show figures crowded the sidewalk, became

Fig. 19. Advertising sheet issued in 1871 by Wm. Demuth & Co. Courtesy Smithsonian Institution.

an attraction, and was known as "the wooden Indian shop."[3] For a period of three or four years, Chichester was the sole wholesale supplier of show figures to the trade, although some of the merchants may have contracted directly with the shipcarvers for an occasional figure for their enterprises. In 1856, a competitor of Chichester came into the business of selling "Indians and Show Figures." His methods were to carry the art of the ship- and now show-figure carver throughout the entire country. His name was Edward Hen.[4]

Edward Hen (1817–1887)

Edward Hen was born in Lorraine, Germany, in 1817. In 1837, he set out for America and after his arrival became an itinerant peddler selling toys, combs, and other toilet articles. By 1840, he had established a novelty and tobacco supply business at 20 Liberty Street under the name of August F. T. Edward Hen. He imported smokers' articles from Europe and his shop became a sort of center of trade for the old-time dealers. The shop continued to grow in popularity and prosperity until a disastrous fire nearly bankrupted its hardworking owner. He reorganized his business, temporarily moving into a vacant store at 29 Liberty Street. Here he remained for a short time until a larger space became available at 23 Liberty Street. He listed his wares, besides tobacconists' supplies, and his business as "Importer fancy goods, gun cutlery, etc."[5]

With Chichester supplying the trade with well-carved and attractive show figures, Hen decided to carry these in stock and approached the shipcarvers with orders.[6] His first advertisement listing his new stock appeared in 1856:

Edward Hen, importer of French & German fancy goods, also smoker's articles, clay pipes, of all kinds, real and imitation meerschaums, hookas, and other Turkish waterpipes, adapted for one or more smokers, amber, meerschaums, horn & china segar tubes, tobacco & snuff boxes, segar cases, matches, Turkish tobacco, walking canes, show figures, Indians, &c &c. 23 Liberty.[7]

Hen was a careful and meticulous businessman whose good sense of public relations aided in bringing him prosperity. He selected his employees for their competency, good character, and keen sense of organization. He befriended the shipcarver Thomas V. Brooks. Brooks's shop supplied Hen with a large number of tobacconists' figures of all types. Among these were "Indians, Turks, Scotchmen, Punches, Sultanas, Etc." By his investments in outside ventures, Edward Hen accumulated great wealth which permitted him to become a large stockholder in many corporations and also to conduct a fair-sized private banking business.

With the expansion of his business, Hen moved into a five-storied brick building at 43 Liberty Street opposite the post office, taking his three

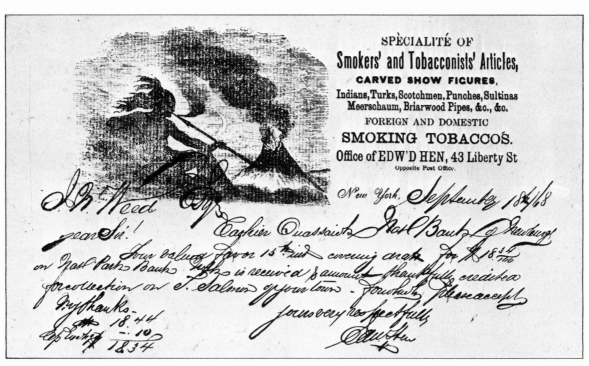

Fig. 18. Billhead with signature of Edward Hen dated September 18, 1868.

nephews into the firm as apprentices (Fig. 18). They served as stock boys and later as clerks, of which there were a dozen in all, under the personal supervision of Hen and his bookkeeper, John Wagner. Hen was an eccentric who lived in his shop, wore the same cloak for twenty-six years, existed on twenty-five cents daily, permitted himself no luxuries, and could be found each afternoon at the brokerage firms of J. P. Goodyear & Company and Vermilye and Company. A bachelor, Hen often visited Brooks at his home at 152 South Third Street in Williamsburgh and aided the shipcarver in his personal real estate investments.[8] Under Hen's direction, the John Wagners invested in real estate. Some deals consummated with Brooks, later developed into legal judgments which in no way affected the personal relationship of Brooks, the Wagners, and Hen.[9]

Edward Hen conducted his own business until May 4, 1887, when he was found dead in his shop. His personal life was kept from the public until his death. The daily newspapers found excellent headline material in the terms of Hen's will, and with the publication of his will on May 9, 1887, devoted columns exploiting in sensational language the details it contained. A special relationship had existed between Hen, John Wagner, and Wagner's wife, Bertha. The will bequeathed

. . . to Mistress Bertha Wagner, wife of John Wagner, now residing at No 12 Market Street in the City of New York . . . all my property and Estate of any and every kind and description and wherever situated. . . .[10]

The estate came to $2,500,000. His nephews and a niece were cut off without a cent, and promptly threatened to break the will or bring to light a more recent one. A compromise was effected on the basis of an equal division of the estate all around.

During his lifetime, Hen frowned upon extravagances and amusements as well as the spending of money for other than dire necessities. In late July, 1887, after the estate was settled, a champagne luncheon was given in the shop. "A dozen clerks who worked for the millionaire enjoyed the luncheon, and when it was over each received a present of a check for six months' salary. In this jolly fashion the firm formally went out of existance."[11]

For a period of twelve years, into and through the Civil War, Chichester and Hen kept the former shipcarvers busy chopping out tobacconists' and other kinds of show figures. Hen's merchandising methods were far too advanced for Chichester, who spent more time at his home in Mount Vernon, New York, than in his shop. Thus, Hen took away most of the local and near-city trade. In 1860, Hen employed William Demuth, who remained with him for two years and who later succeeded Hen in becoming the largest supplier of Indian and show figures to the trade throughout the United States and foreign countries.

William Demuth (1835–1911)

William Demuth was born in Rimbach, near Darmstadt, Germany, on November 1, 1835, and at the age of sixteen came to America, practically penniless. Realizing that to succeed he had to become Americanized, and with his youth to aid him, he studied English with a passion, and mastered the language in a short time. Demuth had various odd jobs until 1858 when he was employed as a clerk. He lived at 95 Rivington Street on the Lower East Side, not far from the yards of the shipbuilders and the shops of the shipcarvers. The following year he moved to 236 Delancey Street. In 1860–1861, after he was employed by Edward Hen as a clerk, he moved to 32 Attorney Street and the following year to 137 Avenue B.[12]

On October 1, 1861, Demuth was married and he and his wife Harriet set up housekeeping in a tiny tenement flat on Avenue B. In 1863, Demuth left Hen to set up his own business, Wm. Demuth & Co., Importers, at 18 Liberty Street, a short distance up the street from his former employer, and became a competitor in the same line of goods. From his crowded flat, he moved to a less crowded one at 97 Allen Street, and in 1864, he moved his shop to more spacious quarters diagonally across the street from Hen's establishment. His trade increased and Demuth was able to move to a more fashionable neighborhood, 329 East 18th Street. In 1865, he took his brother Isaac into the business. By then, the specialty of the firm was pipe manufacture. Like his former employer, Demuth began carrying wooden Indians and show figures for the trade. Though the shipcarvers felt that their tobacconists' and show figures were not to be treated on the same professional level as their ship carvings, nevertheless, Demuth was able to inspire better workmanship, even though the figures sold for less money. He had an appreciation of the carver's art.[13]

In 1869, Demuth moved uptown to an area fast becoming popular with businessmen and expanding at a great rate. He occupied a building at 403 Broadway, with a store and showroom on the street level. Demuth was rapidly becoming the leading pipe merchant in the East with orders coming in from all parts of the country. About a year earlier, Demuth suggested to Morris Seelig, another German immigrant who came to America the same year and who had a zinc foundry in Williamsburgh, that tobacconists' figures be cast in metal and sold from Demuth's shop. Eight models were chosen from wood carvings and then cast in zinc, in a process which Seelig had developed from the discovery of galvano plastics made by Jacobi in Saint Petersburg, Russia. The results were of such distinction that Demuth ordered more sets.[14]

The advantages of the cast-metal figures were several: they could be left out in all kinds of weather; the paint, applied at the time of casting, lasted a long time; the metal could not check or crack in extreme temperatures; and their weight made the possibility of their being carried off unlikely. There were disadvantages as well: if knocked over, they would break which meant that only the foundry would be able to make the repairs; new paint did not stick too well to the metal; they were heavy to handle, unlike the wooden figure that could be moved inside the shop each night; they were more expensive since the cost of the model, the molds, and castings meant more operations and therefore more expenses. Demuth, however, was proud and delighted with his new line and took advantage of a forthcoming event which he felt would provide a showcase for his new line of show figures.

The Thirty-eighth Annual Fair of the American Institute was to be held in the building known as the Empire Skating Rink on Third Avenue between 63rd and 64th Streets, from September 8 to October 31, 1869. In the division known as the "Department of Fine Arts in Education—Group 4—Sculpture, Cameos, Medals, Medallions, Etc. Fine casting in Bronze, Zinc and other metals," was entry No. 91—Group 6—"Eight Metal and Wood Figures for Stores—W. Demuth & Co., 403 Broadway." As such this was the first art exhibition of show figures and cigar-store Indians ever held in the United States, but it was not the first of its kind, as one had been held in London 106 years earlier.[15] For his entries Demuth was awarded a medal, which he promptly displayed and reproduced in his mailings.

The American Institute in the preface to its published catalogue unashamedly admitted:

. . . the managers seek, in these Fairs, to collect such a remarkable group of things brilliant and beautiful as well as useful and to present such attractions as

Art and Music as will draw many thousands of visitors and swell the bank account of the Institute.

The American Institute of the City of New York was incorporated on May 2, 1829. From 1841, the Institute maintained an open exhibition of models and of improvements in manufactures, agriculture, and the arts. In earlier years when the American Institute held its exhibitions at Castle Garden, the managers established boat races to "give the young Whitehall Boatmen an opportunity to try their skill. The principal prize was a new Whitehall boat. These races always created a lively interest."[16] The headquarters of the American Institute were located at Cooper Union where Abraham Lincoln had addressed the assembly on February 27, 1860. Attending the free, evening art school was a young artist in wood who, in a few years, was to become the outstanding carver of tobacconists' and show figures, and who already was supplying Demuth with his carvings. His name was Samuel Anderson Robb.[17]

In 1871, Demuth sent out a single sheet advertisement, which his salesmen also carried and from which orders were taken (Fig. 19). On this sheet were the figures of Gambrinus holding aloft a stein of overflowing beer, with one foot on a keg; a small Indian squaw on a pedestal or stand; a guardsman in a tall shako; and a Chinese figure for tea shops. The advertisement read:

We would respectfully solicit from the Public generally an Inspection of our Large and Varied Assortment of WOODEN SHOW FIGURES, which we are constantly manufacting for all classes of business, such as SEGAR STORES, WINE & LIQUORS, DRUGGISTS, YANKEE NOTIONS, UMBRELLA, CLOTHING, TEA STORES, THEATRES, GARDENS, BANKS, INSURANCE COMPANIES, &c. Before we commenced Manufacturing Show Figures, their use was almost entirely confined to Tobacconists, who displayed before their Stores a figure of what by a great stretch of imagination might have been recognized as an Indian—the workmanship of which, to say the least, was not very artistic. Since then we claim not only to have Manufactured Figures which are both carved and painted in a manner which cannot be excelled, but also to have introduced a number of entirely new and original designs for same, to which we are constantly making additions to suit many other classes of trade (as stated above) besides the Tobacco.

But although our Figures invariably gave full satisfaction, still we wished to make a great improvement in the line, and by the use of some more durable substance than Wood, thus prevent cracking, which will sometimes occur in Wooden Figures, especially when exposed to the climate of our Southern States.

For this purpose, after incurring a heavy outlay for Design, Moulds &c, we commenced the Manufacture of our New METAL SHOW FIGURES (being the first parties in the country to introduce same), which have now been before the public for over two years, during which time we have sent large numbers to all sections of the country without ever having received the slightest word of complaint in regard to them.

We claim for these Figures the following qualities; that they are durable, and as light as wooden figures; are designed and executed in a highly artistic manner; and can be furnished at comparatively low prices.

We are constantly receiving orders for Statues and Emblematic Signs, and can furnish same, of any required design, to order, with promptness.

WILLIAM DEMUTH & CO.
403 Broadway, New York[18]

Demuth was becoming aware of the need to protect his designs—the figures as well as the brands of tobacco—originating with him. In 1869, he applied to the copyright office in Washington, D.C., for the Lurline, Robinson Crusoe, and Santa Claus smoking tobacco.[19] Perhaps he even had figures cut to represent the characters. In 1874, Demuth moved to enlarged quarters at 501 Broadway opening a most attractive showroom and sales office. His pipe business was growing at a rapid rate and he was beginning to feel his opulence. Demuth, who had a fine singing voice, participated in amateur theatrical groups taking the lead parts in musical dramas and light operas. His carver, Samuel Anderson Robb, who was about to open his own shop, also had a fine singing voice and it is possible that many a duet was sung among the wooden Indians, Turks, and Chinese tea figures. Demuth won some notices for his role in "Allemania," as the Lord in "Pinafore," and in "Harmonie." A group known as the "Chestnut Club" which met on Sundays, was partial to Demuth's appearances.[20] This diversion in no way interfered with his business; on the contrary, it extended the reach of his personality and improved his business.

The Demuth showroom was a splendid place to visit with its fitted cabinets, its careful and artistic arrangements of pipes in showcases, and his choicest wood and metal figures (Fig. 20). Two of his favorite figures were the page boy and girl, combination lamp and cigar lighters

Fig. 20. Showroom of Wm. Demuth & Co. at 507 Broadway, New York, about 1887.

FIG. 21

(Fig. 21). These were of wood, glazed to look like stone, on a marbleized wood base supporting the figures in the most splendid colors and striped in the most ornate gold-leafed patterns. A page boy figure still exists and for years has stood in front of Corti's Antiques on Third Avenue at 38th Street in New York. On August 21, 1875, Demuth submitted for copyright "2— Illustrated Catalogues of Smokers Articles & Show Figures" containing thirty show figures and Indians in different styles, for which copyright was granted (Fig. 22). The first eight figures were of wood and the others of metal (Figs. 23, 24). Number 62, also called *Rising Star,* was copyrighted separately in 1874. A female bust for milliners and hairdressers, etc., and a female bust for dressmakers were copyrighted in 1873, and the one-dollar fee for each design was submitted by Mr. Pettigrew of the Wm. Demuth firm. Four more styles of metal bust figures complete the

Fig. 21. Page Boy and Page Girl figures. *Combination lamp and cigar lighters in the Wm. Demuth & Company showroom at 507 Broadway, in 1887. From the tray of fuel, held by each figure, a long metal pipe was fixed with a flame on the far end for smokers to light up.*

Fig. 22. Application for copyright of Illustrated Catalogue of Smokers' Articles and Show Figures by Demuth in 1875.

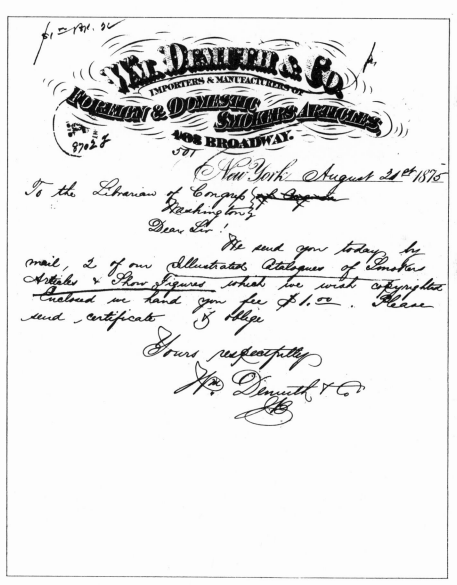

FIG. 22

original group and four additional show figures were added as single sheets issued some years later.[21] It is important to note that in the illustrations the figures usually appear in reverse, as the artist drew them on the engaving plate directly as he saw them. The exceptions are noted with the illustrations.

Demuth also made a small metal counter model with clockwork and a bellows inside the body which blew smoke from a cigarette placed between the lips (Col. Figs. 2a, 2b). In two of the verses of a song called "Punchinello," which was in vogue in the early eighteenth century, Punch says:

> *I'm that little fellow*
> *Call'd Punchinello,*
> *Much beauty about me;*
> *I'm witty and pretty,*
> *And come to delight ye;*
> *You cannot be merry without me.*
>
> *My cap is like a sugar-loaf,*
> *And round my collar I wear a ruff;*
> *I'd strip and shew you my shape in buff,*
> *But fear the ladies would flout me.*
> *My rising back and distorted breast,*
> *Whene'er I shew 'em, become a jest;*
> *And, all in all I am one of the best,*
> *So nobody need doubt me.*[22]

Punch's Judy was not an attractive figure and as far as is known, only one figure of her was made.

There has been a great deal of controversy over the origin of Punch or Pulcinella. Most of it was settled upon the unearthing in Rome in 1727 of an ancient bronze figure of *Maccus*, a character who appeared in satirical dramas called "Atellanae," from the name of the ancient city of Atella.[23] The bronze had a hooked nose, two humps, a mocking, evil and skeptical look, and two silver balls placed at the corners of his lips to increase the size of his mouth. He was shod in a type of shoe with a tie around the ankle.

Another theory had Punch originating from Pulcinella dalla Carceri, a grotesque Italian patriot of the thirteenth century, and still another credited his creation to a sixteenth-century peasant, Puccio d'Aniello, who lived in Acerra, a town near Naples. The Neopolitan Pulcinella, as the character was developed in the theatre, was witty and astute and considered the sensual descendant of Bucco, another character in the "Atellanae"; while Pulcinello, a coarse and stupid character, was accepted as the direct descendant of Maccus. The former type became European, known in France as Polchinelle; in England as Punch, a contraction of Punchinello, and Jack Pudding; in Germany as Hanswurst (Jack Sausage) and Pulzinella; in Holland as Toneelgek; in Spain as Don Christoval Pulichinela; and in the Far East as Karagheus.[24]

ILLUSTRATED CATALOGUE

OF

Smokers' Articles

AND

SHOW FIGURES,

MANUFACTURED AND IMPORTED BY

WM. DEMUTH & CO.,

501 BROADWAY,

Near Broome Street,   **NEW YORK.**

FIG. 23

OFFICE OF

WM. DEMUTH & CO.

MANUFACTURERS OF

METAL & WOODEN SHOW FIGURES,

501 BROADWAY,

NEW YORK.

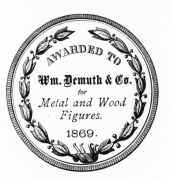

THE vast progress in the manufacture of Show Figures since the time of the old-fashioned Indian scarecrow we claim is mainly due to our improving efforts. The proper proportions of limbs, human expression of face, careful workmanship, and rich painting of our Figures, when first brought before the public, at once distinguished them from the old standard types, and have since preserved them high in public favor.

After a number of years' experience in the manufacture of Wooden Figures, we were induced to make use of a more durable material, and thus remove a difficulty unavoidably adherent to wood; its cracking from exposure to climatic changes; and, under heavy expenditures for designs, moulds, etc., we commenced the manufacture of our Metal Show Figures. During a period of over seven years we have shipped large numbers to all sections of the country; they have resulted in giving the fullest satisfaction to our patrons, and the sale of Metal Figures is now far exceeding that of wooden ones. Their advantages are evident; made in zinc, they combine strength with beauty; they are as light as wooden figures, and considering their everlasting durability, far cheaper.

All figures represented in this catalogue, and many other styles suitable for Drug Stores, Clothing Houses, Notion Houses, Breweries, Banks, Insurance Companies, etc., we keep in stock. In case, however, an order should find us out of a certain figure, or in case we should be called upon to execute a special design, we are always prepared to make them within the shortest possible space of time.

The lowest Net Cash Price is marked under each figure; *charges for packing-case separate, and always at cost.*

Our terms for Show Figures are invariably Net Cash. Parties unknown to us, ordering Figures, are requested to forward a draft with the order as a guarantee of their good faith.

We have spared no labor or expense to render the representation of our Show Figures in this catalogue as true as art can do it, but yet the illustrations fall short of the originals. We trust, however, that the public will appreciate our efforts and award us a liberal patronage.

WM. DEMUTH & CO.

WOODEN FIGURES.

No. 12.

No. 15.

No. 14.

Height of Figure,	-	-	4 ft. 4 in.
Height of Pedestal,	-		1 ft. 10 in.
Total Height,	-	-	6 ft. 2 in.

Price, $33.

No. 11. Same style.

Height of Figure,	-	-	3 ft. 10 in.
Height of Pedestal,	-		2 ft.
Total Height,	-	-	5 ft. 10 in.

Price, $25.

Height of Figure,	-	-	-	5 ft. 10 in.
Height of Pedestal,	-	-	-	1 ft. 2 in.
Total Height,	-	-	-	7 feet.

Price, $60.

Height of Figure,	-	-	5 ft. 4 in.
Height of Pedestal,	-		1 ft. 3 in.
Total Height,	-	-	6 ft. 7 in.

Price, $50.

No. 13. Same Style.

Height of Figure,	-	-	4 ft. 10 in.
Height of Pedestal,	-		1 ft. 7 in.
Total Height,	-	-	6 ft. 5 in.

Price, $42.

Either of the above can be ordered Male or Female.

Indian No. 12 (Fig. 25). A small wooden figure made in great quantities from and before the Civil War period. This style was still being carved with variations in the pose of the right arm and costume, until the turn of the century. Sometimes the chiefs held daggers and the squaws held a rose along with a grouping of cigar boxes, snuff, and other tobacco items in the crook of the left arm. The engravings for this and the two following are not of good quality. The actual carvings are not as crude as shown.

Indian No. 14 (Fig. 25). A life-sized wooden figure also made in great quantities and similar in many details to No. 12. This style was made by several carving shops and was one of the most popular of the tobacconist's figures.

Indian No. 15 (Fig. 25). A tall wooden figure similar to No. 12 also made in a variety of poses, sometimes with a grouping of tobacco rolls, cigars boxes, snuff, and cut plug in the crook of the left arm. All three of the above figures are illustrated in unreversed positions.

WOODEN FIGURES.

Height of Figure,	-	- 5 ft.
Height of Pedestal,	-	9 in.
Total Height,	-	5 ft. 9 in.

Price, $68.

Height of Figure,	-	- 4 ft. 8 in.
Height of Pedestal,	-	1 ft. 3 in.
Total Height,	-	5 ft. 11 in.

Price, $55.

Height of Figure,	-	- 4 ft. 6 in.
Height of Pedestal,	-	1 ft. 6 in.
Total Height,	-	6 feet.

Price, $55.

Turk No. 40 (Fig. 26). This was an early wooden figure as was the Sultana. A fine, larger than life-sized Turk stood for years in front of the Turkish tobacco shop next to C. A. Marsh's drugstore, near the corner of Third Avenue and 125th Street in Manhattan.[26] One quite similar is in the collection of Mr. and Mrs. Bernard Zipkin. An excellent specimen of the Sultana is in the collection of the Shelburne Museum in Vermont. These figures, mostly from the mid-century were made by various carvers in several cities besides New York. Turks are sometimes called Sultans. These are among the rarer of the tobacconist's figures (Col. Figs. 3, 4).

Punch No. 32 (Fig. 26). This was a very popular figure in the 1860s coming in a variety of sizes and shapes, some with huge paunches or noses curved down and around, and most with a lascivious leer to lure the passerby into trying his brand of tobacco.

Girl of the Period No. 51 (Fig. 26). This was a popu-
lar figure during and right after the Civil War and was made in a variety of poses.

One carver said in an interview, "I've never noticed any special demand by Germans for such figures. But Italians and Chinamen show a strong predilection for them. I cannot tell you what they do with them, but I have sold six figures of the Girl of the Period class to Chinese during the last twelve months."[28]

These female figures were also known as "Dolly Vardens," after a character in *Barnaby Rudge*, a Charles Dickens novel of 1841. Dolly Varden, the daughter of Gabriel Varden, a prosperous locksmith, dressed in the latest fashions. One fashion style was so popular that Currier & Ives came out with a print by the same name. The fashion received most note when the "Queen of Burlesque," Lyda Thompson, came to America with her *English Blondes*, stirring at least one publication to note, ". . . her costume which was topped by a small hat trimmed with lace and ribbons and a stuffed squirrel which almost looked her straight in the eye."[29]

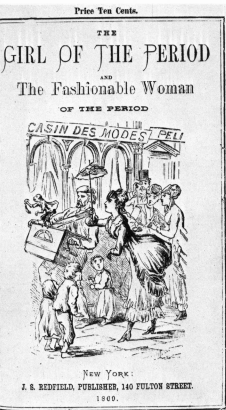

Carved Punches in England have thinner legs and more pronounced features, and sometimes are carved in woods other than white pine or whitewood. An almost perfect specimen of the Demuth wooden Punch, carved by Robb, is in the Van Alstyne Folk Art Collection in the Smithsonian Institution in Washington, D.C.[25]

Long teaser curls hung over her shoulder and she carried a swagger stick. The Grecian bend was all the rage (an exaggerated forward lean, encouraged by the shaped corset.) In 1868, another sedate publication noted:

The girl of the period is a creature who dyes her hair and paints her face, as the first articles of her personal religion; whose sole idea of life is plenty of fun and luxury; and whose dress is the object of such thought and intellect as she possesses. Her main endeavour in this is to outvie her neighbors in the extravagance of fashion. No matter whether, as in the time of crinolines, she sacrificed decency, or, as now, in the time of trains, she sacrifices cleanliness; no matter either, whether she makes herself a nuisance and an inconvenience to every one she meets . . . but she is far too fast and flourishing to be stopped in mid-career by these slow old morals; . . . If there is a reaction against an excess of Rowland's Macassar, and hair shiny and sticky with grease is thought less nice than if left clean and healthily crisp, she dries and frizzes and sticks hers out on end . . . or lets it wander down her back like Madge Wildfire. . . . For it is only the old-fashioned sort, not girls of the period pur sang that marry for love, or put the husband before the banker. But she does not marry easily. Men are afraid of her; and with reason. They may amuse themselves with her for an evening, but they do not take her readily for life. Besides, after all her efforts, she is only a poor copy of the real thing; and the real thing is far more amusing than the copy, because it is real. Men can get that whenever they like.[30]

The following dresses her down best:

> The Girl of the Period
> Oh, she was so utterly utter!
> She couldn't eat plain bread and butter,
> But a nibble she'd take
> At a wafer of cake
> Or the wing of quail for her supper.
>
> Roast beef and plum-pudding she'd sneer at,
> A boiled leg of mutton she'd jeer at,
> But the limb of a frog
> Might her appetite jog,
> Or some delicate bit that came near that (Fig. 27).[31]

The Girl of the Period was made and shipped all over the country and the various carvers outside of New York found it to be in demand by their local tobacconists. Without the cigarette in her hand, she was used by milliners. In dressmakers' shops, her hand held a small metal tray upon which were placed trade cards for the passerby to take (Col. Fig. 5).

WOODEN FIGURES.

No. 54.

No. 33.

THEATRICAL.

CAVALIER.

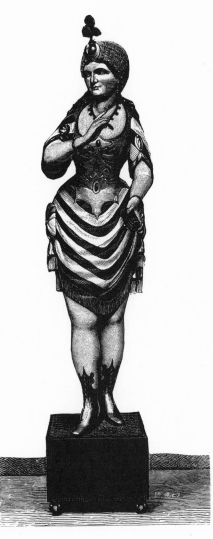

Height of Figure, - - - 5 ft. 8 in.	Height of Figure, - - - 6 ft.
Height of Pedestal, - - - 10 in.	Height of Pedestal, - - - 10 in.
Total Height, - - - 6 ft. 6 in.	Total Height, - - - 6 ft. 10 in.

Price, $90.

Price, $85.

Theatrical Figure No. 54 (Fig. 28). Made as a tobacconist's figure with the bundle of cigars in the right hand, but also used in front of threatres and in lobbies as a decorative attraction.

While thought to be a very daring figure at the time, it was not considered as wicked as the Girl of the Period who smoked cigarettes and lifted her skirt. The girl representing the theatrical figure wore the garments of her profession, which could have been in the circus, on the vaudeville stage, or a curtain raiser in musical plays. Girls that stood at attention with crossed and folded arms, in the attitude of the Captain Jinks (Col. Fig. 6), were quite uncommon. One, carved by H. Matzen, once an apprentice of Julius Theodore Melchers, is in the collection of the Chicago Historical Society and another, carved in Robb's shop, is privately owned. Theatrical figures came in two or three sizes to order. Two such maidens in identical costume appear as curtain raisers in the American Biograph movie short, "The Birth of the Pearl."[34]

Cavalier No. 33 (Fig. 28). A tobacconist's figure in wood, made with slight variations to represent Sir Walter Raleigh; an extremely rare figure today. One figure carved in England and another of American manufacture are in the collection of Brown & Williamson Tobacco Corporation of Louisville, Kentucky.

METAL FIGURES.

No. 49.
GAMBRINUS, OR KING LAGER.

Height of Figure (to top of glass), 6 ft. 7 in.
Height of Pedestal, - - *2 ft. 1 in.*

Total Height, - - - *8 ft. 8 in.*

Price, $250.

No. 50.
SAME STYLE.

Height of Figure (to top of glass), 4 ft. 5 in.
Height of Pedestal, - - *1 ft. 8 in.*

Total Height, - - - *6 ft. 1 in.*

Price, $100.

Gambrinus, or King Lager No. 49 (Fig. 28). An impressive figure in the larger size, especially popular with hofbrau houses until the end of the century and with various breweries throughout the country until 1967. An oversized version was used on top of a Newark, New Jersey, brewery until the building was demolished in the 1950s. This figure and a more youthful Bacchus, holding up oversized and overflowing goblets of beer, were also made by the J. W. Fiske Iron Works of New York (See Fig. 57).

No. 66ᴬ.

INDIAN MAIDEN.

No. 67ᴬ.

AFRICA.

No. 66ᴮ.

No. 67ᴮ.

Entered according to Act of Congress, in the year 1875, by Wᴍ. Dᴇᴍᴜᴛʜ & Co., in the Office of the Librarian of Congress, at Washington, D. C.

Height of Figure, -	2 ft. 11 in.	
Height of Pedestal, -	- 3 ft. 2 in.	
Total Height, -	6 ft. 1 in.	
Price, $28.		
Lettering on pedestal as above, 75 cents extra.		

With Fancy Stand.	
For placing in the Show Window.	
Height of Figure,	2 ft. 11 in.
Height of Stand,	9 in.
Total Height,	3 ft. 8 in.
Price, $26.	

With Fancy Stand.	
For placing in the Show Window.	
Height of Figure,	2 ft. 11 in.
Height of Stand,	9 in.
Total Height,	3 ft. 8 in.
Price, $29.	

Height of Figure, -	2 ft. 11 in.
Height of Pedestal, -	- 3 ft. 2 in.
Total height, -	6 ft. 1 in.
Price, $31.	
Lettering on pedestal as above, 75 cents extra.	

The Africa figure is also admirably adapted for Druggists. The lettering on the banner can be ordered to suit any class of trade, and as it can be altered at pleasure, the banner will be found very useful as a bulletin board.

Indian Maiden No. 66a, No. 66b (Fig. 29). These two metal figures are of the same casting, placed on different stands. The smaller one was for inside the show window, and the one on the larger pedestal was placed outside the shop.

Smokers leaving the shop would occasionally strike their matches against the breast or rear of the figure, prompting a trade publication to print the following rhyme:

> *A girl can flirt and a girl can mash*
> *And a girl can give herself away,*

> *But you can't strike a match*
> *On the seat of her pants,*
> *Because she isn't built that way.*[38]

The figures are rare. One was part of the Anthony W. Pendergast collection but its present whereabouts is unknown.

Africa No. 67a, No. 67b (Figs. 29). These two figures in metal are of the same casting, placed on different pedestals. The smaller one on a fancy stand was for inside the show window, and the one on the larger pedestal was made for outside the shop.

METAL FIGURES.

INDIAN MAIDEN.

SQUAW.

Height of Figure,	-	-	-	-	-	4 ft. 3 in.
Height of Pedestal,	-	-	-	-	-	1 ft. 9 in.
Total Height,	-	-	-	-	-	6 feet.

Price, $40.

They were designed for tobacconists but were also adapted for druggists. The origin and meaning of the headdress is obscure, perhaps derived from an illustration of a brand of tobacco called La Africana, or after the opera "L'Africaine" by Giacomo Meyerbeer, first produced in Paris in 1865 and first performed in the United States on December 1, 1865, at the Academy of Music, New York. Perhaps, the opera was a favorite with Demuth, who honored it with this casting which may represent Selika, the queen. None is known to exist now.

Height of Figure,	-	-	-	-	-	5 ft. 4 in.
Height of Pedestal,	-	-	-	-	-	1 ft. 8 in.
Total Height,	-	-	-	-	-	7 feet.

Price, $65.

Indian Maiden No. 56 (Fig. 30). A small tobacconists' sign made in large quantities. Many of them still survive in fine condition with the original but faded paint. The figure held tobacco leaves in her right hand and had a headdress topped with a grouping of tobacco leaves instead of feathers.

Squaw No. 61 (Fig. 30). A graceful figure with a draped cloak and headdress of tobacco leaves. It was another popular figure which can now be found in various collections throughout the United States. It was also made with papoose.

No. 62.
RISING STAR.

Height of Figure,			*5 ft. 1 in.*
Height of Pedestal,	-	-	*1 ft. 8 in.*
Total Height,	-	-	*6 ft. 9 in.*

PRICE $65.

Rising Star No. 62 (Fig. 31). This figure was copyrighted before the entire catalogue was submitted to the office at the Library of Congress in 1875. The cigar in the right hand and the bundle of cigars in the left shows her to be a tobacconist's figure. The attitude and pose is similar to No. 54 but No. 62 is seven inches smaller and sold for twenty-five dollars less. A plaster figure, similar to this one, was sold at auction in 1956.[36] On the catalogue, Robb himself penciled notes for painting the colors.

No. 63.
SQUAW, WITH PAPPOOSE.

Height of Figure,	-	-	*5 ft. 4 in.*
Height of Pedestal,	-	-	*1 ft. 8 in.*
Total Height,	-	-	*7 feet.*

PRICE, $.70,

Squaw With Pappoose No. 63 (Fig. 31). The same as No. 61 but with pappoose added. There may be some slight differences in the hairlines of the squaws. A fine specimen of this squaw with papoose is in the collection of the Shelburne Museum in Vermont, and another at the Silver Hill Storage area of the Smithsonian Institution. It was also made holding a flaming torch.[37]

METAL FIGURES.

CHINAMAN.

INDIAN.

Entered according to Act of Congress, in the year 1869, by Wм. DEMUTH & Co., in the office of the Librarian of Congress, at Washington, D. C.

Entered according to Act of Congress, in the year 1869, by Wм. DEMUTH & Co., in the office of the Librarian of Congress, at Washington, D. C.

Height of Figure,						4 ft. 4 in.
Height of Pedestal,						1 ft. 8 in.
Total Height,						6 feet.

Height of Figure,						4 ft. 6 in.
Height of Pedestal,						1 ft. 6 in.
Total Height,						6 feet.

Price, $65.

Price, $75.

Chinaman No. 41 (Fig. 32). A small metal figure used in front of tea shops. Several were still in service before 1920 in parts of Brooklyn and Manhattan. One stood in front of the Great Atlantic & Pacific Tea Company's shop on Broadway and Meserole Street in Brooklyn. None is known to be in a major collection.

Indian No. 43 (Fig. 32). A small metal Indian on a variation of the usual pedestal, mounted on wheels. Many of the pedestals of the metal figures are missing today, proving the Demuth contention that metal would outlast the wood. In many instances, the bases of the metal figures along with the plaquettes are missing. Most of the plaquettes read COPYRIGHT 1874 BY WM. DEMUTH & CO. 501 BROADWAY NEW YORK. Others, after 1876, bore the address, 507 BROADWAY NEW YORK, and after 1887 some plaquettes appeared without the copyright date. This is an uncommon figure. Several are known, none in a major collection. One of the international airlines has stationed this figure, molded in fiber glass, in each of its offices throughout the world.

METAL FIGURES.

No. 48.
PAGE.

No. 57.
CAPTAIN JACK.

Entered according to Act of Congress, in the year 1869, by Wm. Demuth & Co., in the Office of the Librarian of Congress, at Washington, D. C.

Height of Figure (to top of Cigars),	- - -	*4 ft. 5 in.*
Height of Pedestal,	- - - - -	*1 ft. 8 in.*
Total Height,	- - - - - -	*6 ft. 1 in.*

IN 3 STYLES:

A—As above engraving. Price, $80.

B—With either a basket of grapes or a mortar at side. A wreath of grape-vine leaves around the head, and holding goblet in raised hand; for liquor and drug stores. Price, $85.

C—Either of the above styles, with a 4-light chandelier, supported in raised hand, to which gas may be attached; a gas-pipe runs through the figure. Price, $90.

The above can be had painted or bronzed, at same price.

Entered according to Act of Congress, in the year 1874, by Wm. Demuth & Co., in the Office of the Librarian o Congress, at Washington, D. C

Height of Figure,	- - - - -	*5 ft. 3 in.*
Height of Pedestal,	- - - - -	*1 ft. 10 in.*
Total Height,	- - - - -	*7 ft. 1 in.*

Price $100.

EITHER PAINTED OR BRONZED.

Page No. 48 (Fig. 33). This figure was made in several styles for liquor and wine shops and drugstores.

Instead of holding cigars the figure held a goblet. At his side was a basket of grapes and a wreath of vine leaves circled his head. With a mortar at his side, he became a druggist's figure. Sometimes his left hand supported a four-light chandelier attached to a gas pipe, which ran through the figure.

The identical figure in wood, hands at the side, was carved at a later date by Samuel A. Robb to serve as corner figures for the Barnum & London circus wagons.

These are now in the Shelburne Museum in Vermont. The Robb shop also carved two other wood corner figures with hands on the hilts of swords. They were on the St. George and the Dragon Pony Float, once part of the Adam Forepaugh's St. George and the Dragon telescoping tableau (Col. Fig. 9).[27] The only known metal figure is in the Merrit Museum.

Captain Jack No. 57 (Fig. 33). A smaller than life-sized metal figure, in a popular pose, also made in wood in many variations of the same pose, and in larger sizes.

METAL FIGURES.

No. 64.
SQUAW.

No. 65.
SQUAW, WITH PAPPOOSE.

Height of Figure,	*5 ft. 10 in.*
Height of Pedestal,	*1 ft. 2 in.*
Total Height,	*7 feet.*

Height of Figure,	*5 ft. 10 in.*
Height of Pedestal,	*1 ft. 2 in.*
Total Height,	*7 feet.*

Price, $85.

Price, $95.

Colonial hero of many adventure stories and dime novels which stirred the imagination of American youth, Captain Jack, was a white settler whose family was massacred by the Indians in the French and Indian War. Swearing vengeance, he disguised himself as an Indian and accomplished remarkable feats. He was also called the "Black Hunter," and the "Black Rifle."[35] Of two such known figures, one is in the Van Alstyne Folk Art Collection, Smithsonian Institution, and the other is in a private collection.

Squaw No. 64 (Fig. 34). A metal figure in a static pose, similar to many which were carved in wood and had more action. The cloak drapes down the back and in most cases its colors have faded and the interesting pattern above the fringed hemline has disappeared, as if it were painted rather than cast. Many are extant.

Squaw With Pappoose No. 65 (Fig. 35). Identical to No. 64 but with pappoose. Decoration and paint were somewhat different. Several are known to be in various collections, some in wood with less elaborate designs on the bodice and skirt. These figures are taller than No. 63.

METAL FIGURES.

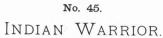

No. 52.

MOORISH QUEEN.

No. 45.

INDIAN WARRIOR.

Height of Figure,	-	-	-	-	5 ft. 5 in.
Height of Pedestal,	-	-	-	1 ft. 10 in.
Total Height,	-	-	-	-	7 ft. 3 in.

Price, $125.

Moorish Queen No. 52 (Fig. 35). A popular metal figure based on an original design of Spring by Tondeur. This was a favorite of Demuth's which he entered, with others, in various expositions throughout the United States. M. Seelig of Williamsburgh may have made the original pattern. The cast was made in his foundry. In the J. L. Mott catalogue of 1890, the height of this figure was given as sixty-four inches, and it sold for $121, bronzed.

Height of Figure,	-	-	-	-	5 ft. 9 in.
Height of Pedestal,	-	-	-	1 ft. 11 in.
Total Height,	-	-	-	-	7 ft. 8 in.

Price, $150.

Indian Warrior No. 45 (Fig. 35). A life-sized metal figure with club, the right foot raised standing on prey, a catamount. Its right hand holds a club and a cloak drapes gracefully off the shoulder, somewhat like a Roman toga.

Examples of this fine figure are not too frequently found and are rarely on their stands. Formerly in the Anthony W. Pendergast collection, the figure with a cracked base and without a stand is now in the storage area of the Smithsonian Institution. Another, in fine condition, is in the Merritt Museum.

METAL FIGURES.

No. 70.

No. 68.

INDIAN HUNTER.

COMICAL BUST.

Entered according to Act of Congress, in the year 1875, by Wм. Dемuтн & Co., in the office of the Librarian of Congress, at Washington, D. Ⴌ.

Entered according to Act of Congress, in the year 1874, by Wм. Dемuтн & Co., in the office of the Librarian of Congress, at Washington, D. C.

Height of Figure,	-	-	-	5 ft. 4 in.
Height of Pedestal,	-	-	1 ft. 8 in.
Total Height,	-	-	-	7 feet.

Price, $80.

FOR THE SHOW-WINDOW.

Height of Figure, - - - - - - - - - 2 feet.

Price, $25.

N. B.—The above engraving shows the feathers somewhat larger than they are on the figure.

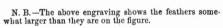

Can be ordered with or without pipe in hand.

Indian Hunter No. 70 (Fig. 36). A medium-sized metal figure in full attire with a voluminous cloak reaching to back of the base. The gun held in his left hand was often appropriated and later replaced with an old cheap Civil War musket. This figure is rarely seen and only one is known to exist—in a private collection.

Comical Bust No. 68 (Fig. 36). A metal figure for the show window, sometimes with pipe in hand.

The figure could be placed on the counter and was an unusual attraction when fitted with bellows and

clockwork, which opened from the back, a lighted cigarette was placed between the lips and the figure would puff out smoke to the action of the hidden bellows. One such bust is in the Dan. J. Friedman collection, Richmond, Virginia. These busts were also made in wood by the Robb shop. One such figure is in a private collection and still another is owned by a New York Second Avenue antiques dealer. In both metal and wood they were painted to life. Usually, a metal plaquette was attached on the back of this figure (See Fig. 49).

METAL FIGURES.

INDIAN CHIEF.

GODDESS OF LIBERTY.

Entered according to Act of Congress, in the year 1872, by WM. DEMUTH & Co., in the office of the Librarian of Congress, at Washington, D. C.

Height of Figure,				6 ft. 7 in.
Height of Pedestal,				1 ft. 11 in.
Total Height,				8 ft. 6 in.

Price, $175.

Height of Figure,				4 ft. 9 in.
Height of Pedestal,				1 ft. 6 in.
Total Height,				6 ft. 3 in.

Price, $105.

Indian Chief No. 53 (Fig. 37). An extremely large figure endowed with great dignity, this was the most famous and popular of all the metal figures. The right hand holds an arrow, the left hand a bow. From his neck is hung a string of bear claws, a mark of bravery. Several metal figures are extant, many without bows and arrows. Some have had the bows replaced by muskets.[32]

Goddess of Liberty No. 58 (Fig. 37). Also known as

Columbia and derived from the French revolutionary figure.

This was an extremely popular figure which served many purposes and various types of patriotic establishments. Demuth issued it in a large size—seventy-three inches high on a four-inch metal base—at the price of $110. Goddesses of Liberty were used as building finials, decorations for recesses in buildings, lawn ornaments for patriotic and fraternal organizations, podium and platform decorations for assemblies, and

METAL FIGURES.

PRICE LIST.

Eagle on Rock, 3 inch
   spread............$1 25
Eagle on Rock, 4 inch
   spread............ 2 25
Eagle on Rock, 7 inch
   spread............. 4 00
Eagle on Rock, 10 inch
   spread............. 6 50
Eagle on Rock, 14 inch
   spread............10 00
Eagle on Rock, 18 inch
   spread............15 00
Eagle on Rock, 22 inch
   spread............15 00
Eagle on Rock, 30 inch
   spread............25 00
Eagle with Shield, 50 inch
   spread............50 00
Eagle on Rock, 54 inch
   spread........ ...... 55 00
Eagle with Ball, 60 inch
   spread...........100 00
Eagle with Ball, 72 inch
   spread...........135 00
Eagle with Ball, 108 inch
   spread...........235 00

Gilded with Gold.

PRICE LIST.

Mortars, 10 inch........$8 00
Mortars, 12 inch...... 10 00
Mortars, 14 inch........15 00
Mortars, 16 inch........20 00
Mortars, 18 inch........25 00
Mortars, 20 inch........30 00
Mortars, 24 inch........40 00
Mortars, 36 inch........90 00
10 inch Mortar with 10
   inch Eagle....... 14 50
12 inch Mortar with 13
   inch Eagle........ 17 00
14 inch Mortar with 14
   inch Eagle....... 24 00
16 inch Mortar with 22
   inch Eagle........ 32 00
20 inch Mortar with 30
   inch Eagle....... 50 00
24 inch Mortar with 31
   inch Eagle....... 70 00
36 inch Mortar with 60
   inch Eagle.... .. 180 00

Gilded with Gold.

No. 69.

CAFFIR SMOKER.

With Smoking Apparatus.

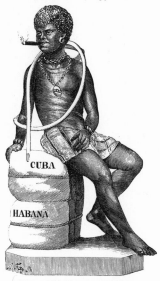

FOR THE SHOW-WINDOW.

Height of Figure, 2 feet 6 inches.

Price, $22.

A pipe or cigar can be placed in the mouth, and by means of a long flexible tube fastened behind, the operator can give the figure the appearance of smoking by drawing on the tube.

LION WITH MORTAR.

Life size, with 30 inch Mortar,   - - - $280
Medium size, with 20 inch Mortar,   - - -   180

Gilded with Gold.

as steamboat, ferry, and pilot-boat deck ornaments (Col. Fig. 7). For a slightly higher price, and with different designs on the shield this figure was offered as a Mexican, Cuban, or any other country's Goddess of Liberty.

Nearly all the foundries had such figures in their catalogues at similar prices. This casting was the best known and perhaps the finest issued. A perfect figure is in The Downtown Gallery, New York (Figs. 45, 46).

Caffir Smoker No. 69 (Fig. 39). The figure represents a member of the South African Bantu tribe known as Kaffirs.

Mainly a display item, it had a pipe or cigar placed in the mouth. By drawing on a long flexible tube that fastened behind, the operator could give the figure the appearance of smoking. Demuth issued cast-metal smoking figures in a smaller size and in a number of interesting figures, including one of Buffalo Bill.

FEMALE INDIAN WITH SPEAR.

SITTING INDIAN.

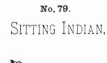

PUCK.

Height of Figure,	*5 ft. 7 in.*
Height of Pedestal,	*1 ft. 8 in.*
Total Height,	*7 ft. 3 in.*

PRICE $80.

Height of Figure,	*2 ft. 8 in.*
Height of Pedestal,	*3 ft. 3 in.*
Total Height,	*5 ft. 11 in.*

PRICE $42.

Height of Figure,	*4 ft. 9 in.*
Height of Pedestal,	*1 ft. 8 in.*
Total Height,	*6 ft. 5 in.*

PRICE $90.

Female Indian With Spear No. 76 (Fig. 40). This figure was added after the 1875 catalogue was printed. The spear was cast separately and added, but few survived the many uses found for it by street urchins and not-too-sober adults. From the casting, it is difficult to know if the figure is indeed female as none of the characteristics are apparent. Two are known in private collections.

Sitting Indian No. 79 (Fig. 40). A small but very graceful tobacconist's figure, admirably suited for placement outdoors near a side window to frame the shop without blocking off window displays.

The figure is sitting on a grouping of a bale of tobacco, pyramiding cigar boxes, snuff, and cut plug. Draped at his feet is a bunch of tobacco leaves and a jar of fine tobacco. The seated figure's turned body with arms to one side give it movement, and the entire composition is well designed. Four are known—one in a private collection, one in the Everhart Museum in Scranton, Pennsylvania, one in the Abby Aldrich Rocke-

feller Folk Art Collection in Williamsburg, Virginia, and one in the Stony Point Folk Art Gallery (See Fig. 44).

Puck (Fig. 41). A cast-metal figure that was popular for a short period of time.[39] This figure was based on the trademark conceived by Joseph Keppler for his weekly satirical magazine, *Puck*. Still standing in front of the old magazine building on Lafayette and Houston Streets, New York, is a large figure made from the wood model by the sculptor, Casper Buberl. This was the only near-nude figure made for Demuth and was a direct copy of the Buberl sculpture. Some poor but equally popular imitations were made in wood. In his left hand, Puck holds a large spearlike version of a pen, as if to prove that the "pen is mightier than the sword." An excellent example of the Demuth figure in original condition is in the Edison Institute, Dearborn, Michigan. It is signed "C. Buberl" and only the tips of the pen are gone (Col. Fig. 8).

METAL BUST FIGURES.

MALE BUSTS.

FEMALE BUSTS.

For Milliners, Dressmakers and Hair-Dressers.

3 kinds of faces.
Measurement around the Chest, 40 inches.
Price, $18.

Metal Bust for Boys' Clothing.
Height, 3 feet, 6 inches.
Price, $15.

Measurement: 24 inches Waist, 34 inches Bust.
Including Metal stand, as shown above, - - Price, $24
With movable arms attached, - - - Price, 36
Either of the above can be had with or without representa-
tion of hair.
With wig of real hair, $10 additional.

Male Busts (Fig. 42). These were made with three different facial hair styles.

A sample of the first type, without Dundreary sideburns (Fig. 43), is in the Costume Division of the Smithsonian Institution on loan from the Van Alstyne Folk Art Collection, and one was found in an amusement park in use as a ball-toss target. The second type appears in an engraving. The boy (Fig. 42) is poorly rendered, although the figure is attractive and in the proper proportions to have taken a full suit of clothes. The third type of male bust is in a private collection.

Female Busts (Fig. 42). For milliners, dressmakers and hairdressers.

Those made without representation of hair were adapted to the rapidly changing styles of hairdressing. At a later period, one French firm was producing busts in competition, which "breathed," by means of a set of bellows and clockwork in the cavity of the chest.[40]

FIG. 43

Fig. 43. Metal Male Bust. *Made for Wm. Demuth and Co. Similar to Figure 42 but without hairpiece and sideburns. Courtesy Smithsonian Institution.*

Fig. 44. Sitting Indian. *Same as No. 79. In cast zinc. Courtesy Stony Point Folk Art Gallery.*

FIG. 44

Figs. 45, 46. Goddess of Liberty. *Same as No. 58. In cast zinc. Height 73 inches. Said to have been used on the pilot boat* Columbia. *Courtesy The Downtown Gallery.*

A facsimile of figure 53 appeared in the Centennial in Philadelphia, the Columbian Exposition in Chicago (Fig. 48), and the 1884–1885 Cotton Exposition in New Orleans, winning two awards. It also won a gold medal at the Paris Exposition.[33] It appears in the J. L. Mott Iron Works' 1890 catalogue of Statuary and Animals, in a seventy-inch size, and the identical size bronzed (No. 53) cost $160. Mott had a factory on Beekman Street, New York, and on Wabash Avenue, Chicago. The figure is also represented in the 1891 catalogue of W. H. Mullins of Salem, Ohio.

A perfect example is in the collection of the American Tobacco Company's offices in New York. It bears a bronze plate placed there by the firm and inscribed, "Longfellow's Indian. This Indian was greatly admired by the famous poet Henry Wadsworth Longfellow and stood for years before a cigar store in Boston, Mass." In the basement storage area of the

Museum of History and Technology of the Smithsonian Institution, in the Van Alstyne Folk Art Collection, is a large wooden figure of the same dimensions as the cast-metal figure, and quite nearly identical in all details. The author noticed some scratches on the stump under the foot. The removal of asphaltum from the incised markings uncovered, "Robb. Manuf. 114 Centre Street." There was a second signature lower on the base (see Fig. 194). This figure was made after 1888 when Robb had moved from 195 Canal Street, Manhattan. Two other wooden figures in smaller sizes are known. One is in the collection of the Henry Francis duPont Winterthur Museum, Winterthur, Delaware, and the other is owned by the Detroit Bank & Trust Company.

Other figures not represented in the catalogue were issued at a later date. One of these in cast zinc was of a seated Negro, a stereotyped carica-ture with the usual expanse of collar and a wide grin. He was cross-legged, and in his right hand between thumb and forefinger, he held a cigar. The left thumb was stuck under the lapel of his tightly buttoned jacket. Under his chin was a jazzbow bowtie. One figure is at the Shelburne Museum in Vermont and another is in the Merritt Museum in Pennsylvania (See Fig. 221).

Fig. 47. *William Demuth in 1886, at the height of his career.*

Since it was impossible for Demuth's salesmen to carry actual samples, orders for the metal and wooden figures were taken from these catalogue pages. Success was immediate. In addition to the show-figure business, Demuth expanded his pipe business which was soon to become the largest in the world. He was fond of sailing, especially on Lake George, New York. He purchased property on its banks and proceeded to build a tow-ered villa near Bolton Landing. Here he entertained his clients in a grand manner and was reputed to be a wonderful host. He had a motor yacht, the *Geneva,* built to his specifications and had Robb make exquisite carvings for the interior and several figures for the top deck. Still later, he had a smaller boat built which he named the *Harriet,* for his new granddaughter.[41] Demuth delighted in having his friends address him as Commodore. He was a handsome man of medium height, usually in excellent spirits, with the confidence and security of a self-made millionaire (Fig. 47). He had a large staff at work in his factory on Thompson Street in New York. Orders came from western towns that cartographers had not yet entered on their maps. His showroom once again moved to larger quarters a few buildings up the street at 507–509 Broadway. He had Robb carve for him a seven-foot-long bent-shank pipe which he hung over the entrance to the showroom and which was to be a landmark for many years.[42] Demuth established branch offices on Madison Street in Chicago and on Pine Street in San Francisco. Many of his Indians and show figures turned up in small towns, a fact which has confused many folk art enthusiasts who did not

FIG. 48

suspect that these were of New York make, but attributed them to local "artists unknown."

Demuth also supplied various other signs such as eagles on balls, lions with mortars, opticians' glasses, and dentists' teeth. These devices came from the Seelig foundry or the Robb carving shop (Fig. 49). Demuth continued to supply figures well into the late 1890s.

William Demuth had three children, Louis, Edgar, and Amy. On his seventieth birthday, a large party was given for him and the program-menu contained several "poems" in English and German extolling the virtues of the guest of honor and recalling his life and successes. Among the guests were Professor Felix Adler, Mr. Isaac Stern, Walter Naumburg, descendents of Carl Schurz, and Leopold Demuth, a brother.[43] Leopold started in the shipping department of the Demuth business and later became manager of the pipe factory which employed one thousand workers producing approximately two hundred thousand units weekly. In later years Demuth would trust the operations of the business to his brother Leopold and his son Louis and spend more time at his Florida home and at his villa at Bolton Landing. At the age of seventy-six on June 29, 1911, Demuth died at his summer retreat. The business was taken over by his son, Louis, who died the following year, leaving the management of the firm in the hand of Leopold. Leopold Demuth died in 1943, having sold the business to Schulte in 1926.[44]

The success of Demuth's cast-metal figures was in large part due to the fine workmanship of the molds and the castings made by M. J. Seelig of Williamsburgh.

Fig. 48. Wm. Demuth & Co. exhibit in Agriculture Hall, Columbian Exposition, Chicago, 1893.

Fig. 49. Plaquette used between 1874 and 1885 on rear of half figures sold by Wm. Demuth & Co.

FIG. 49

FOUNDRIES

M. J. Seelig (1809–?)

Fig. 50. Moritz J. Seelig.

The foundry of Moritz J. Seelig, the Art Establishment, cast almost all of the zinc show figures for William Demuth and many for J. W. Fiske of New York (Fig. 50).

M. J. Seelig was born on December 25, 1809, at Annaberg in Saxony. As a small boy he often visited the family of a woodturner and was fascinated at the wonderful results on the spindle. One year near Christmastime, the various objects resulting from the turner's art left him with a desire to try his boyish skills, especially with plastic materials. Young Moritz made his first attempts at modeling and also became fond of carving. He was apprenticed to a wood-carver and turner and upon the termination of his apprenticeship, he went to Berne, Switzerland. In this congenial and sympathetic environment he was given employment carving decorated flower baskets.[45]

In the spring of 1828, he went to Italy to visit and study the art collections in Genoa, Florence, Rome, and other principal cities. Sculpture attracted him and, in his leisure time, he carved objects in ivory. Frequent attacks of fever forced him to return home, where he soon recovered. Afterward he departed for Warsaw. He participated in the 1830 revolution and received some wounds, spent six weeks in the hospital, and left the city. After his return to Saxony, he visited Dresden where he was permitted to copy models in the Mengs Museum. Some months later, he entered the atelier of Professor Rietschel, and at the same time became a pupil in the Dresden Art Academy, which entitled him to sit in on the lectures on anatomy and art history, as well as to model in the Art Hall.[46]

In Rietschel's atelier at that time were several important works including the monument of King Frederick Augustus, elector of Saxony and founder of the Dresden Library. After a four year's sojourn in Dresden, Seelig went to Professor Schwanthaler in Munich, where he worked on the statuary and other decorations of the Pinakothek (picture gallery), the Glyptothek (little sculpture gallery), the Walhalla, and the Royal Palace.

In 1839, Professor Semper, who had charge of the building of a new theatre, called Seelig to Dresden and commissioned him to make various ornaments and figures, among them the great Gothic fountain on Post Office Square. On the discovery of galvanoplastics (a method of zinc casting), by Jacobi in Petrograd, Seelig saw the great possibilities of a quick and inexpensive form of casting, applied himself with great effort to this method and succeeded in producing the first important work of this kind, a life-size statue of the heavily robed Muse, Melpomene. It was entered in the Industrial Fair in Dresden and received first prize, the grand gold medal worth twenty-five ducats.

After a long series of experiments, Seelig discovered a material for molds, which resisted the action of alkaline solutions, and adapted well to the manufacture of gold and silver ornaments.[47] In addition to his experiments in gold and silver, Seelig concentrated on bronze and zinc castings.

Like so many writers, artists, students, and other revolutionaries, Seelig took part in the unsuccessful Berlin revolution of 1849, and like Julius Theodore Melchers, another sculptor, Seelig was forced to leave Germany, ending his career in Europe. Arriving in New York in 1851, Seelig settled in Williamsburgh, then part of Long Island and now of Brooklyn, seeking ways to employ the new methods in zinc and bronze casting he had perfected in Germany. Since no firm existed for the production of zinc statuary, Seelig concentrated exclusively on producing samples far superior to those in use at that time. In 1852, Seelig was awarded the gold medal for a zinc casting in high relief for the exhibition of the American Institute in Castle Garden. This was the turning point and thereafter he received numerous commissions, for decorations for the Crystal Palace, for dwellings, and for architectural ornaments designed for commercial structures.[48]

Unlike Demuth, Seelig did not become Americanized easily, which was a disadvantage in his many negotiations. Because he could not expand to meet orders, his business suffered. Seelig made some efforts at integrating into his new environment but working in a small area near his home at 201 Ewen Street, and spending most of his time alone limited his contacts with the business world. In 1858, he established his zinc foundry in a small factory on Remsen Street. One attempt at Americanization was to change his name from Moritz to Morris and later to Maurice.[49] Living in a little wooden structure at 194 Lorimer Street, Seelig struggled with his foundry through the Civil War. The depression of 1857–58 nearly ruined him. A lawsuit with an agent lasted for five years and left him in a poor financial state.

In 1861, conditions were again favorable and some recovery was made. With orders coming in, he expanded his foundry, moving to 17 Maujer Street. In 1868–69 with encouragement and business from Demuth, he moved to larger quarters at 115–131 Maujer Street. Among the works produced by Seelig were three figures intended as garden decorations—*Spring, Autumn,* and the *Goddess of Liberty*—which received great praise and brought him many orders, encouraging him to use similar figures in his advertisements (Fig. 5). With this success he introduced new models, among which were Civil War memorials, classic figures and statues, lawn ornaments, his Demuth tobacconists' and show figures, and statues of antiquity. The *Moorish Queen* (See Fig. 35), one of the most popular of the Demuth figures, is based on the *Spring* figure by M. J. Seelig. A fine example, one made in Williamsburgh, Brooklyn, is now in the garden of the Abby Aldrich Rockefeller Folk Art Collection in Williamsburg, Virginia. One of Seelig's best-known zinc castings was of Robert Fulton. The large figure was placed in a niche in front of the facade of the Fulton Ferry Terminal on the Brooklyn side in 1873. The pedestal at Fulton's right was surmounted by a model of *Nassau*, the first steam ferryboat placed on the Fulton Ferry Line. The original model for the figure was made by the sculptor, Casper Buberl, who had also fashioned *Puck* for the Demuth line of show figures. When the terminal was demolished, the figure of Fulton was sent to the Museum of the City of New York where it is currently on view.[50]

In 1877, the Seelig foundry was taken over by Max Fleckenstein and Oscar Neubert, retaining the Seelig name. Neubert ran the foundry as a financially successful enterprise until 1896 when he offered "The Entire Plant For Sale."[51] (Fig. 51.)

The Seelig plant made castings for another firm specializing in iron castings, which was attracted by the success of the cast-zinc figures made for Demuth. This firm, J. W. Fiske, made weathervanes, railings, stable fixtures, and other types of iron items and, for a short time after 1879, produced show figures as well.

J. W. Fiske (1832–1903)

Joseph Winn Fiske was born in Chelmsford, Massachussets, in 1832, remaining there until 1853 when he decided to sell a line of hardware, tools, and other items made of iron in Melbourne, Australia. While in Australia, Fiske also went into the wholesale grocery line, operating from his plant—The Miner's Grocery Warehouse—on Swanton Street in Melbourne. With him in this enterprise as wine, spirit, and provisions merchants were H. W. Hawthorne and W. L. Hall. Five years later, after much experience, he returned to the United States, making plans to establish a factory for the manufacture of ironwork items in New York.[52] After operations began, Fiske devoted himself industriously to the production of fireplace equipment, brackets, and umbrella racks for the home; and for the outdoors, weathervanes, horse stable equipment and garden appliances.

The year 1858 saw the Lincoln-Douglas debates and intensification of the antislavery movement. The completion of the first transatlantic telegraph cable was hailed with wild enthusiasm and hopeful prospects for greater intercontinental commerce and harmony. The effects of the 1857 depression were still being felt but an air of optimism prevailed which encouraged Fiske to seek orders from newer areas. Fiske's offices were at

Fig. 51. Advertisement of M. J. Seelig & Co.

120 Nassau Street and in 1868 he was at 99 Chambers Street, afterward setting up a factory at 21 and 23 Barclay Street in Manhattan. Fiske added architectural ornamental iron and a number of other cast-iron products to his catalogue and increased the volume of his business. His Barclay Street factory spread to include additional space at 26 and 28 Park Place, at the corner of Church Street, adjacent to his plant.

About 1878 or 1879, ten years after Demuth first introduced the metal show figure, Fiske went into the manufacture of cast-metal figures and emblematic signs. There is no record in the copyright office to indicate that Fiske requested protection. Few metal show figures made for Fiske have survived. The attractive iron *Jockey*, while not a show figure, was and has remained a famous symbol, best known as a hitching post. It was also intended for use as a stable and harness-maker's sign. Fiske had a zinc jockey as his own sign and "used to run it out morning and evening. It was on a platform with wheels." The patterns for this and the *Chinaman* were made by Frederick W. Kaiffer who had his own carving shop at 157 Wooster Street in Manhattan.[53]

The engravings, unfortunately, are of poor quality, but the actual figures are most attractive, and show excellent work in the details and construction. It must be remarked that, except where noted, all engravings show the figures reversed, i.e., right is left and left is right. Only the tobacconist's and trade show figures are here represented.

DARKEY.

No. 302.—3 ft. 10 in. high.
One coat paint.......... $50 00
Life color............... 55 00

J.W.FISKE.

JOCKEY.

J.W.FISKE.¥. No. 304.—4 ft. 4 in. high.
One coat paint.......... $60 00
Life color............... 65 00

CHINESE.

No. 303.—4 feet high.
One coat paint.......... $60 00
Life color............... 65 00

J.W. FISKE.

Colored Boy No. 302 (Fig. 52). Called a *Darkey* in Fiske's first issue of this catalogue, it was used primarily as a hitching post.

Chinaman No. 303 (Fig. 52). An interesting figure made for tea and coffee shops
and also adapted as a hitching post. One such figure without the fan is in the
Merritt Museum in Douglasville, Pennsylvania.

Jockey No. 304 (Fig. 52). One of the most popular and copied of all trade signs,
used by harness-makers, saddlery shops, riding habit shops, blacksmiths, and
horseshoers. Also used as a hitching post for horses, as shown. Today, the famous
"21" Club in New York has its stoop decorated with many of these figures wearing
racing stable colors. Reproductions are now sold as garden ornaments.

CAST ZINC FIGURES.

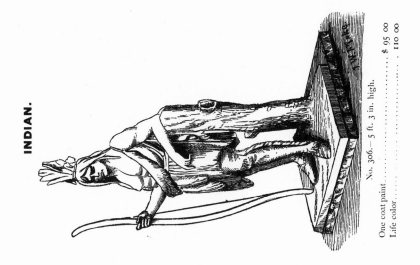

INDIAN.

No. 306.—5 ft. 3 in. high.
One coat paint..............$ 95 00
Life color...............110 00

SAILOR.

No. 305.—5 ft. 4 in. high.
One coat paint..............$ 95 00
Life color...............110 00

Sailor No. 305 (Fig. 53). For use as a ship chandler's sign and in other maritime capacities, it was also intended as a tobacconist's sign. None is known to exist today.

Indian No. 306 (Fig. 53). Like the sailor, this was a "leaner" figure made popular by the tobacconists' figures carved by Thomas V. Brooks between 1855 and 1875 and later. One such figure whose base bore a plate reading "J. W. Fiske, manufacturers, 26–28 Park Place," was sold in 1956 in auction.[54]

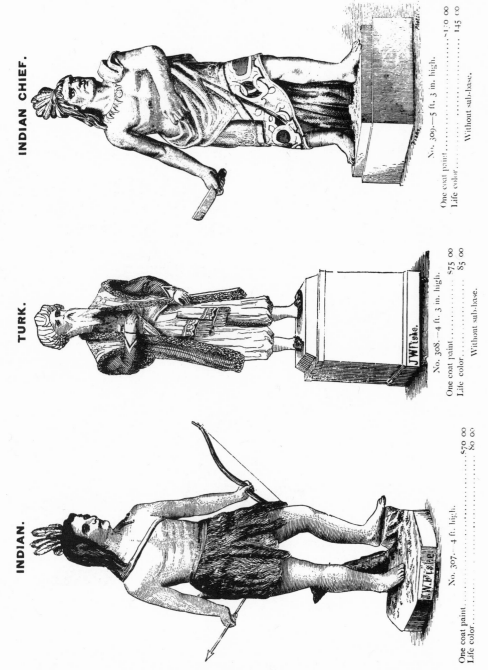

Indian No. 307 (Fig. 54). Another Indian, described in the catalogue as a cigar sign but without the symbols of the trade. No such figure is known to exist.

Turk No. 308 (Fig. 54). This figure was made to hold a long pipe, to be supplied by the purchaser. The name, address, brand of tobacco, or other information could be painted on the base, if requested, at an extra charge. No surviving figure is known.

Indian Chief No. 309 (Fig. 54). A dramatic pose but carrying none of the identifying emblems of the cigar or tobacco trade. No such figure is known to exist.

CAST ZINC CIGAR AND TEA SIGNS.

INDIAN.

No. 312.—3 ft. 4 in. high.
One coat paint............$35 00
Life color................45 00

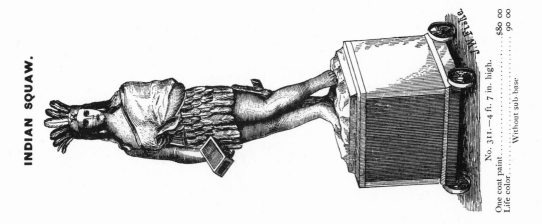

INDIAN SQUAW.

No. 311.—4 ft. 7 in. high.
One coat paint............$80 00
Life color................90 00
Without sub-base

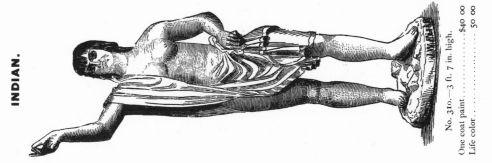

INDIAN.

No. 310.—3 ft. 7 in. high.
One coat paint............$40 00
Life color................50 00

Indian No. 310 (Fig. 55). If the catalogue page did not indicate that this was a cast-zinc cigar-sign, it would be impossible to identify it as such. Like No. 312, it has none of the accessories of the tobacco business.

Indian Squaw No. 311 (Fig. 55). An attractive tobacconist's figure sold without the wheeled pedestal. Painted to life it was $10 etxra. A similar but not exact figure is in the Merritt Museum, Douglasville, Pennsylvania.

Indian No. 312 (Fig. 55). The arm in the engraving is misrepresented. The hand should be shown over the eyes, shading the sun. Like No. 310, this figure has none of the accessories of the tobacconist's trade or tribal dress usually associated with the familiar cigar-store sign.

TURK.

No. 315.—4 ft. 3 in. high.
One coat paint. $75 00
Life color 85 00

J.W. Fiske.

JAPANESE.

No. 314.—4 ft. 7 in. high.
One coat paint. $75 00
Life color. 85 00
Without sub-base.

J.W. Fiske.

CHINESE WOMAN.

No. 313.—4 ft. 3 in. high.
One coat paint. $70 00
Life color. 80 00
Without sub-base.

Chinese Woman No. 313 (Fig. 56). Like No. 303, this figure was to be used in front of tea shops with the brand of tea or the seller's name painted on the wooden base. None is known to exist.

Japanese No. 314 (Fig. 56). Made as a tea-shop sign, the figure is somewhat similar to the tea show figure of Demuth. This figure was used by shops specializing in the Japanese leaf tea. None is known to exist.

Turk No. 315 (Fig. 56). An impressive figure equipped with the hardware of aggression to attract the attention of man and boy, but diminished by its small size. None is known to exist.

BACCHUS. (Cast Zinc.)   **GAMBRINUS.** (Cast Zinc.)

Height to top of head, 2 feet 9 inches.
Height to top of glass, 3 feet 6 inches.
Stump, 12 inches high.
Base, 13x13 inches.

Price, One coat..................$70 00
"   Life color.......................... 75 00

Height to top of head, 2 feet 9 inches.
Height to top of glass, 3 feet 6 inches.
Height of barrel, 10 inches.
Base, 13x13 inches.

Price, One coat...................$70 00
„   Life color............ ...... 75 00

☞Any other size or design of figures modelled to order at short notice on reasonable terms.

Bacchus No. 400 (Fig. 57). This figure was made in two sizes. The smaller intended for use in windows of grog shops, and the larger in saloons, breweries, and for advertising malt products.

Gambrinus No. 401, 402. (Fig. 57). This figure was made in two sizes. The larger one, 123 inches in height, was an imposing figure when used as a building decoration over the Gunther Brewery in Newark, and another used in a hofbrau was so large that a hole had to be cut in the ceiling to accommodate it.[55]

INDIAN HUNTER AND DOG. (Cast Zinc.)

J.W.FISKE N.Y.

	One Coat Paint		Bronzed.
No. 210.—6 feet 6 inches high, with dog,	$275 00		300 00
No. 210½.—6 feet 6 inches high, Indian alone	225 00		250 00

Indian Hunter and Dog No. 210, 210½ (Fig. 58). This engraving shows the figure in its correct position, the dog on the left side. A very handsome and impressive figure, no doubt representing Alexander Pope's "Poor Lo and his faithful dog." An excellent example of this figure is in the Merritt Museum, Douglasville, Pennsylvania. The bronze, *Indian Hunter*, by John Q. A. Ward (1864) may have been its inspiration.

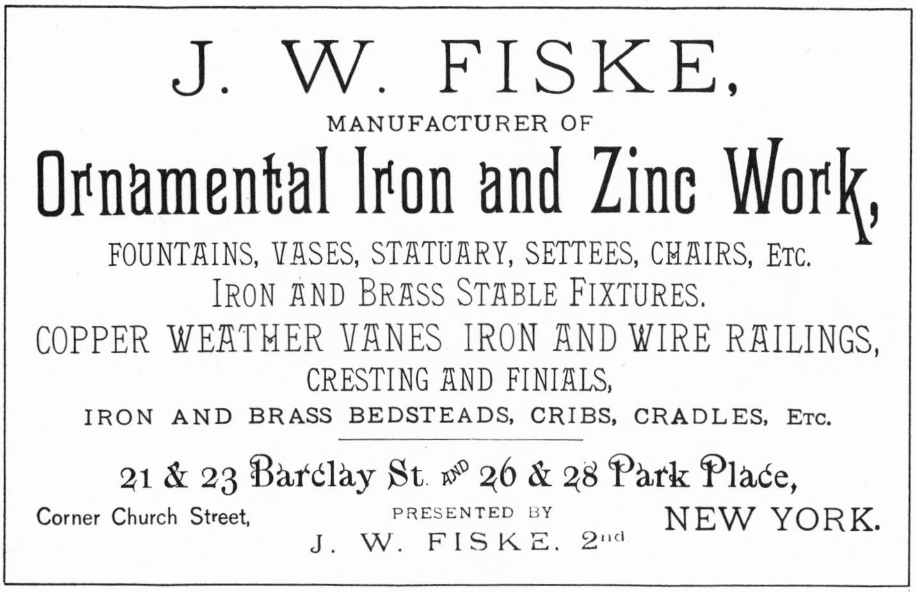
J. W. FISKE,
MANUFACTURER OF
Ornamental Iron and Zinc Work,
FOUNTAINS, VASES, STATUARY, SETTEES, CHAIRS, ETC.
IRON AND BRASS STABLE FIXTURES.
COPPER WEATHER VANES IRON AND WIRE RAILINGS,
CRESTING AND FINIALS,
IRON AND BRASS BEDSTEADS, CRIBS, CRADLES, ETC.

21 & 23 Barclay St. AND 26 & 28 Park Place,
Corner Church Street, PRESENTED BY J. W. FISKE, 2nd NEW YORK.

Fig. 59. Fiske business card.

Later catalogues show that these figures were dropped with the exception of the hitching-post figure. Like Demuth, Fiske issued metal dressmaker and tailor figures, the *Goddess of Liberty*, and the identical figure to *Indian Chief* No. 53, issued by Demuth.

There have been only three company presidents in the century of Fiske's history. The founder served in that capacity until his death in 1903. He was succeeded by his nephew John M. Fiske, who like his brother, Joseph W. Fiske II, came from Boston as a young man to join the firm. Warren R. Fiske, the incumbent, entered the employ of the company in 1911, later becoming secretary and then also the treasurer. He succeeded to the presidency when John M. Fiske died in 1942. Joseph W. Fiske II died in 1930. On May 18, 1956, the firm moved to Paterson, New Jersey. The J. W. Fiske Architectural Metals, Inc., celebrated its one-hundreth anniversary in 1958. The firm still makes weathervanes but is mainly engaged in the making of facades for commercial establishments (Fig. 59).[56]

The Miller, Dubrul & Peters Manufacturing Co.

For a while during the 1880s, The Miller, Dubrul & Peters Manufacturing Co. had some of its usual items cast in metal for resale to customers. These casts included creaseless cigar molds, cigar shapers, cigar cutters, ribbons, and presses. The company maintained factories at 165 to 169 East Pearl Street in Cincinnati, Ohio, and at 413 to 417 East 31st Street in New York City. A single sheet catalogue was issued with the illustration of an Indian on one side and the following message on the other (Figs. 60a, 60b):

Dear Sir:

On the opposite side of this we hand you a picture in color of an *Indian Show Figure*, the manufacture of which we have added to our business.

DEAR SIR:

On the opposite side of this we hand you a picture in colors of an *Indian Show Figure*, the manufacture of which we have added to our business.

This figure is made of Metal throughout, painted in colors true to nature, the design and execution of same in all details has been pronounced perfect by many who are able critics in work of arts.

Especial attention was given by the Artist to the production of a face expressive of all the characteristics of a true

NORTH-AMERICAN INDIAN.

No time or labor was spared in making the figure throughout a work of art; in order to accomplish which museums and private colections were made use of for the dress weapons, etc.

As a figure for advertising purposes, we feel certain its equal has not yet been produced, and it is sure to receive attention by all lovers of Art, and thus accomplish the object of the purchaser more fully and bring his place of business before the public more continuously with better effect and at a less cost than by any other means of advertising.

HEIGHT OF FIGURE, - - - - 6 Feet,
HEIGHT OF PEDESTAL, - - - - 1 Foot 5 Inch.
    TOTAL HEIGHT, - - - - 7 Feet 5 Inch.

⊨PRICE FURNISHED ON APPLICATION.⊣

We call your attention to our latest Catalogue of

Creaseless Cigar Molds, | *Ribbons,*
   Cigar Shapers, | *Presses,*
      Cigar Cutters, | *Etc., Etc., Etc.*

In this Catalogue will be found illustrations of over 1300 Cigar-Shapes, including all the latest sizes with other information, valuable to the enterprising Cigar Manufacturer, which will be mailed on application, free, from either our Cincinnati or New York Factory.   Respectfully Yours,

The Miller, Dubrul & Peters M'f'g Co.

165 TO 169 EAST PEARL ST., | **413 TO 417 EAST 31ST STREET,**
     CINCINNATI. | **NEW YORK.**

FIG. 60a

FIG. 60b

Figs. 60a, 60b. The single sheet catalogue issued by Miller, Dubrul & Peters Manufacturing Company.

This figure is made of Metal throughout, painted in colors true to nature, the design and execution of same in all details has been pronounced perfect by many who are able critics in work of arts.

Especial Attention was given by the Artists to the production of a face expressive of all the characteristics of a true

NORTH-AMERICAN INDIAN

No time or labor was spared in making the figure throughout a work of art; in order to accomplish which museums and private collections were made use of for dress weapons, etc.

As a figure for advertising purposes, we feel certain its equal has not yet been produced, and it is sure to receive attention by all lovers of art, and thus accomplish the object more continuously with better effect and at a less cost than by any other means of advertising.

Height of Figure, ...	6 Feet
Height of Pedestal, ...	1 Foot 5 Inch
Total of Height, ...	7 Feet 5 Inch

Price furnished on Application[57]

At one time, the figure was owned by Anthony W. Pendergast who sold it to C. E. Hegerty of Coalport, Pennsylvania. Another is in a private collection in Texas. Other castings of Indians have casting marks bearing the name of Henry Dibblee Iron Works. In 1879, Dibblee was at 276 Wabash Avenue, Chicago, Illinois.[58]

J. L. Mott Iron Works (c.1875–1939)

Another New York firm, the J. L. Mott Iron Works, was located at 84–90 Beekman Street, with a branch in Chicago at 311 and 313 Wabash Avenue. In its 1890 copyrighted catalogue of statuary and animals appear three figures identical to those in the Demuth catalogue of 1875. These are the *Indian Chief, Moorish Queen,* and *Goddess of Liberty*. The J. L. Mott catalogue lists them as follows:

Indian Chief   Height to top of head—5′ 10″—to top of feathers—6′ 7″
                Base—1′ 6½″ Square—Painted $150.00   Bronzed $160.00
Oriental Girl Height 5′ 4″—base 1′ 5″ Square   Painted $111.00   Bronzed $121.00
Liberty   Height 4′ 11″—base 1′ 3″ x 1′ 3″   Painted one coat $90.00
                Bronzed $100.00

The *Oriental Girl* held a bouquet of flowers in her hand instead of cigars. Liberty was made three different ways by J. L. Mott, with a flagstaff, with a sword, and identical to the Demuth figure. The *Indian Chief* is also identical to a Demuth figure. The Mott catalogue shows the imprint of the firm on the entire bottom of the base and not on a plaquette.[59]

Fig. 61c. *A South Street ship and show-figure carver's shop in 1879. Pencil drawing by H. Murman for Scribner's Monthly.*

4 · The Art of
Show-Figure Carving

THE EIGHTH CENSUS of the United States, taken in 1860, shows that there were 2,269 wood-carvers in the United States and its territories. New York led all other states with 959, Massachusetts was second with 369, and Pennsylvania followed with 340. Maine had 34, as did Kentucky, with Kansas, Florida, Minnesota, and Mississippi and some other states having none. However, the census did not show the specialties of the wood-carvers. In some states at this time, there were a few carvers who limited their work to the ornamentation of ships and the carving of figures for tobacconists and other tradesmen, as signs to be put in front of their shops. Of this small group, those that made the transition from shipcarver to show-figure carving were even fewer. "The art of carving wooden figures is well-nigh as old as the hills, but so few persons are engaged in it that little is known about it. The figures for the most part are used for cigar signs."[1]

According to one carver: "Twelve to fourteen years of apprenticeship is necessary to make a competent workman, and that accounts for the scarcity of good hands, for the wages are low and the demand limited."[2] An examination of census reports for shipcarvers' apprentices finds that most of these names do not appear in subsequent reports, indicating either a casualty or, more likely, a dropout. Another one said, "Learn the trade? . . . Yes, indeed, I've been at it since I was thirteen years old. There are very few in the business. A good man can make four dollars, sometimes five dollars a day, chopping out wooden Indians."[3] That was in 1886. Another commented, "The carvers are paid four dollars a day, but the work is unsteady, and only a poor average is made at the end of the year, as orders come and go irregularly, and a workman may call every day for a month, and find no figure in the embryo stage of order [Fig. 61a]."[4]

In 1886, Samual A. Robb, whose shop was the largest in the city and probably the country, stated; "There never were over a dozen carvers here in New York at one time. There are not over six here now."[5]

For an ordinary six foot Indian, a foot per day is good carving, and painting and finishing runs at the same rate of speed, making twelve days in all. For the larger and elaborate figure a month or more is occupied, according to the degree of finish required. The sizes run from eighteen inches high to eight feet.[6]

The price of these figures varies greatly. You can get a small Indian for $16, or you can indulge your artistic taste up to the tune of $125, Metal figures run up as high as $175.[7]

It is found that Indians are most in demand, but orders from inland cities run close to clowns, betting men, dudes, pucks, and sometimes a Pickwick, or a King, and the price varies from ten dollars to five hundred.[8]

Indian figures are divided into classes. An Indian with his hand shading his eyes is a "scout." If he has a gun, or a bow and arrows in his hand, he is a "hunting chief." If his head, except the scalp lock is shaved and the body partly naked, he is a "Captain Jack." A figure carrying a small basket is a "flower girl," and another nearly similar but with a robe is a "shawl figure." A running posture constitutes a "fly figure." "Fashions in fancies," as the non-Indian figures are called, change greatly. During the war [Civil War] the "Girl of the Period" was in great demand, "Punches" succeeded, and were followed by "Pucks." "Dudes" are just now a drug in the market, as they have been lately supplanted by "baseball players." Ten Indian figures to one fancy is the proportion in which they are sold.[9]

We also take battered and weather-stained figures and put on an ear here or a nose there, or paint a blind eye into life again, rig them out in a brand new suit of clothes, and there they are. . . . Oh, of course styles change, but the genuine old roving redskin with a bad eye and an ugly-looking tomahawk in his hand is the stand-by—that is, in the majority of the eastern and middle States. When you get way out west there is quite a run of just such flash Bowery girls as I am painting up here now. Dudes had quite a go for a while. I have got fully twenty-five dudes planted around in Brooklyn and New York even now, though dudes are on the wane; and Pucks, that were so popular a few years ago, are now so much dead wood on your hands. Scotchman has gone for good, I guess, though I hear he is still all the go over in England. But the plain old war-whoop savage of the plains is the only chap you can bank on as steadily trustworthy. Indian maidens do very well, but not so well as the fine old gore-drinking warriors, with feathers and meat axes.[10]

Fig. 61a. Carver at Work. Harper's Weekly, *January 6, 1883.*

Fig. 61b. Cigar and Tobacco Shop Signs. *Drawn from life by T. Frenzlau. Unidentified shop.* Harper's Weekly, *January 6, 1883.*

The method of show-figure carving was essentially the same as that used in the carving of ships's figures. After creating a design, the carver of tobacconists' figures would cut out a paper or cardboard pattern of a frontal view and another of a side view. These were saved for use when a duplicate figure was ordered. Details could be changed as desired by the tradesmen. Paper and cardboard patterns of the same style of figure were made in different sizes and kept on hand. At one time racks of these patterns of Indians in all sizes and of both sexes were in the shop of Samuel A. Robb. There were also Punches, Pucks, Turks, Sultans, Dundrearys, baseball players, Walter Raleighs, Girls of the Period, dudes, Scotsmen, policemen, theatrical figures, and many others (Fig. 61b).[11]

The wood most used was white pine. The carver would visit the spar yards to select the butt ends of the masts of ships which were the ends left over when the new masts were cut to fit, before being stepped in the vessel. Most of the spars came from the Erie Basin spar yards, and were available in lengths from three to eight feet or longer if the order called for it. The grain was straight, the wood was easily cut and carved, it came in desirable lengths and widths already prepared, and was inexpensive.[12] The wood cut more easily when green than when seasoned and was less liable to split.

While the carving is mostly done by the eye, chalk or pencil lines are drawn on the log for the general contour. The figure, if it is intended to represent a human form, is made eight times the length of the head. . . . The artist begins by making the roughest kind of an outline—a mere suggestion of what the proportions of the figure are to be. In this he is guided by paper patterns. The log is blocked out with the axe into appropriate spaces for the head, the body down to the waist, the portion from there to the knee, the rest of the legs (which are divided at once), and the feet. In its present embryo state the figure to be cut is not very apparent to the eye. The feeling for form in the chopped block is so very elementary as to have complete suggestiveness only for the practiced artist.

A hole is now bored into each end of the prepared log, about five inches deep. Into each of these holes an iron bolt is placed, the projecting parts of which rest on supports, so that the body hangs free. The carver now goes from the general to the particular. The surface of the wood soon becomes chipped up by the chisel, and the log generally takes on more definite form. Then, when the figure is completely evolved, the finishing touches are put on with finer carving tools. Detached hands and arms are made separately and joined on to the body by screws.[13]

The limbs were cut so that the grain would run the long way to prevent their breaking off. When the figure was a very large one, a long pipe was used so that it could be carried by one or more men on each end. Sometimes the pipe or bolt, placed in the center of the log at each end of the figure, could not be removed without splitting the figure and was left in. The hole left by a removed bolt or pipe prompted one of the foremost collectors of tobacconists' figures of recent times to allow oil to seep down into the figure to keep it from drying out and splitting. Actually, linseed oil forms a heavy film at the bottom which keeps it from deeply penetrating the wood; in any case, it could not have penetrated more than another inch or two. Consequently, many figures which this collector treated and which have since entered collections of museums throughout the country, have a residue of linseed oil in the hole in the head.

Sometimes, both figure and shipcarvers prepared sketches or drawings for special figures; or, upon the request of a special client, a sketch complete with colors was prepared for approval. Charles J. Hamilton and John Philip Yaeger left behind such illustrations. William Rush supplied the design of the *Hercules* figurehead for the frigate *Constitution*, and also elaborate designs for the figureheads of six other frigates. Charles J. Dodge supplied a design for a head eighty-seven and one-half inches long, and many sketches by John W. Mason still exist.[14]

Carvers had reference books to which they could refer, and some kept scrapbooks filled with engravings of costumes from all over the world. Others kept pages of animals, historical figures, and statues from antiquity (Fig. 61c).[15] These could serve as reference when a special type of figure was ordered. No doubt, the large number of engravings of eagles available were influential in the carver's rendering of this emblem for the poop decks of steamboats, stern carvings, and escutcheons.

The carver, although capable, did not always produce Indians that could be identified with any particular tribe. Not too much attention was paid to authenticity of costume or headdress, although the paintings of George Catlin were undoubtedly known to most of them. (The exception was

Fig. 61d. Three Squaws. *Carved and painted wood. Formerly in the collection of Anthony W. Pendergast.*

Julius Theodore Melchers, who was an authority on Indian lore and owned a vast collection of Indian artifacts.) In an answer to why this was so, Samuel A. Robb replied: "Fidelity to nature or artistic beauty is not much looked to. That Indian," pointing to a melancholy flat-nosed chief, "was done from life, and we can't sell him. Buyers complain that he is too ugly. What they want is something fine looking and attractive [Figs. 61d, 61e]."[16]

At one time or another, many of the carvers worked in each other's shops, either in the capacity of apprentice, journeyman, shop foreman, or partner. This may account for the similarity in style and appearance of a great number of the existing show figures and was true not only of New York, but also of Baltimore and Detroit, although there was greater individuality in these latter cities. Outside of these three cities, carvers were inclined to follow the styles set by the New York carvers, perhaps to satisfy the demand from the local merchants. In several cases, the style of the carver was so distinctive that it could be identified at once. This was particularly true of Rush, Jobin, Melchers, Yaeger, Brooks, and Robb.

The industrial revolution in America had its effect on the show-figure carving shop as well. Mass production methods were used and the work departmentalized. One man was assigned to chopping the log with an axe, one or two inches from the penciled or chalked line taken from the paper or cardboard pattern. A carver would then take over and bring it to a recognizable form. Another carver would do the finishing. A boy who was paid seventy-five cents a day did the sandpapering, and the figure was given a base with wheels and sent to the paint shop on a different floor.[17] Delivery was made by wagon, if local, and by rail or ship, if out of town.

The typical carver never referred to himself as a sculptor or to the art of carving figures as sculpture. "Sculpturing? No, we don't call it that; just plain chopping."[18] They said they were "cutting," instead of "carving" a figure or figurehead or just a "head." However, the city directories always listed them under the category of "Carvers," or "Show Figure Carvers." Occasionally, when first starting out on his own, the carver would list himself as a "sculptor," as did Charles J. Hamilton and James A. Brooks. Julius Theodore Melchers of Detroit held his talents in high esteem and listed himself all during his career as "sculptor." The most enterprising of the show-figure carvers, Samuel A. Robb, when replying to the question of occupation on his marriage certificate, filled in, "Artist in Wood," from which this book derives its title.[19]

The work of the show-figure carver has been called, "folk art," "advertising art," "decorative art," and "primitive art." There are enough show figures to fit all these labels, and it would not be difficult to find a group of tobacconists' figures that would neatly fit each category. Commercial art would be a correct catchall for most of them as they were created to advertise a product. Whereas the carvers strove for realism to a degree that would class their work as "representational," realism was especially desirable during the period of American art development when professional sculptors, fresh from their visits to the galleries and ateliers of Europe, were infused with the ideals and techniques of the classic and the Beaux Arts movements. Thomas J. White even produced a *Greek Slave* and an *Adam and Eve*.[20]

The large wood sculpture of Julius Theodore Melchers would identify him with those artists trained by a known sculptor rather than by a ship-carver. Louis Jobin of Canada adapted his experience in ship- and show-figure carving to religious carving, a transition from savages to saints. When the show-figure carver was called upon for work of finer quality and a higher degree of art, for which he would be adequately paid for his time and labors, he was capable of fulfilling the requirement. In 1854, when the W. A. Brintzlinghofer tobacco shop in Newark wanted a tobacconist's "statue" of Osceola, the great Seminole chief, Thomas V. Brooks carved this figure at the reputed cost of $750.[21] Melchers also carved a very large Indian, perhaps Chief Keokuk (see Fig. 127), for which he received a large sum. But William Rush had to request from the Select and Common Councils of Philadelphia an equitable price for his wood carving of General Washington:

First the figure is my property and executed by myself some eighteen or nineteen years past. I wish it in a perpetual place in the Hall that it may be said that a prophet may obtain some honor in his native place. I think that you need not have any doubts as to its being a good likeness. I have modelled General Washington

Fig. 61e. Going for His Scalp. *Two inebriated dudes, on being expelled from a Third Avenue Tobacco Store, vent their rage on the harmless Indian sign.* The National Police Gazette, *January 5, 1884.*

in his lifetime frequently in miniature and as large as life. Judge Washington pronounced the figure here alluded to immediately on sight, a better likeness than Stuart's. [Gilbert Stuart, the painter.] Also I am disposed to sell it, if I can obtain a liberal compensation. When the Exchange was building at Baltimore Dr. Dennis Smith offered me $500 which I refused, as it would scarcely pay me for the mere labor of nearly four months. I have been above sixty years in my business and probably have exhibited some humble talents that would entitle me to consideration more than a mere laborer. The figure is excavated and saturated with oil, and would be as durable as any furniture in a room covered from the weather.

The figure, carved in 1814 and now in the Philadelphia Museum of Art, was purchased, "at a price not exceeding $500, the statue of Washington offered for sale by William Rush, Esq., and the same be charged to appropriation No. 21."[22]

The wood portrait by Charles J. Dodge of his father, Jeremiah Dodge, shipcarver, also reveals the portraiture ability of the ship- and show-figure carver (see Fig. 151).

Like artists and sculptors who work in isolation;

The carvers are taciturn men, to whom the constant carving of the stolid Indian features appears to have imparted a solemnity of visage and mind, and if a remark of levity is heard, their expressionless eyes are raised for a moment from the clear-cut wooden face beneath their hands, and dropped again with a wordless air of reproach. Owing to the scarcity of employment, the carvers may be said not to work much, but they chew incessantly, and snuff is, in a large measure their masticatory weakness.

As a rule they take great pride in their work and spend much time in perfecting a feature to their mind, which they could finish in much less time if they were less artistically conscientious.[23]

"Are they Italians who do this artistic work?" "Not a bit of it. Your Italian is good enough in plaster but he's nowhere in wood. They are all Yankees. . . . The foreigners don't catch on, somehow, but the Yankees take to chopping out wooden images just as they do to whittling a pine shingle."[24]

The figure carvers, unlike modelers in clay or other plastic media, were subtractors of the solid. Instead of adding clay upon clay or plaster upon plaster, they cut away from a solid mass. We say that a carving is primitive when it suggests a form, but lacks finishing or details, yet the artisan-craftsman may have had another idea in mind—an economy of time and material—or purely economic reasons if his customer ordered an inexpensive figure.

The sculptors of the 1920s, notably Henry Moore, John B. Flanagan, and William Zorach, picked up this technique of cutting away as little as possible from a block of stone, wood, or plaster. The carver of figureheads and tobacconists' figures tried to create realistic figures within the scope of his ability, and the end results, at times, may be called folk art; but in whatever category his work may be placed, we appreciate its contribution to the varied forms of American sculpture.

Fig. 65. Bandchariot. *Constructed by Fielding Brothers for Adam Forepaugh. Courtesy New-York Historical Society.*

5 · Circus Wagons–
Builders and Carvers

THE CIRCUS originated with the Romans to celebrate the consecration of the gods. The first circus built in Rome was undertaken by Lucius Tarquin, fifth king of Rome. The Circus Parade or Pomp consisted of a procession with sacrifices offered to the gods and was the forerunner of the Circus Parade as we knew it earlier in this century. A ceremony preceded the games which consisted of seven kinds of exercises. The first was a contest—combat with sword or club or with a pike; the second was a foot race; the third, dance; the fourth, competition with the discus or quoits; and the fifth, a horse race and exercises in horsemanship in which the young people of Rome participated. The sixth consisted of chariot races with two or four horses; the seventh, combats between gladiators on foot, and between men and wild beasts (Fig. 62). Much later, another type of exercise was introduced—the arena was flooded and naval battles took place.[1]

With the decline and fall of the Roman Empire, the circus and its parade disappeared for nearly a millennium. The spirit of the circus was

Fig. 62. Roman Circus

reborn in England with the introduction of fairs, traveling jugglers, acrobats, musicians, and trained animal acts. In 1133, King Henry I gave a charter for Bartholomew Fair to Rayer, a monk who was once a court jester. It endured for seven centuries and was proclaimed for the last time in 1855.[2] By then, the procession or circus parade in America was just beginning to get rolling.

On April 13, 1796, Jacob Crowninshield, a native of Salem, Massachusetts, captain of the ship *America*, sailed into New York harbor with a strange cargo—a three-year-old female elephant, the first to be seen in this country. The elephant, bought in India for $450, was sold for $10,000 to a Philadelphian named Owen, who took it on tours of the cities and towns on the eastern seaboard until about 1818. By the 1820s, many shows with wild, exotic animals in cages were on the road.[3] By 1828, Buckley and Wicks's Circus ventured out into the eastern areas with forty horses, eight wagons, thirty-five people, and a tent of seventy-five feet diameter accommodating eighty-eight spectators. For the next twenty or more years, the cage wagons were strong but simple affairs of light construction and with no ornamentation. As early as 1837, Purdy and Welch seem to have been the first of the traveling shows to travel with a band and a show parade.[4]

Parades were not unknown in early America. There were historical parades, political parades, military parades, and parades for other special occasions. The circus parade was among the most colorful and the most exciting to the senses; the sight of wild beasts in their cages or on foot, the roars of strange animals, the sound of bands, and the special smells. Isaac A. Van Amburgh, who astonished the country by entering a cage of wild animals on the stage of the Richmond Hill Theatre in New York in 1833, formed his own company, which he took on tour. On April 20, 1845, Van Amburgh's Triumphal Car passed down Broadway in New York, and an existing lithograph shows it in front of the Astor House, on the west side of Broadway, between Vesey and Barclay Streets. Also called a "Roman Chariot or, Imperial State Carriage and Throne," this bandwagon was twenty feet long, seventeen feet high, and the first of the telescoping circus wagons. The canopy, topped by a carved eagle, was supported by a dolphin on each side and could be lowered for passing under bridges.

The *Armamaxa* or *Imperial Persian Chariot* (Fig. 63) was introduced at the Bowery Amphitheatre (more accurately known as the New York Amphitheatre) at Number 37 Bowery, just above Bayard Street and a short distance below where Chichester was to open his "wooden Indian store." This large bandwagon had as its main feature two huge dragons carved for the front. A driver sat on a bench held between their upswept wings. Drawn by thirty horses, the chariot was manufactured by John Stephenson at 47 East 27th Street between what is now Madison and Fourth Avenues. He constructed the chariot for the Welch, Delevan & Nathan National Circus in 1846 or early 1847. The carvings were made by John L. Cromwell with the assistance of those working in his shop, one of whom was Thomas V. Brooks, almost at the end of his apprenticeship and about to open his own shop.[5] According to the advertisement:

This gorgeous Chariot, from the manufactory of J. Stephenson & Co., 27th St. New York has just been completed. For its graceful portions, exquisite workmanship, and brilliant emblazonry it has never been equalled either in ancient or modern times. It is said to be fashioned after the model of the Imperial Chariots of Persia, during the reign of Cyrus the Great. The sides of the chariot are divided into six panels, separated by richly gilded scroll work in the style of Louis XIV. The scroll work is bordered by beautiful frill moulding, and runs along the top as well as the bottom of the chariot. The seat of the charioteer is covered with a rich hammercloth of purple velvet trimmed with deep silver fringe, pendant from a border of blue and yellow velvet, the whole decorated with eagles, equestrian figures, stars and flowers, wrought in gold and silver. The carioteer appears borne along between the expanded wings of two mighty dragons, apparently of massive gold, which crouch above the fore wheels of the chariot.[6]

The descriptions as well as the carvings were a forerunner of the art of the copywriter and the carver.

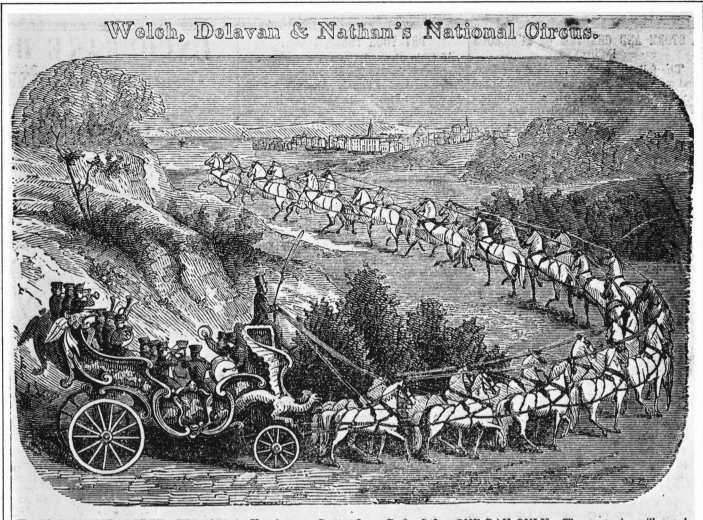

J. W. BANCKER, AGENT.—Will exhibit in **Xenia, on Saturday, July 8th.** ONE DAY ONLY. The procession will parade through town at about 10 o'clock, A. M. Admission **25** cents—no half price. Open at 2½ and 7½ o'clock, P. M.

THE ARMAMAXA, *Or Imperial Persian Chariot, Drawn by 30 Horses.*—This gorgeous Chariot, from the manufactory of J. Stephenson & Co., 27th St., New York, has just been completed. For its graceful portions, exquisite workmanship, and brilliant emblazonry it has never been equalled either in ancient or modern times. It is said to be fashioned after the model of the Imperial Chariots of Persia, during the reign of Cyrus the Great. The sides of the Chariot are divided into six panels, separated by richly gilded scroll work in the style of Louis XIV. The scroll work is bordered by beautiful frill moulding, and runs along the top as well as the bottom of the Chariot. The seat of the Charioteer is covered with a rich hammer-cloth of purple velvet trimmed with deep silver fringe, pendant from a border of blue and yellow velvet, the whole decorated with eagles, equestrian figures, stars and flowers, wrought in gold and silver. The Charioteer appears borne along between the expanded wings of two mighty dragons, apparently of massive gold, which couch above the fore wheels of the Chariot.

THE PERFORMANCE, &C.—A very brief description of the names and position of these nonpariels, of professional skill, may be needful to the public, who wish to understand their proper standing and pretensions. The Equestrian Manager, to whom is entrusted the arrangement and order of the scenes, acts, professional Pageants and general Cavalcade, is MR. J. J. NATHANS, of the highest celebrity as a superior *two and four horse rider.* This gentleman's style is manly, energetic and masterly. In his scenes of Centaur and Infant Achilles he is assisted by FRANK PASTOR, a most interesting and highly gifted child. This Infant Artist, will appear on his flying courser in an act entitled *Nimrod Junior,* in which he will justify the remarks of the press, that for grace, beauty and courage, he is the most wonderful child in the world. This miniature prodigy will, with his yet younger and smaller BROTHER WILLIAM, be introduced by his instructor, J. J. Nathans, in a series of personal gymnastics.

YOUTHFUL RICHARD RIVERS.—Whose professional path has literally been strewn with garlands, medals and tokens of approbation, stands confessedly forth as a model of excellence in the foremost class of Equestrianism.

IL SIGNOR GERMANI, the great rider of Italy ; whose horse gallops a different course from any other in the ring, will after his own singular school, appear in an Equestrian act, representing the Hindoo Miracles of an East India juggler, attired in the exact costume and caste of his tribe, with an Orrery of Golden Globes and Sacred Daggers, the Sacred Vase of Destiny and Fated Bullet. A very novel and most agreeable episode will be introduced with the two LEARNED DOGS of Signor Germani. They can comprehend and perform a variety of feats and tricks, too extraordinary to be believed unless witnessed. They may truly be pronounced the greatest wonders of the age.

WASHINGTON CHAMBERS, will for the first time in this country, ride and enact the beautiful personation of the Beguln of Mexico, Gen. Taylor, Jaikes, a Yankee Volunteer, Santa Anna, and the Genius of Freedom, bearing on its flag the memorable resolve of " We never surrender."

JAMES HAWKINS, a very celebrated equestrian in Roman and Grecian characters, especially in the double scene of the Two Gladiators of Cæsar, acted and rode with J. J. Nathans.

MR. E. WOOD, will give his terrific act of the Wild Indian of the Prairie, in which he will introduce those astonishing feats of equestrianism so peculiar to these tribes, and of which travelers give such wonderful and most incredible accounts.

GEORGE DUNBAR.—His scene of Personal Position is of the most finished and wonderful class. His skill in Equilibrium and Power of Balance exceeds all professors who have gone before him.

MR. FRANK BROWER, is the Merryman Buffo of the Equestrian Arena Entertainments.

MR. N. JOHNSON, RING MASTER, of the Equestrian Scenes. His Orical Pageants and Grand Cavalcades are relieved by COMIC CONCERTS, for which the following eminent Vocal and Instrumental Performers have been engaged, and whose correct delineations of character give life to their Ethiopian extravaganzas.

| T. BROWER, | J. MALLORY, | NEIL JEMIESON, | TONY GERMON. |

To render the entertainment free from tediousness they will be relieved with BALLETS of all descriptions, including the peculiar *pas de danse,* fashionable in the West Indies.

This Company will perform in Cincinnati the 1st, 3d, 4th and 5th ; Hamilton the 6th ; Lebanon the 7th ; and Dayton the 10th of July.

XENIA, June 29th, 1848. (1w)

In 1850, C. C. Quick & Co.'s "Mammoth Menagerie" exhibited an "Automatodeon" or mechanical band, "the most extraordinary invention of the age, performing as it does all the various functions of a full orchestra, whether of Brass, Reed or String instruments with the most perfect accuracy. The splendid machine will be drawn on a magnificent van drawn by Elephants and Camels." The instrument was, no doubt, an orchestrion played by a roller organ, turned by hand, the forerunner of the calliope.[7] No information as to the maker or carver appears in the advertisement. However, the Franconis, descendents of Antoine Franconi, Parisian showman and founder of the Cirque Olympic, omitted nothing in their advertisement which appeared in the Springfield *Daily Post*, July 23, 1853, under the heading, "Franconi's Colossal Hippodrome":

Colossal Car of the Muses! drawn by twelve beautiful horses . . . this exquisitely wrought vehicle was built in the city of Paris at immense cost. It is constructed upon the model of the Ancient Triumphal Cars, and presents such a style of classic elegance and massive decoration as has never been witnessed since the Roman Empire. The carriage which is thirty feet in length, displays upon pedestals erected at each extremity, groups of life-sized statues of the nine Muses, led by Apollo, finely chiseled and arranged in the following order, on the front pedestal is grouped, with appropriate emblems and in varied and graceful attitudes, *Calliope, Euterpe, Melpomene* and *Urania*, at the other end are *Thalia, Clio, Terpsichore, Erato* and *Polyhymnia*. The centre piece is a sublime allegory representing the aspiration of the Arts to Glory. The Arts are illustrated by *four beautiful girls,* with garlands revolving around the figure of Glory, who stands erect upon a Grecian altar, holding aloft three civic or laurel crowns. The last named group is moved by machinery attached to the wheels of the car and produces as the vehicle proceeds a most magnificent and magical effect. The figures comprised in the above beautiful Tableaux are the work of the celebrated Sculptor Octavini Gori, and are faithful copies from the famous groups at the Vatican. The wheels and carriage of this consummate work of art are massive, deeply carved and ornamented with gold and scarlet.

In 1851, the Spaulding & Rogers Circus introduced the forty-horse hitch which drew the *Apollonicon.* "The Spirit of '76—GEN WASHINGTON—and MAD ANTHONY WAYNE. The APOLLONICON drawn by FORTY HORSES, FOUR ABREAST driven by one man, will enter the town on the day of exhibition."[8] Spaulding & Rogers claimed to be the first company that placed their show and wagons on railroad cars which could be switched off at the places of performances.

By the middle of the 1850s the band chariot and ornamental wagons were part of the circus. A free street parade preceded the performance. While the Stephenson shop was capable of producing these wagons, its specialty was in transport with a vastly different undercarriage. Another shop, operated by the Fieldings, was better equipped to construct these wagons.

Fig. 63. The Armamaxa, or Imperial Persian Chariot. *With the Welch, Delevan & Nathan's National Circus at Xenia, Ohio, July 8, 1848. The earliest recorded circus band chariot made in America. Constructed in the shop of John Stephenson on 27th Street, New York. The wagon was 20 feet long, 17 feet high and the carvings were done by John L. Cromwell. Courtesy Richard E. Conover.*

Fig. 64. Van Amburgh & Co.'s Great Golden Chariot. *The carvings are probably by Thomas V. Brooks. Constructed by Fielding Brothers in New York, c. 1868. Courtesy Richard E. Conover.*

Fielding Brothers

In 1842, Jeremiah Fielding, a ship carpenter, was established at 18 Houston Street and his brother Robert was a porter at 202 Houston Street in New York. George Fielding, a son of Jeremiah, established his first shop in 1843 at 206 Houston Street, and in 1846 was a coachmaker at 27th Street near Fourth Avenue, quite close to the Stephenson shop. George Fielding and his brother Charles remained at the 27th Street shop until 1855 when they moved to larger quarters at 130 East 41st Street between Lexington and Third Avenues. At this time, Robert J. Fielding joined the firm. In 1859, the firm was listed as Fielding Brothers with George and Robert J. Fielding at its head.[9] In 1856 or perhaps earlier, Fielding Brothers built a combination band and advertising wagon for the Lee & Bennett Circus. In 1859, the J. M. Nixon and Company Circus had constructed by Fielding Brothers a wagon with carvings probably by Thomas V. Brooks.[10]

In 1863, their first advertisement appeared mentioning circus wagons: "FIELDING BROTHERS, OMNIBUS MANUFACTORY, 130 and 132 East Forty-First Street, near Third Avenue. All kinds of Express, Mineral-Water,

Circus, Menagerie and Business Wagons made to order."[11] That year a long chariot for Thayer & Noyes may have come from their factory, and in 1865, Alexander Robinson had a new Fielding chariot for his show. In 1866, they constructed a wagon for the Van Amburgh Circus and one for the Thompson, Smith and Howes Circus. In 1867, a bandchariot was built for J. M. French and Company Circus.[12] A wagon made for the Van Amburgh Circus in 1868 by the Fieldings was somewhat similar to the Triumphal Car of 1845. This bandwagon, known as the Van Amburgh's Golden Chariot had an oversized figure of an armed warrior thrusting his spear into the mouth of a beast (Fig. 64). Over the rear wheel was the relief figure of a Roman gladiator prying open the mouth of a lion. In all probability the canopy tilted forward to allow passage under bridges. In 1867, Fielding Brothers also constructed a new $2,000 performing den for Adam Forepaugh.[13] In 1870, a long bandchariot was delivered to Lewis B. Lent (Fig. 65) and in 1872 the firm was engaged in constructing sixteen cages for John O'Brien; the following year Fielding made eight cages for Adam Forepaugh.[14]

In 1864, Seth B. Howes returned from England after a stay of seven years with his Great European Circus, bringing with him the first tableaux wagons Americans had ever seen. The carvings were quite different from those made by the shipcarvers who had made the carved work for Stephenson and Fielding. The Americans tried to create an overall effect without the great attention to small details, the enormous amount of ornamentation around mirrors, the infinite number of scrolls in minute detail and bunched-up carving in the rococo style. The Howes wagons could be distinguished by these very effects. To some extent these wagons did have an influence on the new concept of circus wagon design, especially the Howes Globe Tableau, so called because of the large sphere mounted on top of the wagon, upon which sat a living, robed, female figure. The entire superstructure could be lowered into the body of the wagon. While this wagon was not in the style of European circus wagons, a news item in the New York *Clipper* of 1877 notes: "Fielding Brothers are building a fine chariot for Adam Forepaugh, somewhat similar to the one brought from abroad by the Howes London Circus."[15]

By 1877, Fielding Brothers no longer listed themselves as carriage makers but wagon builders. The wagon under construction for Adam Forepaugh was quite similar to the Howes Globe Tableau, except for details on the skyboards, the corner dragons and most noticeably in the tableau, which had four carved sitting lions guarding the rider seated on top of the globe and four carved corner figures. On the side, were carved in high relief five maidens (Fig. 66). This wagon, in recent years, has been misnamed *The Five Graces*. The intention of the designer was to divide everything into fours—not fives. The globe represented the four continents, the four carved sitting lions each guarding a continent, the four carved corner figures representing the four races of man. On the side are

Fig. 66. Globe chariot. *Constructed for Adam Forepaugh in 1877 by Fielding Brothers of New York. Shown with the upper structure removed and converted into a bandwagon. The figures on the side panel represent the four seasons with the Goddess of Liberty in the center. Photograph taken at the Forepaugh quarters in Philadelphia in 1888. Courtesy McCaddon Collection, Princeton University Library.*

Fig. 67. The superstructure removed from the Adam Forepaugh Globe Chariot and mounted on a wagon. Photograph taken at the Forepaugh Quarters in Philadelphia in 1888. Courtesy McCaddon Collection, Princeton University Library.

presented spring, summer, fall, and winter—the four seasons centered by Columbia, or the Goddess of Liberty, sword at side. There were four mirrors, two on each side, as well as four dragons, one at each corner guarding the substructure. In four plaques, two on each side, are the fruits of the earth, denoting fecundity.

The extreme height of this tableaux managed to get it ensnarled in telegraph and telephone wires.[16] About 1882, the Globe Tableau with the four corner figures and four lions was removed and mounted on a light-wheeled wagon (Fig. 67). The original wagon was equipped with seats and converted into Band Wagon No. 1. The Globe Tableau with the four lions and four figures was badly damaged in a train wreck on September 19, 1889, at Scarsboro, Iowa. After repairs were made it served for another four years, after which all traces of it were lost.[17] Band Wagon No. 1, under its assumed name, has survived, and is now part of the collection at the Ringling Circus Museum in Sarasota, Florida.

In 1877, after Samuel A. Robb opened his carving shop at 195 Canal Street, Thomas V. Brooks had moved his shop from South Street to 211 Hudson Street, spending a large amount of time making plans for his moving to Chicago. Cromwell had died in 1873. The carvings for the Forepaugh Globe Tableau, in all probability, were made in Robb's shop, with the assistance of Thomas J. White and other carvers. The corner figures are not too different from their tobacconists' figures. Another Forepaugh tableau, the St. George and the Dragon, made in 1881 was acknowledged by Robb as having been made in his shop.[18]

From 1879 through 1880–1881, a large reshuffling of circus holdings took place. James A. Bailey and his partner, James E. Cooper, bought out the Howes Great London Circus and Sanger's Royal British Menagerie, creating a huge circus enterprise in competition with the financially troubled P. T. Barnum. In 1880, Bailey bought out Cooper's interest for $40,000 and that year he was joined by James L. Hutchinson. On March 10, 1880, at the winter quarters of the Bailey enterprises, a baby elephant was born, the first in captivity in America. Barnum wired Bailey offering $100,000 for the elephant. Bailey not only sent the great Barnum a terse refusal but immediately publicized Barnum's telegram to his own advantage. This climaxed the rivalry between the two great circus impresarios and also brought them together in a business transaction resulting in a combination of the Barnum, Bailey & Hutchinson interests, which became known as Barnum & London.[19] James A. Bailey, described as the "greatest managerial genius and organizer the circus has ever known,"[20] handled an amazing amount of detail which included the ordering of wagons, carvings, all supplies, and hundreds of other large and small matters. His address books show that he could select a supplier of oats or a calliope player in almost any part of the country; the orderliness of his entries indicates a well-organized mind. The new association with P. T. Barnum required a large number of wagons. For the next ten years, Fielding Brothers and their carvers were kept occupied creating their most fanciful wagons, some of which have survived to this day.

In the fall of 1881, Robb's shop was commissioned to turn out a large number of carvings for a new group of circus wagons known as Tableaux Dens. *Harper's Weekly* reported:

One shop in New York made forty figures, costing from $25 to $100 each, for a circus last winter. They were figures of gods and goddesses, and beasts, birds, and reptiles, and were fastened on the golden chariots that appear in the street processions. When they are to be placed on the sides of chariots, half-figures are used, but when they are to be placed on the corners they are carved complete, and afterward cut out in the back to fit.[21]

Many of the corner figures were on foliated bases, others on a scroll, not unlike the figureheads, but in an upright position. Gods and goddesses were corner figures inspired by events in mythology, birds were on the aviary cage wagon, crocodiles and snakes were on the reptile cage (Fig.

Fig. 68. Barnum & Bailey tableaux dens at the Bridgeport, Connecticut, winter quarters. Courtesy McCaddon Collection, Princeton University Library.

68), and carved beasts represented the various wild species exhibited in the street parades. The wagons came from the Fielding Brothers wagon shop which built five tableaux dens during this period for Barnum, Bailey and Hutchinson. These were part of the twelve tableaux dens or cage wagons they built over the next few years.[22]

In 1882, George Fielding died. His will designated his wife Matilda as the executrix of his estate. Fielding had various properties on East 41st Street between Third and Second Avenues, and an estate at Ocean Grove, New Jersey. These he left to his wife, including one-third of his half-interest in the wagon factory. His sons, James E. Fielding and Frank T. Fielding, each held another one-third of the one-half interest. Robert Fielding, the brother and partner, reorganized the firm, changing its name to Fielding & Co. In the reorganization, a business was set up at 661 Washington Street, by the sons of George Fielding, but it lasted only one year.[23] In 1883–1884, George Schuchman joined Fielding & Co. as a partner, and the firm's name changed to Fielding & Schuchman. In 1885–1886, the firm moved to Broadway and 35th Street under the name of "George W. Fielding, Carriages," and within the year went out of business. Most of the circus wagon business went to the Sebastian Manufacturing Company.

Sebastian Wagon Company

In 1853, Jacob Sebastian listed himself as a wheelwright, with his shop at 218 Third Avenue, New York, and his home just across the street at 211 Third Avenue. He made wheels, light carriages, and iron parts for carriages and heavier commercial wagons. In 1858, he was listed as a smith, and with Louis Saul he set up a partnership, the firm being known as Sebastian & Saul, at 700 Third Avenue near East 46th Street. Sebastian's partner changed his name to Saal and the firm's name was accordingly changed. In 1863, they started making wagons. By 1867 they had expanded their business, occupying 700, 702, and 704 Third Avenue between 47th and 48th Streets in Manhattan. Here they manufactured "Wagons of every description—made to order and warranted. Painting, Trimming and Repairing done promptly, and in style and price that will ensure satisfaction.[24]

In 1874, the partners separated. Saal moved into the Fielding building at 134 East 41st Street and probably advised Fielding in the construction of heavy wagons. Sebastian took over a brick building at 204 East 43rd Street near Third Avenue. By 1876, Sebastian had expanded, taking over 206, 208, and 210 East 43rd Street. First building heavy wagons, trucks, and carts, by 1878 Sebastian was producing circus wagons as stated in his advertisement:[25]

Established 1854

JACOB SEBASTIAN

Manufacturer of WAGON TRUCKS and CARTS

Brewers' and Circus Wagons A Specialty

204, 206, 208, 210 East 43rd St., New York

On September 18, 1884, Jacob Sebastian, the wagon builder, died, leaving three daughters and two sons, one a minor, as survivors of his estate which included the wagon factory. During 1884–1885, a reorganization took place in which Anton Sebastian, one of the sons, became a stockholder in the new corporation that was formed with Henry M. Haar, Charles A. Stadler, and William Hoffman, the latter representing the major beer brewers in New York. The firm was renamed The Sebastian Manufacturing Company, and was guaranteed "existence for forty-nine years for the purpose of carrying on and conducting business of manufacturing wagons, carriages etc. and all the appurtenances thereto, and article of like description." The amount of capital stock was $80,000 divided into 800 shares; a par value of $100 each. The new group was a two-thirds owner having paid $21,400 in stock or, 214 shares as well as a sum of $36,000 toward the discharge of a debt owed by Jacob Sebastian. The new owners read like a *Who's Who* in the brewery world; Jacob Ruppert, George Ehret, The F & M Schaeffer Brewing Company, Adolph Hupfel, Charles A. Stadler, and others.[26] The purchase and continued operation of the wagon company by the brewers assured them of the wagons they needed and of control over the price and the market. After 1885, with Fielding no longer in business, the Sebastian Manufacturing Company had a monopoly on the circus wagon business and on the manufacture of all the brewery wagons in greater New York. Two years later they acquired additional property at 223 East 43rd Street, enlarging their wagon-building operation.

About 1878 or 1880, Adam Forepaugh, who may have been dissatisfied with the construction of the Globe Tableau made by Fielding, switched to Sebastian, who was better equipped to handle the manufacture of heavy wagons. Forepaugh placed an order for a huge telescoping tableau of St. George and the Dragon (Col. Fig. 9).

Fig. 69. Old Santa Claus. *Pony-drawn parade float, part of the 1883 fairy tale series. A live costumed Santa occupied the back seat. Courtesy McCaddon Collection, Princeton University Library.*

Fig. 70. The Old Woman That Lived In A Shoe. *Pony-drawn float, part of the 1883 fairy tale series. Still surviving at the Circus World Museum at Baraboo, Wisconsin. Courtesy McCaddon Collection, Princeton University Library.*

Fig. 71. Mother Goose. *Pony-drawn float, part of the 1886–1888 fairy tale series. Still surviving at the Circus World Museum, Baraboo. Courtesy McCaddon Collection, Princeton University Library.*

About 1883, two tableaux wagons were ordered by Barnum & London based on themes from nursery rhymes: Old Santa Claus and The Old Woman Who Lived in a Shoe. They were to be of a size to be drawn by a team of matched ponies and became known as the *Allegorical Pony-Drawn Parade Floats* (Figs. 69, 70).[27] Five more were to follow and possibly seven. Between the years 1886 and 1888, the other five were made. While it is possible that Fielding may have made the first two wagons, it can be assumed that Sebastian made all the others: *Mother Goose, Bluebeard, Little Red Riding Hood, Cinderella* (Col. Fig. 10), and *Sinbad the Sailor* (Figs. 71, 72, 73, 74, 75). A Barnum & Bailey two-sheet lithograph issued for the 1889 winter season in London, under the

Fig. 72. Bluebeard. *Pony-drawn
float, part of the 1886–1888 fairy
tale series. Courtesy McCaddon
Collection, Princeton University
Library.*

Fig. 73. Little Red Riding Hood.
*Pony-drawn float, part of the
1886–1888 fairy tale series.
Courtesy Roy F. Arnold.*

FIG. 72

FIG. 73

FIG. 74

Fig. 74. Cinderella. *Pony-drawn
float, part of the 1886–1888 fairy
tale series (See Col. Fig. 10).
Still surviving at the Circus World
Museum in Baraboo. Courtesy
McCaddon Collection, Princeton
University Library.*

title "Childhood's Fairyland and Nursery Rhymes. . . . Illustrated By Picturesque Moving Tableaux in the Spectacular Procession," shows *Robinson Crusoe* and *Sleeping Beauty* floats as part of the procession. However, no other record of them has ever turned up and it is doubtful if they were made. The carved figures for the pony-drawn tableau, as well as the original mud boards and platform trim were made in the shop of Samuel A. Robb. Two years later, Frank W. Weitenkampf, a *New York Times* reporter, interviewing Robb noted that:

> P. T. Barnum has been supplied with a number of wooden figures which appear in his street parades. They are all life size or larger, and include Bluebeard, Cinderella, Mother Goose, Sinbad the Sailor, Red Riding Hood, and The Old Woman That Lived in a Shoe. . . . The figures on Barnum's vans are also carved in wood. . . . Nearly all these figures came from Robb's shop and many of them are Thomas White's handiwork.[28]

These floats had fancy wheels which were replaced at some time with simpler ones. After the 1898–1902 European tour, it was found that only four from the original seven had returned: *Mother Goose, Bluebeard,*

Fig. 75. Sinbad the Sailor. *Pony-drawn float, part of the 1886–1888 fairy tale series. Courtesy McCaddon Collection, Princeton University Library.*

Little Red Riding Hood, and *Cinderella.* Another pony float, a two-headed dragon from a former Howes wagon, also returned. Of the four pony-drawn tableaux wagons, old *Santa Claus* was left to rot on the winter quarters lot of the Robbins Brothers Circus at Granger, Iowa, during the 1932 season. *Cinderella, Mother Goose,* and *The Old Woman That Lived in a Shoe* were bought in 1935 by the Cole Brothers Circus. All three, in restored condition, are now part of the collection of the Circus World Museum in Baraboo, Wisconsin.

At the end of the 1889 tour, Barnum & Bailey shipped their show to England where it had a successful season. In 1890, Adam Forepaugh died and on April 7, 1891, P. T. Barnum was dead. In 1894, when the Forepaugh show was bought by Cooper and Bailey and transferred with all its rolling stock to the Buffalo Bill Wild West Shows, the Forepaugh title combined with that of Sells Bros. circus.

In 1891, Bailey decided to put new flash into the street parades, a series of tableaux would be designed in an inexpensive manner to create the illusion of opulence and grandeur. This was to be achieved by covering the existing cage wagons with painted canvas drops depicting popular children's stories and fairy tales as well as notable events in American history. On a platform on top of the wagons, the main characters in costume were to be posed in the most dramatic episode of each story. Several designers were employed to provide ideas and sketches. Howard Davie submitted a set of watercolors and pencil sketches, as did Alfred Edel and Samuel A. Robb. Harry Ogden submitted the designs for the wardrobe which eventually was furnished by Browning King & Co. of New York.[29] Depicted on canvas and hung from the sides of the wagons were *Beauty and the Beast, Bluebeard, Puss in Boots, Aladdin, Ali Baba and the Forty Thieves, The Queen of Hearts, Toys and Games, Nursery Rhymes,* and *Sleeping Beauty* (Col. Figs. 11–16). In the historical series were *Landing of the Pilgrims, Captain Smith's Rescue by Pocahontas, Wm. Penn's Treaty with the Indians, Signing of the Declaration of Independence,* and *Washington's Inauguration.*

The following year, *The Fall of Nineveh,* a huge biblical spectacle, was staged and in 1893, *The American Revolution—Scenes and Battles of 1776.* The economic depression of the early 1890s also affected the Bailey holdings and no wagons were added or made for some time.

On July 12, 1893, the Sebastian Manufacturing Company petitioned the New York Supreme Court for permission to change its name to the Sebastian Wagon Company and on August 19 permission was granted.[30] The firm had expanded under the ownership of the combined brewers of New York, purchasing property at 217 to 223 East 43rd Street and to the rear at 202 East 44th Street between Third and Second Avenues.

By 1895, the Ringling Brothers Circus had made a great impression on the American public and had become a serious competitor of the Bailey interests. The 1890s had not produced the vast profits of earlier years, turning Bailey's thoughts to pastures that were greener with dollar bills. Because the 1890 tour of England had been a great success, a tour of Europe was given serious consideration. The year 1898, an exception, had been one of the most financially rewarding for Bailey, who then decided upon the European tour. He formed a corporation, Barnum & Bailey, Ltd., and issued stock to finance the enterprise.

Having in previous years visited Australia, South America and London with the reward of immense success, the public of its native land was quite prepared to hear any project it might announce without great surprise. But the public of Europe was ignorant of its actual scope and enterprise. True, those interested in tented exhibitions knew in a general way that it was in reality the greatest show on earth, but its truthful statements of its actual dimensions and quality were usually smiled at as simply instances of Yankee exaggeration. When they learned that it intended to tour practically the whole of Europe they were astounded at what they considered to be sheer American audacity. They had hundreds of tented shows in their own countries. This American concern could not hope to compete with them, nor would it dare assert a superiority over all of them.

Thus reported the new enterprise in its own publication a few years later.[31]

The tour of Europe was indeed a success. Its advent in London was contemporaneous with the Spanish-American War. Certain problems did present themselves during the tour, especially in Vienna during the 1900 season when it was found that the Rotunde was not equipped with a heating plant and one had to be installed at great expense. Likewise, for the 1901–1902 winter season in Paris, the Galerie des Machines had to be equipped for the Circus' occupancy of nearly four months. In spite of these and other inconveniences, the tour was proving to be profitable, and in 1902, in preparation for the homecoming the following year, Bailey ordered from the Sebastian Wagon Company a large number of parade wagons with which to make his triumphal return to America after an absence of five years.

On January 14, 1902, Bailey entered into a contract with the Sebastian Wagon Company for the construction of four tableaux cars, six racing chariots, and eight additional tableaux cars, stipulating that the work was to be completed and ready for delivery about the month of December, 1902.[32] Later, on June 17, 1902, the contract was amended to include a new bandwagon, making a total of thirteen large and elaborately carved vehicles to be produced within a ten-month period.

The designs for the four continental groups did not originate with the Barnum & Bailey designers nor with Robb but actually are scaled-down copies of the corner figures of the Prince Albert Memorial in Hyde Park, South Kensington, London, built on the actual site of the 1851 International Exhibition inspired by the Prince Consort. Upon the death of Prince Albert in 1861, as a commemoration, it was proposed that a huge obelisk with a group of statuary at the base be erected. This was abandoned chiefly because of the difficulty of excavating a monolith; instead, a hall and a monument were proposed but were also rejected. Queen Victoria proposed a grouping which included a statue of the Prince. In a competition, in which six designs were submitted, that of Gilbert Scott was chosen. The critics were unmerciful but after an expenditure of £130,000 and twenty years for completion, some of the critics had softened their judgments while some maintained their original objection:

It would seem hardly worthwhile to describe in any detail this monument, the biggest and probably the best-known in London: but a short attempt, for the benefit of those who have never seen it should be made.

Imagine then a huge square-spread canopy, decorated with gold and mosaics, above a great gilt seated figure of the Prince Consort holding in his hand the catalogue of the 1851 Exhibition. Round the base of the pedestal is a marble frieze in high relief of 178 portrait figures, representing all the arts since the days of Pharaoh, and projecting from the corners thereof are four marble groups representing Agriculture, Manufacture, Commerce, and Engineering. The somewhat gaudy pedestal, covered with coats of arms and typical nineteenth century decorations, rests on a spacious pink, black, and white platform approached by four flights of granite steps, and at the four flights of granite steps, and at the four corners of the steps are big marble groups of Europe, Asia, Africa, and America. The height of the whole memorial is 175 feet, and it took ten years to construct. . . the big central figure by J. H. Foley, though much sneered at, is good, and so is the "Asia" group, by the same artist. "Africa" (by W. Theed) runs it close, and "America" (by J. Bell) is fairly lively; but "Europe" (by P. MacDowell) is a most depressing and inferior work. It is characteristic of the time that, except for the negro and perhaps the Chinaman, all the nations depicted in the group are purely European type and build. . .[33]

The memorial was opened in July, 1877 and the statue of the Prince unveiled on March 9, 1876. At the time of its erection it was called a "wedding cake," or "A confection of gingerbread which ought to be under a glass case on a giant's mantlepiece."[34]

The *Four Continents Tableaux* were given meanings different from those on the Memorial and also colored to suit both press agent and pageantry:

EUROPE—is the first continental float. The general color scheme is white, red and gold. The body of the float is surrounded by representations of all the nationalities

FIG. 76

of Europe in bas-relief. The central figures on the float are golden statues of heroic size. In the center of the group is "Europa" seated upon a mammoth golden bull. Grouped around her are allegorical statues of "Commerce," "Justice," "Philosophy," and "The Arts." Situated at different points upon the float are great pilasters flying the banners of the nations of Europe. In addition to the statuary there are a number of living figures who wear costumes designed and executed with absolute correctness, representing the four crack infantry regiments of Europe, namely the Grenadier Guards of England, Infantry of the Line of Germany, Infantry of the Line of France and the Russian Imperial Guards. The driver of the float is a typical English coachman in royal livery. Accompanying the float are six outriders representing the knighthood of Europe [Fig. 76].

ASIA—The color scheme of this float is red and blue. The central figure of the group, a golden statue of heroic size, is an oriental houri lifting her veil. She is seated upon a recumbent elephant. Grouped around her are a Chinaman, an Arab, a Parsee, and a Persian. The body of the float is surrounded with panels holding a typical vignette in bas-relief representing all the nationalities of Asia. The living figures represent soldiers of Japan, China, India, and Asia Minor. The driver is a Persian. The six mounted outriders are Persian soldiers [Figs. 77a, 77b].

AMERICA—The general color scheme is blue and gold. The central figure of the heroic group of golden statuary is "America," seated upon a buffalo. Grouped around her are Columbia, Canada, an Aztec, and a pioneer. The living figures are an Indian chief, Canadian snowshoer, a Gaucho, and a Mexican. The drivers are a cowboy and a scout. The six outriders are American soldiers in Khaki [Figs. 78a, 78b].[35]

AFRICA—The general color scheme is green and gold. The central figure is an Egyptian seated upon a camel couchant. She is surrounded by a group comprising

FIG. 77a

Figs. 76, 77a, 77b. The Four Continents/Tableaux Wagons: Europe (Fig. 76), Asia (Figs. 77a, 77b), Photographs: McCaddon Collection, Princeton University Library, Roy F. Arnold, and Richard E. Conover.

FIG. 77b

FIG. 79a

FIG. 78a

Figs. 78a, 78b, 79a, 79b. The Four Continents/Tableaux Wagons: America (Figs. 78a, 78b), and Africa (Figs. 79a, 79b). Photographs: McCaddon Collections, Princeton University Library, Roy F. Arnold, and Richard E. Conover.

FIG. 78b

a Soudanese, a negro, a fellah, and a Riffian Arab. The driver is an Egyptian. The living figures are soldiers of Egypt, Morocco, Nubia, and the Transvaal. The six outriders are Egyptian soldiers. The panels surrounding the float are filled with vignettes in bas-relief of all nationalities of Africa [Figs. 79a, 79b].

The Golden Age of Chivalry wagon (Fig. 80) was originally designed with carved dragons in deep relief as side panels, one on each side of the wagon. Small carvings were made as samples. The results may not have had the dramatic effect required and a single-bodied, two–headed monster was decided upon. Robb and his carvers created one of the most astonishing circus wagons to parade the streets. The finished wagon in the Sebastian factory just barely cleared the rafters. It was described in the Barnum & Bailey publication as follows:

GOLDEN AGE OF CHIVALRY—The general scheme of this, the most magnificent float ever constructed, is green and red and gold. The entire float is surmounted by a double-headed dragon, with protruding tongues and fangs and blazing nostrils. Reclining upon the back of the dragon is a captive maiden. Upon her either side is a Knight Templar coming to her rescue. The driver of the float is a medieval servitor, while the six mounted outriders are medieval knights [Col. Fig. 17]."[36]

Sometime before 1910, the necks of the dragons were shortened by nearly fifteen inches, while the tail was adjusted in a similar manner to

FIG. 79b

Fig. 80. The Golden Age of Chivalry Tableau Wagon. *A live captive maiden sat between the wings of the dragon, guarded on either side by a Knight Templar. Upon completion in the Sebastian Wagon Company's factory on East 43rd Street, 1902.*

accommodate their loading on flatcars for rail transport. In December, 1925, it was sold with a group of twenty-one wagons to George Christy who abandoned it in Bridgeport. During 1933, it was purchased by Whitlock, Inc. of New Haven, dealers in antiques, from the lot owner in Fairfield, Connecticut, where the wagons had been moved. It was then sold to an automobile museum in Princeton, Massachusetts. In 1965, it was purchased by Gene Zimmerman, an automobile collector, and in 1968, was acquired by Marshall Field & Company of Chicago who has loaned it to the Circus World Museum of Baraboo, Wisconsin. Accurate restorations were undertaken, directed by Charles P. Fox, Director of the Museum, bringing it back to its original condition.

One of the greatest contributions to American circus pageantry was the massive bandwagon drawn by a team of forty matched bay horses under the reins of one driver. The *Two Hemispheres* (Fig. 81), twenty-eight feet long, ten feet six inches high, and eight feet wide, was designed by Harry Ogden. The wagon with its forty-horse hitch and the sound of the hooves striking cobblestones mixed with the brassy notes of a march struck up by the band is a memory only the older generations can enjoy.

This is unquestionably the most enormous float ever built for any purpose in the world. It is not only the greatest in size, but the noblest in conception, design and execution. The general color scheme is gold. The central figure upon either side is one of the Two Hemispheres. Upon them is reproduced in bas-relief the continents. Upon either side of each of the hemispheres there are about quadruple life-size lions and bears. In front there are great eagles while the rear comprises huge elephants with uplifted trunks. Upon the side of the Eastern Hemisphere there are mounted high in the air exquisitely carved coats of arms of Great Britain, France, Germany, Austria, Belgium, and Italy. Upon the side of the Western Hemisphere there are the coats of arms of Chili, the Argentine Republic, Brazil, Mexico, Canada, and the United States. The reproduction of these coats of arms is absolutely perfect and no finer specimens of the art of wood-carving can be seen anywhere in the world. This float is so vast in size and enormous in weight that it requires a team of forty horses hitched abreast in quaternions.[37]

This was the last of the thirteen wagons carved in Robb's shop. Possibly, with time running out, some of the medallions or coats of arms, and other parts of the carved sides may have been subcontracted to the sign shop of Spanjer Brothers of Newark, New Jersey, and supervised by Robb; for Spanjer later used these medallions in its catalog. The wagon was in continuous service in the Barnum & Bailey parades until the firm was absorbed by the Ringling Brothers. For many years the wagon along with many others was abandoned in Bridgeport, Connecticut. This, with others, was acquired by Fred Buchanan and was used in the Robbins Bros. Circus,

Fig. 81. Two Hemispheres Tableau Wagon. *Pulled by a forty-horse hitch in a street parade. The wagon is now at the Circus Hall of Fame in Sarasota, Florida. Photograph: courtesy of Roy F. Arnold.*

then left to the exposure of the elements at Granger, Iowa. The Iowa Circus Fans, under the leadership of Jacob A. Wagner, moved the wagon into an exhibition building on the Iowa State Fair Grounds. It was eventually acquired by the Circus Hall of Fame in Sarasota, Florida, where it remains on public exhibition.

The remaining six tableaux, with the exception of the *Imperial Chariot*, were hardly as elaborate as the others because the costumes and the living characters on top of the wagons would be too distracting. With its two frontal pylons burning incense and with peacock-feathered fans over the elevated throne bearing the queen, with handmaidens dressed in shimmering silk and guarded by elephant tusks, the *Triumphal Car of the Balkis* did not require extensive carvings. The *Throne Tableau Car* (Fig. 82), *Our Country* (Fig. 83), *Funny Folks*, and *Fairy Tales* were also designed for the living characters to be the focus of attention.

The Sebastian Wagon Company, Robb and his carvers, the painters and carpenters, and all other people involved in producing these wagons were under tremendous pressure to have them ready at the Bridgeport quarters for the press to preview the wagons before the 1903 season opened. Tody Hamilton, Barnum & Bailey's "mobilizer of adjectives and promoter of publicity,"[38] had arranged to have the press at the Bridgeport Winter Quarters on March 2, 1903. The New York *Daily Tribune* reported the following day, under the headline "Newspaper Men Visit Circus Winter Quarters in Bridgeport":

Tody Hamilton, Barnum & Bailey's irrepressible but genial press agent yesterday took eighty-six representatives of the leading newspapers of the country (circus count) to the winter quarters of the show at Bridgeport, Connecticut to show them the new attractions to be exhibited this season after an absence of five years from the United States. The party boarded the parlor car Sapphire at the Grand Central Station at 9 o'clock and landed in Bridgeport an hour later. . . . The party was to have been met at the station by the new $18,000 gold chariot drawn by forty bay horses, hitched four abreast, and a brass band accompanied by gayly caparisoned outriders, but the charioteer decided that the gold paint and varnish were not hard enough and carriages were provided instead. On the way, "Tody" explained that there were twenty-eight other chariots, "charming, captivating, colossal and of countless cost," but the paint was not dry enough on any of them. The party later saw the chariots, certainly deserving of all that "Tody" had said of them. All are new and resplendent in gold and rich colors and the cheapest of them is said to have cost $4,000.[39]

Over this article was a photograph of the *Two Hemispheres* with a caption, "The $18,000 Golden Chariot Two Hemispheres." The actual cost of the wagons is not known. Records of partial payments exist but no record of cost or invoice have come to light. The cost of the *Two Hemispheres* wagon may have been less than half the price publicized.

In the *Realm of Marvels*, which was sold to the public on opening day, March 18, 1903, the pride of the Barnum & Bailey press agent in present-

FIG. 82

Fig. 82. Throne Tableau Car. *One of the thirteen circus wagons made by the Sebastian Wagon Company in 1902 for the 1903 homecoming of the Barnum & Bailey Circus. Photograph: courtesy Roy F. Arnold.*

Fig. 83. Our Country Tableau Wagon. *The live figures on top represent the important presidents in American history. Photograph: courtesy Richard E. Conover.*

FIG. 83

ing the wagons to the public was written up under the title, "Colossal Works of Art—Ambitious Creations of American Studios and Ateliers."

The one feature that will at once command the greatest attention will be the superb array of not less than twenty-nine new chariots, tableau cars and floats. It is entirely without exaggeration to state that any one of these twenty-nine splendid items of the parade are finer, more artistic, more costly and, in the case of at least half of them, twice as large as anything that has ever been seen before in any street parade given by a circus. As an evidence of this fact they are the first items of street pageantry worthy of detailed description. They were constructed by the greatest builders of enormous vans in America, the Sebastian Works in New York City, from designs supplied by the leading artists of the day in America and Europe and adapted from some of the greatest works in sculpture of the masters, old and new, of that art in the world's history. The wood carving is easily the finest that has ever been executed in America, and as an entirety it has never been excelled, if equaled, anywhere in the world. This carving was done in the mammoth atelier of Mr. S. A. Robb and required the combined efforts for more than one year of some twenty-five of the very best leaders of the wood-carving craft in this country.[40]

On Wednesday, March 18, 1903, the circus opened at Madison Square Garden. The following day, the New York *Daily Tribune* reported, "And yesterday began the circus. Without parade it came, a sorry handicap on any circus even 'the greatest show on earth.' " The show did open with a parade in the arena, called "The Tribute of Balkis," but the grand street parade with all the new wagons was to wait until better weather and until the varnish, paint, and gold leaf had properly set.

During this time while Robb was hard at work rushing to get the carvings done for the order of thirteen wagons, Sebastian received an order from Major Gordon W. Lillie, better known as "Pawnee Bill," for one new bandwagon and one Japanese wagon, with delivery specified for the spring of 1903. The bandwagon was to be twenty-one feet long by ten feet high. One side was to depict Columbus discovering America, after the painting *The Landing of Columbus*, by John Vanderlyn (1775–1852) (Col. Fig. 18A); and the other, Pocahontas saving the life of John Smith (Figs. 84,

FIG. 84

FIG. 85

Figs. 84, 85. Side panels for the Pawnee Bill Bandwagon No. 80 in the process of being carved in the Robb shop in the Sebastian Wagon Company during the spring of 1903. One panel depicts the landing of Columbus and the other, Pocahontas saving the life of John Smith.

FIG. 86   **FIG. 87**   **FIG. 88**

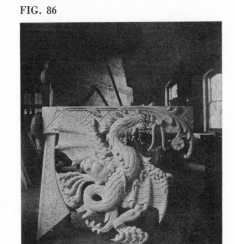

Figs. 86, 87, 88. Dragons and center panel from the Pawnee Bill Japanese wagon in the Robb shop in the Sebastian Wagon Company, spring 1903.

85; Col. Fig. 18B). The photographs from Robb's files show the side boards in the process of being carved and smoothed after the initial roughing in. The Japanese wagon had two sets of exquisitely carved dragons (Figs. 86, 87) and on each side a panel with carved figures of an oriental male and female (Fig. 88). The completed wagon was on parade in Kansas City sometime between 1904 and 1910 (Fig. 89). The *Pawnee Bill Bandwagon No. 80* was used on his show until 1909, then it went to the Mighty Haag Circus which used it through 1914; to Miller Bros. to the 101 Ranch Real Wild West Show from 1925 to 1931; and later to the Bill Hames family which donated it to the Circus World Museum in Baraboo, in 1962. Col. Figs. 18A and 18B show the wagon on the Wisconsin lot in 1965, ready for the parade through Milwaukee.[41] Fortunately, the invoice for the two wagons has been preserved. From it we learn that the price was $7,312 for the two and that the carved background of the Japanese wagon, exclusive of the figures but including the gilding, was $120 (Fig. 90).

In 1906, James A. Bailey, one of the greatest names in American circus

Fig. 89. Pawnee Bill Japanese wagon on parade in Kansas City between 1904 and 1910. Photograph: courtesy J. Beggs.

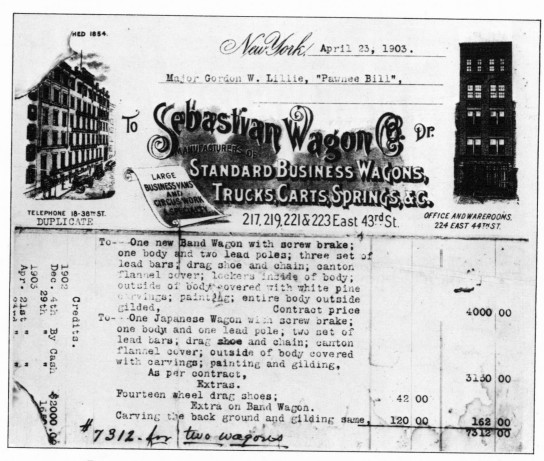

Fig. 90. Invoice from Sebastian Wagon Company to Major Gordon W. Lillie, for the two Pawnee Bill circus wagons. Courtesy Circus World Museum, Baraboo, Wisconsin.

history died, and in the following year, Ringling Brothers purchased the physical properties of the Barnum & Bailey circus. Both operated as separate shows until 1918 when they combined to form the Ringling Bros. and Barnum & Bailey Circus.[42] In 1907, the Sebastian Wagon Company, which hadn't made a circus wagon since the 1902 series, sold their 43rd and 44th Street property to James C. Fargo of the American Express Company, moving to 422 East 54th Street, a property running from East 53rd through East 54th Streets occupying six lots on which was a large factory. With the auto truck coming into use, the large brewery wagons with their teams of dray horses and the cobbled streets were beginning to pass out of the scene, but there was enough need for the huge wagon to keep the factory in operation for another thirteen years.

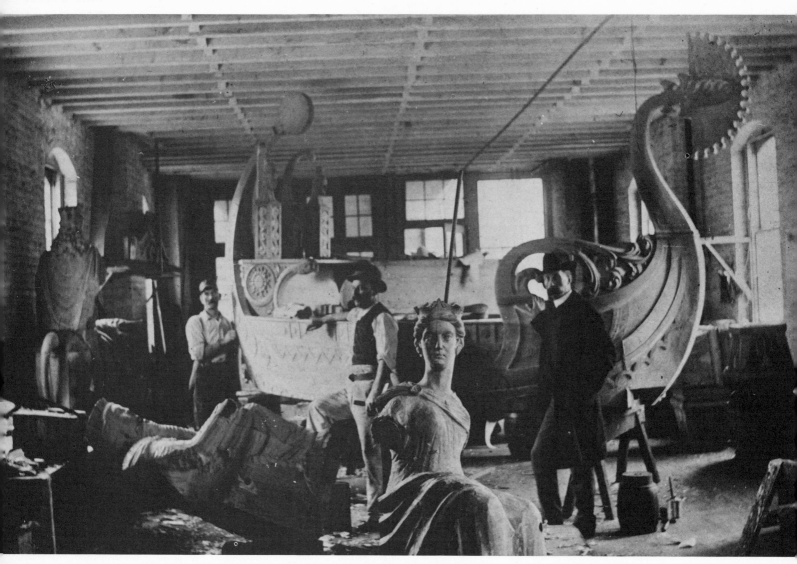

Fig. 197. Interior of the Robb carving shop in the Sebastian Wagon Company at 232 East 43rd Street in Manhattan, 1902. Samuel A. Robb is in center, Charles A. Stadler, is at the right, helper at left is unidentified. In the center is the nearly completed Phoenician Galley; to the left, against the wall, is Europa seated on the Bull; and in the foreground, two figures from the Europe Tableau. Note the pipes sticking out from heads, a technique used by carvers for easier moving and turning.

COLOR SECTION

Side panel of America wagon made for the Barnum & Bailey Circus. Carved in the Robb shop at the Sebastian Wagon Company on East 43rd Street, Manhattan, 1902.

Col. Fig. 1a. Indian Squaw. *Carved and painted wood. Height 49 inches. Said to have been made in Freehold, New Jersey, by an American slave. Courtesy New York Historical Association, Cooperstown.*

Col. Fig. 1b. Squaw with Crossed
Legs. *Carved and painted wood.*
Height 6 feet 4 inches on base 12½
inches, c. 1880–1895. From the
Edwin P. S. Newman Estate.

FIG. 2b

FIG. 2a

Col. Fig. 2a. Punch. *Painted and cast zinc. Height 24 inches. Made by M. J. Seelig for Wm. Demuth. Used as window attraction. Smoke was blown into a tube and out through cigar. Courtesy L. C. Hegarty Collection.*

Col. Fig. 2b. Punch *(close-up view). Carved and painted wood. Height 4 feet 9 inches. Collection Smithsonian Institution.*

FIG. 3

FIG. 4

Col. Fig. 3. Turk. *Carved and painted wood. Courtesy Abby Aldrich Rockefeller Folk Art Collection.*

Col. Fig. 4. Sultan. *Tobacconist's figure. Carved and painted wood. Height 76 inches. Courtesy Abby Aldrich Rockefeller Folk Art Collection.*

FIG. 6

FIG. 5

Col. Fig. 5. Lady of Fashion. *Carved and painted wood. Overall size 67½ inches. Made to sell Cuban cigars, c. 1885. Courtesy Abby Aldrich Rockefeller Folk Art Collection.*

Col. Fig. 6. Theatrical figure. *Carved and painted wood. Height 61 inches, base 20 inches. Carved in the Robb shop, c. 1888. Courtesy Dr. Wm. S. Greenspon Collection.*

FIG. 7

FIG. 8

Col. Fig. 7. Goddess of Liberty.
Tobacconist's figure. Carved and painted
wood. Height 56½ inches, base 17½
inches. Incised on upper edge of base, Robb
MANU'F'R. 114 CENTRE ST. N.Y.
c. 1888–1902. Courtesy Henry Ford Museum.

Col. Fig. 8. Puck. Painted and cast zinc.
Height 57½ inches, wood base 18½ inches.
Also the trademark of Joseph Keppler's
satirical magazine, Puck. Made by M. J.
Seelig for Wm. Demuth. Placquette reads:
Patented Dec. 12, 1881. Incised on base: C.
Buberl, sculpt. Courtesy Henry Ford Museum.

Col. Fig. 9. Lion and Mirror Bandwagon No. 1. *Once part of the St. George and the Dragon Tableau. Made for Adam Forepaugh Circus in 1879 by Jacob Sebastian, carved in the Robb shop at 195 Canal Street, New York. Wagon is 23 feet long, 10 feet high, and weighs 6 tons. Courtesy Circus World Museum, Baraboo, Wisconsin.*

Col. Fig. 10. Cinderella. *Pony-drawn parade float made for Barnum & London, 1886–1888. Carved in the Robb shop, probably the work of Thomas J. White. Courtesy Circus World Museum, Baraboo, Wisconsin.*

Col. Figs. 11–16. Original watercolor
sketches for the 1891 Barnum & Bailey
street parade. Photographs: Ernst Beadle.

Col. Fig. 17. The Golden Age of Chivalry. *One of thirteen wagons carved in the Robb shop at the Sebastian Wagon Company on East 43rd Street, New York. Made for Barnum & Bailey in 1902–1903. Courtesy Circus World Museum, Baraboo, Wisconsin*

Col. Figs. 18a, 18b. Bandwagon No. 80. *Carved in the Robb shop at the Sebastian Wagon Company on East 43rd Street, New York, in 1902. One side (18a) depicts The Landing of Columbus and the other (18b), Pocahontas saving the life of Captain John Smith. Courtesy Circus World Museum, Baraboo, Wisconsin.*

FIG. 18a

FIG. 18b

Col. Fig. 19. Brother Jonathan. *Carved and painted wood. Height 76 inches, base 16 inches. The predecessor of Uncle Sam, used as a tobacconist's or clothier's figure. The left hand usually held a satchel. Courtesy Henry Ford Museum.*

Col. Fig. 20. Dude or Racetrack Tout. *Carved and painted wood. Height 72 inches, c. 1886. Courtesy Abby Aldrich Rockefeller Folk Art Collection.*

Col. Fig. 21. Indian Chief with Tomahawk. Carved in the style of John L. Cromwell, New York. c. 1855. Painted and carved wood. Overall size 82 inches. Courtesy Smithsonian Institution.

Col. Fig. 22. Indian Chief with Pipe. *Painted and carved wood. Height 78 inches, base 22 inches. The identical figure appears on Robb's trade card (See Fig. 188). Courtesy The Van Alstyne Folk Art Collection, Smithsonian Institution.*

Col. Fig. 23. Tobacconist's Indian. *Carved in the Robb shop, c. 1890– 1905. Carved and painted wood. Life-size bust, lower section destroyed in fire. Courtesy Shelburne Museum. Photograph: Einars J. Mengis.*

Col. Fig. 24. Baseball Player. *Tobacconist's figure. Carved and painted wood. Height 50 inches, base 23 inches. Incised on base,* Robb MANU'F'R. 114 CENTRE ST. N.Y. *Courtesy Carl W. Haffenreffer Collection. Photograph: Ernst Beadle.*

Col. Fig. 25. Eagle. *Carved and gold-leafed wood. Used as a sample by Samuel A. Robb. Courtesy Dr. and Mrs. Walter Liebling Collection. Photograph: Arnold Rosenberg.*

6 · Artists in Wood

AS WE HAVE SAID, from Maine to Maryland during the nineteenth century, the coastline was dotted with shipbuilding centers. The shipcarvers' shops were near the shipbuilding yards to supply the carved decorative work required. Occasionally, the carver was called upon to execute a figure for a tradesman— usually a tobacconist who wanted an Indian, a Mercury, or some other kind of figure which he thought could be identified with the wares inside his shop. One of the earliest shipbuilding centers was Philadelphia, which also had the distinction of being the home of America's first native sculptor.

PHILADELPHIA

William Rush (1756–1833)

Few citizens of Philadelphia are more deserving of commendation for their excellence in their profession than this gentleman, as a shipcarver. In his skill in his art he surpasses any other American, and probably any other shipcarver in the world! He gives more grace and character to his figures than are to be found in any other wooden designs.[1]

So wrote J. F. Watson in his *Annals of Philadelphia*. That William Rush was the foremost wood-carver of his day can be proven by the existing specimens. Like many another shipcarver, Rush was the son of a ship carpenter and at an early age displayed a talent for carving. He was born on July 4, 1756, to Joseph Rush and Rebecca Lincoln, who was remotely related to the family of Abraham Lincoln.[2] A cousin was Dr. Benjamin Rush, a signer of the Declaration of Independence. "From his youth he was fond of ships and used, when a boy, to pass his time in the garret in cutting out ships from blocks of wood and to exercise himself in drawing figures in chalk and paints."[3]

Rush's father sought to divert William's taste to plain ship carpentry, and in this, the father was encouraged by his associates. There were no statuary, no art galleries, no elaborate books on art, that the youth might take advantage of, and that his artistic impulses were not destroyed by environment and circumstances is a matter for wonder.[4]

According to J. F: Watson's *Annals:*

When of a proper age he followed his inclination in engaging his term of apprenticeship with Edward Cutbush, from London, the then best carver of his day. He was a man of spirited execution, but inharmonious proportions. Walking attitudes were then unknown; but all rested astride the cutwater. When Rush first saw, on a foreign vessel, a walking figure, he instantly conceived the design of more tasteful and graceful figures than had been before executed. He instantly surpassed his master; and having once opened his mind to the contemplation and study of such attitudes and figures as he saw in nature, he was very soon enabled to surpass all his former performances. Then his figures began to excite admiration in foreign ports. The figure of the "Indian Trader" to the ship *William Penn* (the Trader was dressed in Indian habiliments) excited great observation in London. The carvers there would come in boats and lay near the ship, and sketch designs from it. They even came to take casts, of plaster of Paris, from the head. This was directly after the Revolution, when she was commanded by Captain Josiah. When he carved a river god as the figure for the ship *Ganges*, the Hindoos came off in numerous boats to pay their admiration and perhaps reverence to the various emblems in the trail of the image. On one occasion, the house of Nicklin and Griffeth actually had orders from England, to Rush (nearly forty years ago), to carve two figures for two ships building there. One was a female personation of commerce. The duties in that case cost more than the first cost of the images themselves! A fine Indian figure, in Rush's best style, might be preserved in some public edifice for many centuries to come; even as he carved the full statue of Washington . . .[5]

At the outbreak of the Revolution Rush volunteered, and on September 9, 1777, he was commissioned as an Ensign in the Fourth Regiment of Foot, in Captain Philip Wagener's Company under Lt. Colonel Wills, Philadelphia Militia.[6] After the War for Independence, Rush may have been working as a journeyman, but in 1791, he billed John Ross for carving for the ship *Sally*, completed in his own shop.

About this time Charles Willson Peale, the portrait painter, made a futile effort at organizing an art school to give young talented students a proper education in the arts. In 1794, William Rush, Giuseppe Cerracchi, the Italian sculptor who had come to America in 1791 with a grand design for a colossal *Liberty*, and others assisted Peale in establishing the first art school in America, the Columbianum. A dispute over the posing of live models caused its failure. In December, 1805, the Pennsylvania Academy of Fine Arts was founded. William Rush and Peale were among the members elected to the first board of directors. Benjamin H. Latrobe, the leading architect in America at that time, was selected to design a building for the school. It was to be built on the north side of Chestnut Street between 10th and 11th streets.[7]

In an oration delivered before the Society of Artists in 1811, Benjamin H. Latrobe spoke about Rush's figures for the prows of vessels:

There is motion in his figures that is incontrovertible; they seem rather to draw the ship after them than to impel the vessel. Many are of exquisite beauty. I have not seen one on which there is not the stamp of genius.[8]

Rush's reputation as a shipcarver was earned in 1794, when the newly established Navy of the United States commissioned him to design the figureheads for six frigates. He himself carved the figureheads for the *Chesapeake*, the *John Adams*, the *Congress*, and the *Constellation*.[9] "The figureheads were nine feet high and could be removed, for repair or in action."[10]

At the beginning of the nineteenth century, Rush carved a number of figures not made for ships. Latrobe had designed the New Theatre on Chestnut Street with niches for large sculptures. In 1808, Rush carved two figures, *Comedy* and *Tragedy*, about which "Poulson's Advertiser" of April 2, 1808 reported:

William Rush, Esq. of this city, has recently completed two elegant figures, (Comedy and Tragedy) for the proprietors of the Philadelphia Theatre, to be placed in niches in front of that building on Chestnut Street. In the execution of this work the genius of the artist is truly portrayed; he has done himself honor and added to that of his country.[11]

The figures (Fig. 91) were saved from a fire in 1820 and were used in the structure which replaced the burnt theatre. Sometime later in the century the figures were removed to the grounds of the Edwin Forrest Home for Aged Actors in the suburbs of Philadelphia at Holmesburg; they are now in the Pennsylvania Academy of the Fine Arts, on loan from the Philadelphia Museum of Art. These figures were really architectural ornaments although they served the purpose of show figures as well. In spite of the exposure to the elements, these wood figures have held up and are in excellent condition.

One of the most famous of the Rush carvings is the *Water Nymph and*

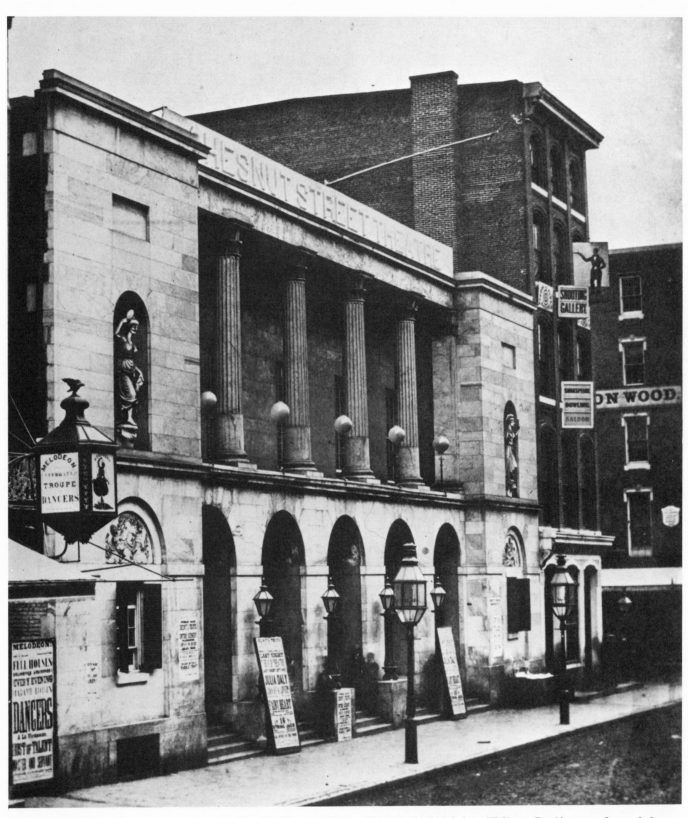

Fig. 91. Chestnut Street Theatre, Philadelphia. William Rush's carved wood figures of Comedy *and* Tragedy *fill the niches on the second story. Photograph: courtesy Mrs. Edward R. Furst.*

the Bittern, once referred to as *Leda and the Swan,* which inspired Thomas Eakins's *William Rush Carving the Allegorical Figure of the Schuylkill.* The canvas depicts Rush carving a wooden figure whose full form is revealed beneath clinging wet garments, while the nude model stands near by, guarded by a knitting chaperon. On its shoulder, the figure had a bittern. From a pipe in the bird's beak, water spouted over the figure. Executed in 1809 for the fountain of the Center Square Water Works, the carving shocked staid officeholders and citizenry. The carving of the wet drapery and the delicate pose and sensitivity of the statue earned the praise of the knowledgeable citizenry, however. About 1854, the wood began to deteriorate and a casting in bronze was made. Today, only the original wood head remains. Rush executed two allegorical figures, representing the Schuylkill River, for the Fairmount Water Works. *The Schuylkill Freed* and *The Schuylkill Chained* are presently in the Philadelphia Museum of Art on loan by the Commissioners of Fairmont Park. Three figures, *Faith, Hope,* and *Charity,* by Rush, were commissioned for the Chestnut Street Masonic Hall and are now owned by the Free and Accepted Masons of Philadelphia.

A boy's eye view of the shop is given in Abraham Ritter's *Merchants of Philadelphia:*

Mr. Rush's studio and workshop was a two-story frame building, No. 172 North Front Street, near Key's alley. . . . There was a log under the front window, upon which we little boys on our way to school climbed and peeped under his window, wondering at the transformation of unwrought timber unto the form and appearance of human beings. Mr. Rush was rather below middle height, but well-formed, genteel in appearance, and very intelligent in countenance. . .[12]

Rush was constantly employed and had sufficient work for his apprentices, journeyman, and for his equal partner, his son, John.

My force consists of my son who is an equal partner—one journeyman and myself—I have to labor through the greatest part of the business I would willingly employ more hands but they are not to be had—I expect one more hand in the course of ten or twelve days who has been with me all the spring and summer at present in the country.[13]

Among Rush's apprentices were two carvers who later set up their own shops in New York, Daniel N. Train, who received some fame for carving the ornaments for the ship *Adams,* a sloop of war; and Thomas Millard, Jr., who turned out many show figures. Another was John Brown who went to Baltimore to execute heads for the sloops of war *Maryland* and *Patapsco;* also, a Mr. Bids, who was either an apprentice or a journeyman.[14] No doubt, there were others, as Rush's fame attracted talented and ambitious youths from distant cities.

Rush worked mainly in pine, it was plentiful, easy to work, inexpensive, and came in large logs, saving time and labor in laminating sections to proportions needed. Rush also modeled in clay, having been taught by

Fig. 92. Self-portrait. *Sculpted by William Rush. Terra-cotta, life size, c. 1830. Courtesy The Pennsylvania Academy of Fine Arts.*

Joseph Wright about the time of the Revolution. Rush did many fine works in this medium including a self-portrait (Fig. 92). It may have been carved in wood originally, and a cast made later, but only the cast survives today.

The bust is a unique and curious work. The head is of the strong Revolutionary type and rises from what appears to be a rough, knotty, log, over which a pine sprig, has fallen. Its needles mingling with the artist's long, thin locks. Though the modeling is dry and liberal, the character of the head is excellent and there is no question of its truth. The fine old head is turned vigorously to the right, the pose is strong and despite the grotesqueness of the wood-carver's fancy, the whole effect is one of power.[15]

While Rush had commissions for busts, idealized figures, and other types of carvings, his mainstay was the carving of ship's figures and ornaments and tobacconists' figures. The nature of the work did not always call for great works of art. In an interview for the Philadelphia *Evening Bulletin,* a carver who remembered Rush reported:

Rush did an immense amount of sculpture carving, not all of it of the first class, but the best of it equal, I think I am right in saying, to the best that ever has been produced . . . even if it was for the most part given to the making of ship and tobacconists' figures.

"Are there any of his tobacconists' figures left?"

I know of a few . . . it is the fate of sculptures of this nature to be given over to house painters for refurbishing, and when they get old they hardly ever look as they should and as the carver intended them to look. The Third Street *Indian* is disfigured in his present dress of paint, and the Market Street *Mercury* looks like a soldier in his red and yellow instead of being in pure white as the sculptor meant him to be.[16]

The *Mercury* in the collection of the Maryland Historical Society is dark brown, with signs of faded colors beneath the surface (Fig. 93). There are cracks in the figure and part of the extended arm is broken. The left hand is a replacement. Considering the years of exposure to the elements, the figure has weathered well enough. Everything about it suggests the work of William Rush.

William Rush died on January 17, 1833, at the age of seventy-seven and was buried in Woodlands Cemetery. His son, John, took over the busi-

Fig. 93. Mercury. *Carved by William Rush. Height 38 inches, base 13 inches, c. 1830. Stood in front of the tobacco shop of John Foble in Cambridge, Maryland. Courtesy Maryland Historical Society.*

ness, establishing his shop at 469 North Front Street near the screwdock on Beach Street. The influence of Rush's work was to be seen in the carvings of the men who came after him.

Other Philadelphia Carvers

A ship's officer holding a sextant to his eye was carved by Samuel H. Sailor (Fig. 94). A familiar shop sign, it endured the elements and time, and is still in service over the doorway of Riggs & Brother's nautical instrument and watch shop at 110 Market Street, Philadelphia. An almost identical figure, but with cigars in his right hand and a box of cigars under his left arm, is in the Mercer Museum in Doylestown, Pennsylvania. This is also the work of Samuel Sailor, who carved ships' and tobacconists' figures from 1858 to about 1885, in Philadelphia. In 1857, his shop was at 103 Harmony Street and he was listed as "Carver & Designer for stoves, railings, etc." Later he moved to 128 South Second Street.[17]

At 717 Sansom Street from 1883 to 1902, a man named James Brown was also carving "garden ornaments, steamboat eagles, figures, church ornaments, pompeys, and cigar Indians." One of his steamboat figures is in a New York collection.[18]

By 1892, the disappearance of tobacconists' figures from the streets of Philadelphia prompted a reporter from *The Times* of that city to write:

Many once familiar devices for advertising have been laid on the shelf forever and have become obsolete. Foremost among the recently rejected methods of catching trade is the cigar-store Indian, at one time the most frequent and conspicuous character of sign in this city, but which has now almost entirely disappeared and, within a few years, will be seen no more.

We all know the carved wooden figures which have been used for generations as the peculiar and individual sign of the tobacco shop. So familiar in times past has every one become with the cigar-store Indian that we have forgotten to look for them. Thus the majority of pedestrians have failed to notice the disappearance of these figures from most of our cigar stores throughout the city. Today not one in twenty cigar stores is so designated, while in times past every cigar store, large or small, was decorated with some character of Pompey. There is not now any man, so far as the writer can determine, who makes a business of carving these wooden figures. There used to be a place on Third Street near Walnut street, where many of them were turned out, but the proprietor of this shop the other day said: "I have no Indians or Pompeys now in stock, in fact, there is no call for them. The demand for this character of signs is now entirely from the rural districts or country towns and this trade is pretty well-supplied by the second-hand figures cast off from our city stores."

A man up Third street, who runs a cigar store and deals in these second-hand figures, when asked the cause of the disappearance of the Pompey, said that the reasons were many. "In the first place a Pompey was an expensive affair, costing all the way from $25 to $200. A good figure, in fact, could not be bought for much less than $75, and this amount of money was necessarily a serious expenditure for a man commencing the tobacco business in a small way, and the advantages to be derived from it were in no ways proportionate. Then, too, many new devices in the way of advertising have been invented by our wholesale cigar and tobacco dealers, and, as trade was directed to them by the wholesalers, the retail men have not felt it necessary to expend any large amount of money on individual advertising. Furthermore, the Pompeys became so common that they entirely lost their individuality and attractiveness and thus failed of their purpose."

Several large retail cigar dealers all gave pretty much the same explanations. When one of these men was asked how it would be possible to procure one of these figures should a demand arise for it, he replied that there was a firm in New York who, in connection with the manufacture of pipes [Demuth] also carved cigar-store figures and, he continued "most of our ship carvers here in this city will get you one up to order."[19]

One metal figure from the Demuth warehouse, No. 45, an *Indian Warrior*, was still in use at the time the reporter and artist noted it for their story (Fig. 95). Another the *Forty-Niner*, was, according to *The Times*, "clad in a flannel shirt of flaming red with baggy trousers stuffed into tremendous cowhide boots, on his head a disreputable slouch hat. In one hand he holds a pick, while the other supports, in his mouth, a tremendous pipe" (Fig. 96).[20] Unmentioned by the article, but now at the Mercer Museum, is a very large figure of Buffalo Bill that also came from the streets of Philadelphia.

The Times article continued:

The familiar Punch advertised *The Times* [Fig. 97] and Brother Jonathan must not be overlooked in this mention of the tobacconist's signs. Every one has seen pictures of "Yankee Doodle" as represented in Children's books, and after this pattern Brother Jonathan is always costumed. In his hand he usually carries a patent traveling bag upon which is painted the name of a celebrated brand of cigars to be secured within. . . . [Fig. 98; Col. Fig. 19.] Then there is the drum major [Fig. 99] with high bearskin shako on head and a costume which is composed of a brilliant red coat covered by much gold lace, and blue trousers banded with a broad strip of gold. Poised aloft he holds his baton as if as a

Figs. 95, 96, 97. A group of tobacconists' figures to be seen in the streets of Philadelphia in 1892.

FIG. 95

FIG. 96

FIG. 97

THE NOBLE RED MAN.

THE FORTY-NINER.

PUNCH.

notice to the public that as soon as they step inside the band will commence to play, "and all, ladies and gentlemen, for the small sum of a nickel." Then there is the sight of the "English swell of the Dundreary type with immense auburn whiskers, with a self-complacent, imbecile smile on his florid face. He was generally clad in a light blue cutaway coat and buff, baggy trousers, while upon his head was a shiny tile and in one hand he carried a natty cane and the other a cigar or cigarette" [Fig. 100.][21]

Among the figures that served as tobacconists' signs was an Indian with shield and spear by an unknown carver. It was at Bush & Trexler's shop from the middle of the nineteenth century but was hacked to pieces and burned by its owner in 1914.[22]

Francis Jacob Deker was a Philadelphia carver who cut wood into small blocks to laminate for the carving of large tobacconists' Indians. When he arrived in Philadelphia from Austria, he changed his name from Decker and opened a carving shop in his home at 2332 Seybert. In 1888, Deker did some figures for shops along with his cabinetmaking. In 1898, he continued in the same line of work from the shop in his home at 1435 North 29th Street. One of his figures stood in front of the Charles Seiders's shop at Fourth and Arch Streets.[23]

On Race Street is a wooden figure of a Negress holding a torch aloft "Liberty Frightnin' de World." This is a relic of slave days surely. By the way, I wonder if the torch of Liberty which while enlightening the world, throws the goddess herself into deep shadow, is symbolical of the fact that Liberty gets very little credit for what she does.[24]

And, as our 1892 correspondent from *The Times* of Philadelphia concluded his article on the cigar-store Indians of that city, "It seems a pity that the cigar-store Pompey has gone out of style, as he was a characteristic and attractive method of advertising and certainly a great advantage over the swinging sign nuisance of today."[25]

BROTHER JONATHAN.

FIG. 98

Figs. 98, 99, 100. A group of tobacconists' figures to be seen in the streets of Philadelphia in 1892.

FIG. 99

THE STYLE IN THE ARMY.

FIG. 100

LORD DUNDREARY.

BALTIMORE

From the beginning to the end of the nineteenth century, Maryland, with its English traditions, had creditable works of art strung along streets and post roads in the form of inn and tavern signs. Conestoga wagons, drawn by teams of six and eight horses, might pass *The Golden Horse, The White Swan, The Black Bear, The Open Hand, The Seven Stars, The Wheatfield Inn,* and many other signs. One of the most famous was *The General Wayne,* showing "Mad Anthony" full length, dressed in his continental uniform. This Baltimore sign, one of the last of its kind, hung from its iron frame, until the end of the nineteenth century, watching wagons and stages give way to street cars and locomotives. The sign of *The Indian Queen,* which had accommodations for "two hundred guests with bells in every room," was a natural starting place for General Andrew Jackson and his guest, the Indian Chief Blackhawk, in their tour of Baltimore.[1]

In ports along the eastern seacoast and in foreign ports, Baltimore's ships were easily recognized by their nameboards and figureheads. The Patapsco River and the harbor with its crowded wharves, its warehouses, and busy water traffic were surrounded by a growing city once called the "Liverpool of America."[2] It was here that the *Constellation* was built. Its figurehead, *Nature,* was supplied by William Rush. Here, Rush's apprentice John Brown set up his own carving shop and here, too, the Baltimore Clippers started out on their race to fame. In 1851, R. and E. Bell built the clipper *Seaman's Bride* for Thomas J. Handy of New York. The eagle figurehead was carved by James Randolph whose shop was near the wharves. He carved the heads for fifteen major vessels and many smaller ones, including *Toothpick,* renamed *Kate Hooper,* and the *Flying Childers.* For the clipper *Canvas Back,* he carved an entire flock of Maryland ducks in flight. James Mullen, also of Baltimore, executed the carvings for the clippers *Rattler* and the *Spirit of the Time;* while James Mullen of O carved the figurehead of a half-nude woman holding a dove to her breast for the clipper, *Carrier Dove.*[3]

Baltimore was long known as a city where the tobacco industry required "warehouses in different sections of the city," and where the

. . . tobacco marketed in Baltimore goes to Germany and France to be converted into moist cigars, or into the stringy smoking material in which the Gaul so much delights. The tobacco and cigar manufactories in the city employ thousands of workmen.[4]

Rolling Road, and others so called, were once used to roll tobacco in barrels downhill to the harbor to be loaded on ships. Tobacco was a large industry and the symbol of the trade, the tobacconist's figure, was said to have been in use in Baltimore from right after the American Revolution.[5]

In 1849, a carver named Philip Yaeger had a shop at 30 Fell Street and was attempting to compete with the already established shipcarvers. Though he had difficulty with the English language and had been at carving for only two years, he found enough work in the shipyards to encourage his continuing the craft. He offered his skills to various businesses outside the shipyards, among which was the growing tobacco trade.

John Philip Yaeger (1823–1899)

John Philip Yaeger was born in Germany on August 18, 1823, to John Jäger and Catherine Schawler. In his youth, he showed some talent for carving and art, but, following the wishes of his parents, he studied for the priesthood.

In 1846, at the age of twenty-three, he set out for Montreal with his two brothers in a sailing vessel. The ship encountered a terrible storm which threw the steerage passengers into a panic. As a divinity student, Yaeger prevailed upon his shipmates for order, faith, and prayers, which were rewarded with a change of wind and a calm sea. Upon arriving safely in Montreal, he continued his studies while his brothers, with no previous experience, attempted to breed racehorses and lost all their savings. After nine months, John Philip Yaeger left Montreal to go to Baltimore.

John Philip took up residence in the East Baltimore section among the large German population. His strong predilection for the arts took much time from his divinity studies, and by 1848, he was totally engaged as a carver and decorator. He became active in the social life of the community and met Catherine Hartman whom he married. In 1849, his wife gave birth to a son, Louis Emmanuel, but both of them died soon afterward. In his shop near the waterfront, John Philip did church- and shipcarving and also some forms for castings. He continued to take an active part in the community life and made many friends among the German businessmen and professional people. Among the merchants were toy, shoe, and tobacco traders who provided him with orders for signs and figures.

As a widower, Yaeger was introduced to many eligible women and in time found that three women were in love with him. In a most democratic manner, touched with the sense of humor for which he was later known, he informed each of the ladies that he would put their names on slips of paper in a bowl, cover his eyes, reach in, and pull out the name of his bride-to-be. He pulled out the name of Eva Catherine Popp, who indeed did become his wife and eventually bore him eleven children.[6]

By 1853, Yaeger had established a shop at the corner of Lombard and Concord Streets, where he conducted his business as a plain, ornamental, and fancy carver, for architectural and ship work; he also made molds

Fig. 101. Yaeger advertisement from Baltimore business directory of 1853–1854.

for castings and sculpture. He took a large advertisement in the business directory (Fig. 101) for 1853–1854. He moved his family to 106 East Baltimore and, after some attempts at Americanization, he took one step which cleared up the confusion over the spelling and pronunciation of his name, changing it permanently from Jäger or Yager to Yaeger. From 1855 to 1858, his shop was at the northwest corner of Baltimore and Frederick and thereafter at 5 East Lafayette between Bridge and Front Streets.

During the Civil War, Baltimore was a busy place and afforded the carver and woodworker a fair amount of employment. This came in handy as Yaeger then had six children to support with another on the way, and he had to keep busy to maintain his family. By his own account, he did all kinds of carving, especially for ships and tobacconists, in and near the Baltimore harbor.[7] In 1870, he moved to 39 Albemarle and the following year to 21 Albemarle; then in 1872, he moved to 41 Albemarle where he remained for a few years. The shadow of the Merchant's Shot Tower, nearly two hundred and fifty feet high, always fell on his shop, so he said—perhaps meaning that he was always at or near the waterfront (Fig. 102).[8] In 1880, Yaeger was at 41 East Lombard, but in 1887 he moved into a large house at 919 East Lombard near Exeter Street. The house had three large cellars which he used as storage areas for his finished work. Upstairs were two huge rooms which he used as his workshop. The living quarters for his large family were at the opposite end of the house, enabling him to conduct business without interference from domestic affairs.

Yaeger produced a large variety of tobacconists' figures in different

Fig. 102. Merchant's Shot Tower on the street of signs, Baltimore, 1875.

sizes. Among his tallest is the well-known figure of *Lo* which stood at 1000 East Pratt Street, the cigar store owned by Joseph Klein. The figure is 76½ inches high on a thirteen-inch base and was donated to the Maryland Historical Society in 1952 (Fig. 103).[9] A similar carving by Yaeger stood at the intersection of Baltimore and Liberty Streets but was destroyed in the fire of 1904, which burned a large section of downtown Baltimore and a large number of carved figures with it.[10] Another very tall squaw in a pose similar to *Lo* was owned by Edwin P. S. Newman, a Washington, D.C., collector, who bought many figures from Baltimore tobacconists' shops before 1920. On April 20, 1968, upon his death, Newman's collection of forty figures was sold at public auction in New York. In that collection were at least three other known Yaeger figures.

Fig. 103. Lo. Carved by John Philip Yaeger of Baltimore, c. 1878. Height 76½ inches, base 13 inches. Front of Joseph Klein's Cigar Store at 1000 East Pratt Street, Baltimore. Now in the Maryland Historical Society. Photograph: courtesy Sunpapers.

Fig. 104. Tobacconist's Figure. Carved by John Philip Yaeger of Baltimore, Maryland, c. 1876. From a pose by his daughter, Eva Isabelle, with her Juliet cap. Height 55 inches, base 14 inches. in the Maryland Historical Society.

In the Van Alstyne Folk Art Collection at the Smithsonian Institution in Washington, D.C., are two fine figures, both squaws, one with a papoose. Both are in the Silver Hill, Maryland, storage facility building. In the basement of the Maryland Historical Society in Baltimore is a carving (Fig. 104) that is evidently a portrait of Yaeger's eighth child and one of his favorites, Eva Isabelle. Height fifty-five inches on a fourteen-inch base. She had a favorite beanie or Juliet cap which managed to get into this figure of an Indian maiden. The incised heart on the Indian's bodice, beautifully designed in relationship to the entire area, has not been explained. It may have been Yaeger's way of saying she was his sweetheart, or it may have been the symbol of one of the many popular brands of tobacco.[11] In a drawing made by Yaeger, probably for the carving of a plaque, a younger Eva Isabelle wearing the same beanie sits astride the back of a cow and wrestles with its horn (Fig. 105). Eva Isabelle spent many an hour with "papa" in his workshop, and on occasion helped him sandpaper. One of her big sanding jobs was the altar of St. Vincent's church on Front Street, which was made piece by piece in Yaeger's workshop and assembled on location.

Yaeger worked in pine and hickory from spars obtained at the spar yard and evidently preferred working on over-sized carvings. A penciled

Fig. 105. Drawing of Eva Isabelle Yaeger. From sketchbook of John Philip Yaeger.

Fig. 106. Drawing of Perseus chopping off Medusa's head. From sketchbook of John Philip Yaeger.

drawing of a stern board, twelve feet by nineteen feet, is in his scrapbook in which he pasted engravings of the many races of people, their costumes, and other items used as references in his carvings. There is also a clipping from the Baltimore *Morning Herald* of Saturday, January 20, 1894, which shows quite prominently the scroll carving on the bow of the U.S. Cruiser *Montgomery*. The name of Philip Hichborn, Chief Constructor, U.S.N., appears in Yaeger's faded writing on the edge of the clipping. Perhaps the carving was one of Yaeger's. Another sketch by Yaeger shows a figure of Perseus in the act of chopping off the head of Medusa (Fig. 106). Another figure carved by Yaeger was once in the Pendergast Collection (Fig. 107).

For a period of time, Yaeger's son, Charles Philip, worked with him as an apprentice wood-carver. Another son, Louis G., was apprenticed as a coach painter. Each son used his specialty to help prepare the tobacconists' figures for the market. In 1893, Louis died. Yaeger had lost two other sons in previous years.[12] On July 20, 1893, Yaeger wrote a long letter to his favorite daughter, reviewing many of the family problems and interspersed with his wry humor:

It is very hot yet in the City but I have a good load of work from Ganter which refresh me— . . . I should think being August 18 next 70 years and so called over

Fig. 108. John Philip Yaeger,
1823–1899.

Fig. 107. Tobacconist's Squaw.
Carved by John Philip Yaeger,
Baltimore, Maryland, c. 1886.
Present location of figure
unknown. Photograph: courtesy
Sunpapers.

the death line. . . I have done enough. Willie goes out at 6 A.M. and coming home 11 or 12 P.M. Marie is singing washing and scrubbing all day. Marie sorting Carpet Strips and I cutting ships as usual. rent is paid—I have $10 over cash— have a month's expenses to cover outstanding to collect what more I want—2 meals —2 newspapers to read—2 glas bier and plenty of work, a good wife one day and a scolding woman for the next two days because for change etc. etc. hoping my health will continue for a while as will my humor and wishing the same to you. I remain yours in love—Jno Philip Yaeger.[13]

His health held up, as did his sense of humor, until his death on March 23, 1899 (Fig. 108).

William Teubner, Jr. (1857–1926)

William Teubner came to America in the early 1850s and settled in the German community of Baltimore. His training in Europe as a carver and cabinetmaker gained him immediate employment until 1855, when he decided to open his own shop at German and Sharp, making his home at 225 Saratoga. He engaged for some time in carving patterns for castings, institutional furniture, tobacconists' figures, and all kinds of architectural and shipcarving, mainly for smaller vessels. On November 27, 1857, his first child, William Teubner, Jr., was born. The boy attended one of the many German private institutions instead of Baltimore's public schools.[14]

Young William, like his father, showed talent at an early age. Taken into his father's shop as an apprentice, he learned the craft of the carver, and the handling of the various assignments that came into the shop. In 1874, the Teubners moved to 2 Fayette near Charles in downtown Baltimore, where they did some church work, furniture carving, patterns, figure carving, eagles, and shipwork. The nature of the shipwork is unknown. But at this time, "More than a thousand vessels arrive at Baltimore yearly. . . . Eight hundred little schooners and three thousand small-boats are engaged. . . ."[15] These may have provided his shop with some of the carved work.

In 1883, Teubner, Jr., moved to his own shop at 506 Callendar Alley, near St. Paul's Cemetery. Here, he obtained work similar to his father's.

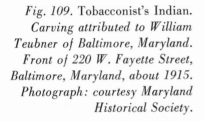

Fig. 109. Tobacconist's Indian. *Carving attributed to William Teubner of Baltimore, Maryland. Front of 220 W. Fayette Street, Baltimore, Maryland, about 1915. Photograph: courtesy Maryland Historical Society.*

In 1878, he married Mary Catherine Towson and in time there were four-teen children, of whom at least one, Charles W. Teubner, was listed as a "helper." Among the items made in his shop were the benches in the Senate, tobacconists' figures, clock cases, candlesticks, and furniture. There is no documentation for a family claim that Teubner carved the paddle-box decorations for the *Emma Giles*.

Two figures have been attributed to William Teubner, the father or son. One is a tall, distinguished figure which stood in front of Pressler's Vienna Restaurant at 220 West Fayette Street in Baltimore and was for many years a landmark on the Atlantic City boardwalk in front of number 121, Schwartz's Antique Shop (Fig. 109). The other is a smaller figure, which was bought in Baltimore by the late collector Edwin P. S. Newman of Washington, D.C., sometime before 1920.[16]

William Teubner, Jr., died on April 22, 1927, at the age of sixty-nine. Another member of the family, Gordon E. Teubner, still follows the tradition of the wood craftsman.

Other Baltimore Carvers

It is estimated that in the 1870s there were approximately eight hundred wooden Indian and tobacconists' figures in Baltimore.[17] Many carvings made in earlier years had come from other places like New York and Philadelphia.[18] There were at least four carvers besides Yaeger and Teubner turning out figures in Baltimore: James Campbell, a shipcarver; a tobacconist who had a large stock of tobacconists' figures and whose sign on West Fayette Street read "F. Dreves"; and Pierre G. Gaspari, who had been at 31 South Calvert for some years as an importer and manufacturer of meerschaum pipes, cigars, and fancy goods, and as a carver. Gaspari started his business in 1861 on West Baltimore Street and, in 1864, moved to South Street. Gaspari carried a large stock of all kinds of show figures and, while he was listed as a carver,[19] it is difficult to visualize his conducting a tobacconist shop while carving a stock of nearly two hundred figures —a full year's work for a group of four experienced carvers. Gaspari noted that he had a manufacturing branch in New York, which probably did most of his figures, except for those he may have purchased from the local carvers.[20]

Richard Callanan, shipcarver, had his shop at 19 Philpot in 1867. He was listed as a shipcarver at 74 Block in 1883 and at 1426 Block from 1896 to 1901. No show figures have been attributed to him, but it is possible that he helped supply the many that dotted the streets of Baltimore.[21] A figure from the Newman Collection (Fig. 110) sold at auction in New York in 1968 for $4,100, the highest price paid for a single figure. It came from the Baltimore area and was carved in the last quarter of the nineteenth century, but the carver is unidentified.[22]

Fig. 110. Tobacconist's Indian. *Carver unidentified, from the Baltimore area, c. 1870. Height 62 inches. Established record price of $4,100 at auction in 1968. Photograph Taylor & Dull.*

WASHINGTON, D.C.

Charles J. Hamilton (1832–?)

FIG. 111a

Charles J. Hamilton was born in Philadelphia in 1832, one year before the death of William Rush. In 1855, at the age of twenty-three, he was listed as a carver at 423 North 11th Street in Philadelphia. The following year, he listed himself as a sculptor at 431 North 11 ab. Poplar. In 1857, he changed his address to 783 Coates and the following year to 1214 Girard Avenue. By then Hamilton was married and had two children.[1]

In 1859, he moved with his family to 133 G Street North, Washington, D.C. He went into partnership with Elias W. Hadden, also a carver, and they established a shop at E Street North, about 13th Street West. Hamilton's wife, Leila, younger by four years, gave birth to another child in 1859.[2]

During his stay in Washington, D.C., Hamilton turned out carved work for tobacconists. In 1859, he supplied a druggist in the "Old Union Building" with a carving of a Negro in a huge mortar. Two watercolor and pencil drawings, front and side views, were prepared for this carving (Figs. 111a, 111b). The side view illustration has the inked notation, "Old Union Building, for W. C. 1859." Hamilton's signature is in the lower left-hand corner. Hamilton illustrated seven other figures—two views of a Turk (Figs. 112, 113), a Sultana (Fig. 114), an odd dwarf carrying a sign with "Medium" (Fig. 115), a squaw (Fig. 116), an Indian and a

Figs. 111a, 111b. Ink and pencil watercolors for a figure by Charles J. Hamilton, carved for a druggist in the old Union Building, Washington, D.C., in 1859. Original in author's collection.

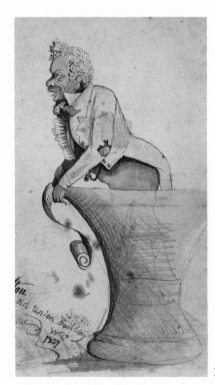

FIG. 111b

Fig. 112. Watercolor and ink and pencil sketch for tobacconist's figure by Charles J. Hamilton, Washington, D.C., from 1859 to 1865. Courtesy Home Insurance Company

FIG. 114

FIG. 115

FIG. 116

Figs. 113, 114, 115, 116, 117, 118, 119. Watercolor and ink and pencil sketches for tobacconists' figures by Charles J. Hamilton, Washington, D.C., from 1859 to 1865. Courtesy Home Insurance Company

tobacco plant (Fig. 117), a Punch (Fig. 118), and a sketch of a smoking Negro standing on a pedestal marked "Signs" (Fig. 119). These sketches turned up in 1921 at an auction by Samuel T. Freeman & Company of Philadelphia. Three portfolios of watercolors were offered in this sale; one contained the sketches of James Hamilton, the nineteenth-century marine painter of Philadelphia, and the others were by Charles J. Hamilton. In one of his portfolios were renderings of tombstone and monument designs, which may indicate that Hamilton had prepared sketches for monument carvers or did this kind of carving himself. The other portfolio contained approximately thirty-five renderings of tobacconists' signs, of which only ten drawings are now extant. At the time of the auction none of the watercolors brought more than one dollar and thirty cents.[3]

In 1865, Hamilton terminated his partnership with Hadden. Between

FIG. 113

FIG. 117

FIG. 118

FIG. 119

1872 and 1873, he turned up in Charleston, South Carolina. He resided at 76 Rutledge Avenue and listed his occupation as a "Painter." He did an oil on canvas of "Charleston Square," a very lively primitive painting which retained the style and feeling of his tobacconists' figure sketches. The painting is in the Abby Aldrich Rockefeller Folk Art Collection and is signed, "C. J. Hamilton, Artist, 1872." Another signed Hamilton painting is a most stylized still life, signed in the same manner but with no date or title. The painting is in the collection of the Addison Gallery of American Art, Phillips Academy, Andover, Massachusetts. No signed carvings by Hamilton have come to light.

In 1881, Hamilton returned to Washington, D.C. He lived at 1536 I Street N.W. with a member of his family, Leila A. Hamilton, who was employed as a clerk in the Treasury Department.[4]

DETROIT

Julius Theodore Melchers (1829–1909)

From the middle nineteenth through the twentieth centuries no American wood-carver received as much recognition during his lifetime as Julius Theodore Melchers (Fig. 120). Melchers, who had his training abroad, influenced a large number of American artists and wood-carvers in Detroit, Michigan.

He was born in Soest, Prussia, in 1829. His mother was of French-Dutch origin, the daughter of the burgomaster of Rees in the Netherlands and also a descendant of Doctor Heyman who is a figure in a fragment of a burnt Rembrandt in the Amsterdam Museum. On his father's side, Melchers was related to an eighteenth-century cardinal and an archbishop.[1]

At fifteen years of age, he was apprenticed to Minsterman, a sculptor and master wood-carver. In his youth Melchers engaged in revolutionary activity. When the rebellion of 1848 failed, he, along with thousands of his compatriots, was forced to leave his homeland. He settled in Paris where he studied in academies and private schools under Carpeaux and Etex. His active engagement in politics during that time resulted in his involuntary removal to England in 1851. For one year he obtained work as a modeler in the Crystal Palace and then left for America. While in New York, he was employed in various occupations which gave him a precarious livelihood. On learning that many of his compatriots and a few of his fellow revolutionaries had settled in Detroit, he moved to that city in 1852.[2]

Melchers received a hearty welcome from his fellow countrymen in Detroit. In 1848 they had organized the Harmonie Society, which he joined, and he soon became one of its best singers. Word spread that Melchers was searching for work but the talents of the artist-sculptor were not in great demand. Art appreciation was at a very low ebb in Detroit

Fig. 120. Julius Theodore Melchers, 1829–1909. Photograph: courtesy John William Stroh.

at this time; architecturally, the city was backward; shipbuilding had not yet reached its later strides; and there was no tobacco industry to require the skills of the carver. Melchers was first employed by Henry Weber but the nature of the work he did is unknown. Bishop Lefevre was the first to recognize Melchers's talents and gave him some important church commissions.[3] In 1855 Melchers was at 150 Beaubien. By 1857 he had moved to 122 Congress East, listing himself as a "sculptor and carver."

George B. Catlin, in an article for the Detroit *News* on January 4, 1925, stated:

Down on Woodward Avenue, a few doors north of the Mariner's Church, Isaac S. Miller had a little tobacco factory and retail shop which was the beginning of the tobacco industry in Detroit. Mr. Melchers's first commission was the carving of a wooden Indian of a design which would appeal to the passer-by. It was to be an erect and alert figure of a wooden Indian holding out a bundle of wooden cigars in his left hand while his right held in reserve a tommyhawk as if to give each wayfarer his choice of punishments. Mr. Melchers took the job with misgivings but turned out a highly creditable figure of an Indian, life size. Mr. Miller was delighted with it and had it painted in gaudy colors, and when Mr. Melchers went to look at his finished product as it was placed on a pedestal in front of the tobacco shop he gave it one wild look, threw up his hands and exclaimed: "Mein Gott, and dis is art, in America!"

But this was only the beginning of art in Detroit for Mr. Melchers. Other tobacco shops were opened and each of them wanted a wooden Indian. Dealers out in the state came to buy tobacco and were captivated by the Miller advertising design, so the wooden Indian became a conventional necessity for tobacco stores, and Mr. Melchers was so overwhelmed for a time with orders of duplication that he came to loathe his calling. But the creation of wooden Indians earned bread and butter, and a man must live.[4]

In an interview by J. H. Junkin for the Detroit *News Tribune*, July 23, 1899, Melchers gave his views on Indians and his early start:

"We don't know how long the Indian has been used as a tobacco sign. Before I left Germany, which was in 1849, pictures of Indians were hung up in tobacco shops, and were pasted on packages of tobacco. The first wooden Indians I saw were merely profiles, sawed out of a board, and painted to represent Indians. When I came to Detroit, in 1852, a few rudely carved and badly painted signs were found at the stores. The first work I did in Detroit was to carve a little chief, about five feet high. I hired an Indian to put on a lot of savage finery and pose as a model. It was no trouble to get an Indian model in those days. Give one of them a lunch and a glass of beer and he was happy. He would pose all day, if I wanted him to. When I got the image done I received $55 for it, and spent the money for a boat and a gun, and went exploring."

"Where did you explore, Mr. Melchers?"

"Oh, I'm the greatest explorer in this region. I explored the River Rouge. I'm the first white man that ever saw the lotus beds on the Rouge and knew what they were. Many of the people in Detroit don't know that there are lotus flowers along that stream, but there are many acres of them about the mouth of the Roulo Creek.

"Then I carved more Indians. I bought a lot of old masts at the old Clark drydock. There's no timber like an old mast for carving. It is straight-grained, and so thoroughly seasoned with its many years of exposure on the deck of a ship that there is no danger of its cracking. I carved all sorts of Indians. Big Indians, chiefs, and Indian queens. Sometimes the images represented real characters but they were oftener ideal figures."

"What prices did you get for the Indians?"

"From $5 to $150. The highest price was for a very large Indian I made for a man in Chicago. Sometimes a cigar dealer wanted a classical figure instead of an Indian. We carved several of them with slight variations to indicate the cigar business. A statue of Pomona with a handful of cigars insteads of apples, or Ceres, holding a bunch of tobacco leaves, instead of wheat, was a striking sign, and indicated classical proclivities on the part of the proprietor. Sometimes a patriotic fellow wanted a Goddess of Liberty or Uncle Sam. I have made several Brother Jonathans for customers with strong Yankee sentiments. Along in the '70s the fancy figure known as the 'Girl of the Period' was quite popular."

The "Girl of the Period" of which Mr. Melchers spoke was dressed in a style in vogue about 1873 with the "Grecian bend," high heeled shoes and a natty little cap, with a squirrel perched upon the top of it. A "Girl of the Period" still stands in front of the Old Sol cigar factory at 188 Randolph Street, but some sign painter who had a job of painting it evidently mistook her for an Indian squaw and decorated it according to his idea of a female aborigine.

"In late years," said Mr. Melchers, " a great many images have been made in a factory in New York, where each image is carved in several pieces—legs, arms, and heads being made separately and put together with glue and dowl pins. I always carved my images in one piece, except extending arms or projections that were too great for the dimensions of the leg. These factories have made a great many cast-iron figures, carving one in wood first, for a pattern. In this way they have made a great deal of money. But there is little demand for any of them now."

"Why is the Indian disappearing, Mr. Melchers?"

"I think that Yankee thrift has done it. The American merchants are pretty shrewd businessmen, and there is a demand for space on sidewalks for fruit and news stands and many other kinds of business. The Italians pay good rent for the space, and there is no room for the signs."

"The Italians have crowded the Indians out, you think?"

"That's the idea, exactly. Just as the white race has crowded the real Indians off the face of the Earth."

Mr. Melchers has long made a study of Indian character and customs and has the largest and best collection of Indian curiosities in the state. Many of them he gathered himself, and the rest formed the collection of Gen. David S. Stanley, who led the expedition which explored Yellowstone region in 1873, and was the best informed man regarding the Indian tribes in the United States. Mr. Melchers purchased Gen. Stanley's entire collection several years ago. . . . Many of the articles are wonderful examples . . . among them is a buckskin and hunting shirt which belonged to Black Hawk, the famous chief of the Sacs and Foxes . . .[5]

The carving of wooden Indians was only one phase of Melchers's work; his experience at modeling in plaster and his education as a sculptor and artist stood him in good stead, and various jobs came to him requiring these skills. Feeling somewhat secure, in 1858 Melchers married Mary Bangetor, who was born in Buffalo, New York. Many of the veterans of the unsuccessful German revolution of 1848 formed a group known as the "48ers" and with the outbreak of the Civil War in 1861, these liberty-loving Detroiters played gallant roles in the "War of the States." Before the Civil War, Melchers took in a few art students, some of whom became his apprentices in his little workshop at 83 Randolph Street near Jefferson. Young men with talent for drawing sought him out for instruction. Many of these were employed elsewhere through the week and were too tired to attend classes at night, so Melchers started conducting Sunday morning classes at the old Arbeiter Hall and had a large number of students.

It may be said without exaggeration that out of Julius Melchers's studio and his Sunday morning classes came much of Detroit's artistic development during the succeeding thirty-five years. Practically all the well-known artists who have come out of Detroit, and some of them are world-famous, had their early instruction and their basic ideas of art out of the Melchers's School. When he found an apt pupil who took his work seriously, the old master would rub his hands and chuckle with delight. At the sight of a meritorious piece of work he would indulge in an expansive smile, grip the student by the shoulder and shout: "Gut, boy gans gut; maybe you'll be a real artist some day." But if he caught one of them skylarking and disturbing the others or doing a slovenly bit of work, he would fly into a rage and denounce him, sometimes ending his censure with a hearty box on the ear of the offender.[6]

Melchers was a rigid and exacting instructor of the old school. He kept his apprentices working hard at the bench for nine hours a day and demanded that they continue their studies at home after the day's work. At the end of four years of apprenticeship, he would decide if the student's ability warranted continuation in the profession, always with a warning that if they wanted to grow rich or become a success in the eyes of the world during their lifetime they had better take up some other work; that the world regarded originality with suspicion and often with hostility.[7]

Soon after the Civil War, the city of Detroit resumed the task of building its City Hall, which was delayed by the war. By 1870, the work was well advanced, and the architect's plans called for four statues to be placed at the corners of the central towers. Fourteen feet high, these figures were to represent Justice, Industry, Art, and Commerce. Melchers was selected to do the carving. A shed was erected on a plot and here he carved the figures from blocks of Cleveland sandstone. Upon completion, they were derricked into position around the tower. The architect's plans called for four other statues in niches; two on the east front and two on the west. These were not filled until fourteen years later when Bela Hubbard, a pioneer citizen and a man of culture and wealth, offered to bear the cost. He suggested that the four figures represent Cadillac, the founder of the city; LaSalle, the first white man to navigate the Detroit River; Father Marquette, the first missionary to the Indians of Michigan; and Father Gabriel Richard, pastor of St. Anne's Church, for thirty-four years respected by Catholics and Protestants, and the only priest who was ever elected a representative to the Congress of the United States.

Fig. 121. Jefferson and Randolph Streets, Detroit, about 1898. Melchers' studio is behind the Brush Street horsecar with his wall sign above. Courtesy Burton Historical Collection, Detroit Public Library. Photograph: J. Klima, Jr.

Hubbard asked John M. Donaldson, a Detroit architect with broad experience to design the figures. Donaldson consented only on condition that the carving be done by Julius Melchers. Donaldson made the model for the statue of Father Marquette. The other three models as well as the carving of all four in stone were done by Melchers. As the work was too large to be executed at Melchers's studio on Randolph Street, it was done at his home at 340 Fort Street East.[8]

Melchers's workshop constituted the ground floor of half a small brick building with alley windows (Fig. 121). The shop was filled with plaster casts, drawings, designs, and half-finished carvings of all types (Fig. 122). He turned out architectural carvings, decorative plaster molds, busts, eagles, tobacconists' figures, steamboat and ship carvings, and various types of church carvings.[9] For over thirty-six years Melchers advertised yearly, in the Detroit city directories, his skills as a "Sculptor, Modeler and Wood Carver," and his "Figures for Tobacco Signs Always on hand or made to order: Ornaments for Churches; Carving for Vessels, Build-

Labels within the drawing:
BUST OF JULIUS MELCHERS

A CORNER IN THE STUDIO

SCULPTORS AT WORK.

SCULPTOR JULIUS MELCHERS AND HIS WORKSHOP.

Fig. 122. Drawings of Melchers' studio as pictured in the Detroit-News Tribune, August 22, 1897.

ing, Furniture; Ornamental Patterns for Casting."[10] "His charges were moderate but, if somebody offered Melchers a commission and haggled about the price he would give way to righteous indignation and tell his clients to look elsewhere."[11] A bill dated May 21, 1878, to D. Bethune Duffield for a plaster bust of the client shows the charges to have been $50 (Fig. 123).

In 1890, Melchers took a former apprentice into the business as a partner and his ads read, "Melchers & Siebert, Sculptors, Modellers and Wood Carvers, 83 Randolph Street." Henry A. Siebert was one of the several Detroit modelers and pattern makers who received nearly all his training from Melchers. The partnership lasted only until the end of 1895 when Melchers listed his work as modelmaker and wood-carver at 83 Randolph Street.[12]

Melchers had several competitors; two of the better known were Theodore Crongeyer, a "Designer, Sculptor and Carver in Wood," at 55

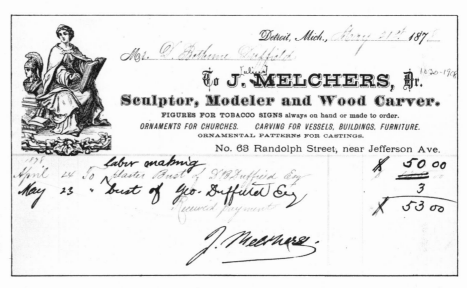

Fig. 123. Invoice of Julius Theodore Melchers, May 21, 1878. Courtesy Burton Historical Collection, Detroit Public Library.

Farmer, and also Ferdinand Lapp, a "Carver, Sculptor and Designer," at 72 Congress Street East. Lapp also conducted classes in drawing at his studio on the third floor.[13] Melchers had very little respect for one of these men. He expressed his sentiments in an interview as follows:

Mr. Melchers takes the pride out of art triflers, if they have any pride. He humiliates them by exposing their deceitful purposes. His words are one long clear call back to art for art's sake. A sham artist or a make-believe sculptor, of whom there are many in Detroit, no doubt, listening to Mr. Melchers' talk, would, if they had any brains, throw his tools into the river, give up his pretenses and go to work. In another connection mentioning a Detroit Sculptor, he said, "He is the worst enemy I have in the world. If I made a bid of $5 on some work, and he hears of it he will say: 'What, Melchers bids $5? Then I'll bid $2.50.' But the fellow is good in his art and I respect him for that, all the same."[14]

Melchers's most famous and illustrious student was his own son. When a son was born to his wife Mary in 1860, he named him Garibaldi after the Italian revolutionary leader who conducted a long struggle for Italian unity in an effort to unite his people divided since the days of Napoleon Bonaparte. Gari, as he was known to his friends, came under his father's rigid schooling when he first showed signs of artistic ability. He took to his work with great enthusiasm which delighted his strict instructor. He would point out his boy in a corner, "That piece *Night* is by him.[15] If it had been made by Gen. Alger's son, don't you know, the papers would be full of it? If there were a rich young man in Detroit who could carve like Henry or any of my boys, it would be considered almost a miracle."[16]

Gari was in Europe seven years with the best teachers and while he was away he often wrote to me and said: "Papa, I can sell a picture for so much. Do you think I had better take the time?" "Bah!" was what I would think, "What is the use? Every picture made for mere money is of no account for art!" I insisted that my Gari work without thought of pay, for the seven years of apprenticeship. That is the trouble with us Americans! We are always thinking of price, cost, sell, and all that. We move about too much, we are here now, in London next month, in Paris in the fall, and so on. The American art student gets about so far and then stops. He is usually on the very edge of a career, when he rushes at something else. He wants to make money, you see. I taught my Gari not to care a straw for flattering words. What good would columns in the papers be if he disappointed expectations? He wrote me repeatedly saying: "Papa, I won't have any puffery; I don't want a line in the papers; it will do me no good." Gari Melchers went on to win the Legion of Honor and the endearing respect of his father and of the entire city of Detroit.[17]

Toward the end of the century, Melchers had little work, and went to his studio as a matter of routine, for only a few hours each day. He still took in apprentices who were subjected to the usual Melchers standard of discipline and adherence to the principles of art. "I don't take boys who have not the real art spirit; I have no time to fool; I want thorough boys or none at all." He referred to himself as "the old man who is merely a wood-carver."[18] Without doubt, Melchers's wood carvings are among our finest. His figures, usually elongated, had an air of elegance. The poses are simple and straightforward, the figures perfectly proportioned with a great amount of dignity, and meticulous attention is paid to small details. Tobacconists' Indians carved by Melchers were, in most cases, authentically costumed, reflecting his knowledge of American Indians. These are not the works of a primitive carver, but of the experienced sculptor with a classical education in the arts.

During the year 1900, Melchers gave up his workshop on Randolph Street and confined his activities to his home at 73 Seyburn Avenue. On May 28, 1907, Melchers suffered a stroke that deprived him of speech and affected the use of an arm. He had been ailing for three years and the stroke was not unexpected. Two years later on January 14, 1909, apoplexy struck, and Detroit lost a great citizen and its finest sculptor. In

1909, the many friends and former pupils of Melchers commissioned the famous architectural sculptor, Adolph Alexander Weinman, to design a large, bronze bas-relief plaque in memory of the artist-sculptor-wood-carver and musician of early Detroit. It was dedicated and placed at the Detroit Institute of Art in 1910.[19]

Fortunately, several important Melchers's wood carvings still survive. Although time, fire, and the elements worked against his tobacconists' figures, some have endured and are now, in most cases, in museums. One of these figures, a tall Indian, slightly over seventy-two inches, is signed by Melchers with a script M in the center of the medal hanging from its neck (Fig. 124). The whole figure is carefully planned with the directional visual devices of folds in the robe to break up the straight vertical direction of the feathered headdress and the feathered belt. This carving is in the collection of the New York Historical Association in Cooperstown, New York.

Another figure, nearly eighty-four inches high has a large amount of incised ornamentation. In the half-moon neck ornament it bears the incised script capitals K. J., which is supposedly Kunstler Julius (artist Julius) or more likely Kapitan Jack, the germanic for Captain Jack (Fig. 125). This figure was made in 1867 for Schott Brothers of Lincoln, Il-

FIG. 125

FIG. 124

Fig. 124. Signed tobacconist's figure by Julius Theodore Melchers. Height 73 inches. Courtesy New York Historical Association, Cooperstown, New York.

Fig. 125. Captain Jack Figure. Photograph taken in 1950 by A. W. Pendergast. Letters K. J. incised in neck ornament. Courtesy John William Stroh Collection.

Fig. 126. Captain Jack *or* Chief Red Jacket. *Carved by Julius Theodore Melchers, c. 1867. Front of the Schott Brothers' Tobacco Shop in Lincoln, Illinois, 1895.*

linois, at a cost of $367, including crating. The photograph (Fig. 126) of Kapitan Jack in front of the Schott Bros. shop was taken near the end of the nineteenth century.[20] A quite similar half-sized Melchers figure was once in the A.W. Pendergast collection. Undoubtedly, one of the finest carvings of a wooden Indian and probably the best made by Melchers, is a very tall figure of Chief Keokuk, of the Sauks and Fox tribes, now in the New-York Historical Society's collection (Fig. 127). The figure stands eighty-four inches high on a seven-inch base. The carving is nearly identical to a daguerreotype from which engravings of the Chief were later made. The figure is in near-perfect condition, and like the other known figures by Melchers has the dark brown color of faded varnish.

The story of Keokuk is a fascinating one.

Keokuk (the Watchful Fox) was not a hereditary chieftain, but attained the chieftaincy of the Sauk nation by courage, military skill, eloquence, superb physical appearance, and a deep knowledge of human nature. Born in Saukenuk, in 1788, to humble parents, he was a born horseman and great admirer of the beautiful; "his weak points were whiskey, women and horses."[21]

At fifteen he was as bold as any man and the most daring horseman of his nation. His fondness for horses made him an excellent judge and the best of trainers. When just fifteen years old, he was permitted the honor of accompanying the warriors of his tribe on the warpath against their natural enemies, the feared and powerful Sioux, whose name means the enemy. In the skirmish between the bands of both tribes, a burly Sioux brave, seeing this haughty boy mounted on a magnificent pony, took a fancy to the pony, and attempted to kill the lad. The Sioux were admitted to be the best horsemen among all the Indian nations, and an encounter with them on their level was shunned. Keokuk "placed his lance at proper rest, and rushed at the Sioux with the speed of the wind. With equal fury on came the Sioux. The encounter was fierce and short. Keokuk's lance passed through the breast of the Sioux who fell from his horse carrying with him his opponent's spear, which had pierced his heart."[22]

The act of courage and strength gained for Keokuk a powerful reputation that started him on his way to eventual chieftaincy.

A great feast was given at which he was admitted a member of the braves. Within a few years he advanced to chief of the fourth grade, or the Eagle, which he occupied in 1812, when Chief Black Hawk left Saukenuk with 200 braves to join the British. The history of Keokuk reads like the best of the Wild West novels. He became a great statesman, a friend of the white man, and a legend in his own time. "He usually wore a robe elaborately ornamented with porcupine quill, and the gaudy colored feathers of the wild drake and other richly plumaged birds."[23] Numerous paintings by many artists exist of Keokuk, most famous is the painting by George Catlin. In 1837, when Keokuk with his wife and son, accompanied by Black Hawk and other Sauk chiefs, were in the city of

Fig. 127. Keokuk. *Chief of the Sauks and Foxes. Carved portrait by Julius Theodore Melchers. Height 83½ inches, base 7 inches. Courtesy New-York Historical Society.*

New York, they attended a public lecture given by Catlin on North American Indians. He exhibited his paintings of the most illustrious Indians and when he displayed his painting of Keokuk mounted on his favorite horse:

> They [the Indians] all sprang up and hailed it with a piercing yell. When the noise subsided, Keokuk arose and addressed the audience in these words: "My friends, I hope you will pardon my men for making so much noise, as they were very much excited by seeing me on my favorite war-horse, which they all recognized in a moment."[24]

Keokuk died in 1848 at the Sauk reservation on the Marie de Cygnes, or Mother of Swans River, Franklin County in the state of Kansas.

On the Melchers's figure of Keokuk, in a carved thonged basket on the medal is incised an arrow hung from the neck. He used this device on another of his figures.

In some collections there are tobacconists' figures which were made in the Melchers's workshop in his style, but which are not by his hand. Some are either too rigid or awkward in pose, irregular in proportion, or unprofessional in execution.

> I made Black Hawks, Pontiacs, Hiawathas, and Pocahontases. The first Hiawatha I carved was for Danile Scotten, when he brought out his Hiawatha brand of fine cut. But I made Indians only when there was a lack of other work, or to keep my apprentices employed. I made the models, and they cut out the image. They liked this work as it gave them practice in study of figures.[25]

Another of Melchers's figures is seventy-two inches high on an eight and one-half inch stand (Fig. 128). In one hand are tied tobacco leaves and it probably once held a musket or bow in the right hand now missing. Melchers cut thin folds in the robe, and the area from waist to hemline in front is decorated with more thin folds, to break up the long blank space. The headdress feathers fall gracefully about the head and the fine incised feathers call attention to the face. The figure is privately owned. On May 21, 1872, Melchers patented a horse's head hitching post and an illustrated advertisement appeared in the Detroit *Post* of July 1, 1872.

In Detroit in the 1870s, many tobacconists' figures could be found in the streets. G. W. Pattison & Co.'s Old Book Store at 63 Griswold Street had a figure in front (Fig. 129). The squaw, advertising pipes and cigars, appear to be much like the *Princess of the Ottawas*, also of Detroit and attributed to Melchers (Fig. 130). It had an inscription painted on its side after 1937 listing the names and dates of its owners. The earliest owner was McKune, 1870–1875, followed by John Meyers, 1875–1901, then Baxter, 1901–1908, and finally John Kenny, 1908–1933. The figure has none of the characteristics of the Melchers carvings and may

FIG. 128

Fig. 128. Tobacconist's Figure. *Carved by Julius Theodore Melchers. Height 71 inches. Right hand once held bow or musket. Photograph: Taylor & Dull.*

Fig. 129. Squaw. *Probably by Julius Theodore Melchers, c. mid-1870s. Front of 63 Griswold Street, Detroit. Courtesy Burton Historical Collection, Detroit Public Library.*

Fig. 130. Princess of the Ottawas. *Attributed to Julius Theodore Melchers, c. 1870. Height 51 inches, base 17 inches. Courtesy Virginia Museum of Fine Arts, Richmond.*

FIG. 130

FIG. 129

have been made by another of the Detroit carvers or by one of Melchers's assistants. It is in the Virginia Museum of Fine Arts in Richmond.

Melchers carved the state's Coat of Arms for the Michigan Centennial Building in Philadelphia in 1876.[26] In 1906, he carved a new seal for the city of Detroit.

Theodore Crongeyer

Theodore Crongeyer, like Melchers, came to America before the Civil War and settled in the refugee German colony of Detroit. By that time, Melchers was well established and Crongeyer found work slow in coming in. In 1871, there were three shops in Detroit manufacturing wooden Indians for tobacco signs. Crongeyer, who free-lanced, was one of these manufacturers.[27] In 1872, he listed himself as a wood-carver, boarding at 239 Jefferson Avenue. In 1873, he went into partnership with Henry Schmitz. The firm was listed as "Schmitz & Crongeyer, Carvers," each working from his home. The partnership lasted only one year during which time Crongeyer met Ferdinand Averbeck. Averbeck had more business experience, and he and Crongeyer set up a new partnership. Their shop was at 49 Farmer Street in Detroit, and an advertisement taken in the city directory for 1874–1875 read "Crongeyer & Averbeck, House & Ship Carvers, Designers & Modelers—Ornamental Patterns, Carved Signs, Old Ship carving regilded."[28]

The partnership lasted a little over a year. Crongeyer then moved the shop to 55 Farmer Street where he remained for the next sixteen years. Here he made patterns for architectural interiors, ship carvings, tobacconists' figures, and some church work in figures and altars. He continued listing himself as a sculptor until 1879 and thereafter as a "wood-carver." After 1880, he produced mostly carved signs, some cabinet work, a few ship carvings, and figures for the tobacconists. Crongeyer continued this work until 1893, when he was made a deputy sheriff and gave up his workshop on Farmer Street. After 1896–1897 Crongeyer returned to his skills as a woodworker, taking on mostly cabinetmaking with his son. In 1910, he received an appointment in some capacity in the Department of Public Works.[29]

Crongeyer's style of wood carving shows the traditional German schooling. He paid a great deal of attention to small details and broke up the large surfaces with some decorative elements. Crongeyer may have had his apprenticeship under a German shipcarver accounting for similarities in their styles. A tobacconist's figure of an Indian Maiden (Fig. 131), now owned by the Henry Ford Museum at Dearborn, has a brass plaquette, 1¼ inches by 3¼ inches, fastened to the base and is inscribed, "T. Crongeyer, 235 Jeff. Av. Detroit, Mich" (Fig. 132). The figure is fifty-two inches in height overall and dates to 1873, the year Crongeyer was in partnership with Henry Schmitz.

FIG. 132

FIG. 131

Fig. 131. Tobacconist's Indian. *Carved by Theodore Crongeyer, Detroit, 1873. Collection Henry Ford Museum & Greenfield Village. Photograph: courtesy Norman Flayderman.*

Fig. 132. *Brass plaquette on base of Fig. 131, revealed when paint was removed.*

SOME OF DETROIT'S TOBACCO SIGNS.

Girl of the Period.
Indian Queen at 34 Lafayette avenue.

Oriental Flower Girl.
Indian 49 years old.

Fig. 133. Some of Detroit's tobacco signs in 1899.

Other Detroit Carvers

Two Detroit carvers may have contributed to the gallery of tobacconists' figures: Anthony Osebold, Jr., who was at 366 Division Street, and was listed in 1882 as a "Sculptor and carver, statues in wood, stone, marble, also church furniture";[30] and, Charles Guhle at 207 Champlain, "Wood carver and ornamental designer," listed in 1888.[31]

In 1899, the oldest cigar-store Indian in Detroit, known to have been in constant use since 1850, stood in front of the Cabinet cigar store at

36 Monroe Avenue. Beside it stood a "Colossal figure of Atlas performing his arduous contract of holding up the earth."[32] Two doors away, at No. 40, was an iron figure representing an oriental girl holding a bundle of cigars. A Detroit *News Tribune* artist went about town sketching these figures on a hot summer's day in 1899 (Fig. 133).[33]

ASHLAND, WISCONSIN

Herman Kruschke (Dates Unknown)

On Sunday, August 21, 1932, the Washington *Star* ran a two-column story in the magazine section under the headline, "Cigar-Store Indian Becomes a Valuable Relic." The photograph used to illustrate the Indian showed a long-braided brave dressed in fringed deerskins holding or leaning on a huge cigar (Fig. 134).

There's Bob Parsons, pioneer tobacco dealer at Ashland, Wisconsin, whose store still is guarded, after 40 years, by fierce-eyed chief Sitting Bull. Parsons is intensely proud of his Indian.

Fig. 134. Chief Sitting Bull. *Carved by Herman Kruschke, c. 1882. Front of the tobacco shop of Bob Parsons, Ashland, Wisconsin.*

"Sitting Bull is an exact model of the great chief who ruled the Dakota Plains when white men first pushed beyond the Mississippi River," says Parsons. "He was carved for me by hand from white pine by Herman Kruschke, a woodworker at Ashland, half a century ago."

Conclusive proof that Sitting Bull is, indeed, a realistic model was provided some years ago when Buffalo Bill and his Wild West Show played Ashland. Somewhat bored, the Western Indians were marching by Parsons' Shop when they saw the giant wooded chieftain.

With loud war whoops they deserted the parade and surrounded the statue of their old chief. Finally they were herded back into line, but between performances they were to be seen grouped wonderingly about their revered leader.

The region around Ashland was once the assembly ground for Chippewa and Sioux tribes. When Sitting Bull had been at his present location a number of years, Indians of the region decided to make a treaty before him. A hundred Sioux and Chippewa braves, fierce-looking warriors with lean horses, grouped themselves about the wooded model of Sitting Bull while the ceremony solemnly was executed.[1]

In 1888 the carver, Herman Kruschke, was engaged in making church decorations, scroll sawings, newels, and railings at 408 Ninth Avenue West, maintaining his residence in the same building. In 1890, he was making office fixtures and also had a planing mill. In 1893, Kruschke entered into partnership with Julius Kinkel, manufacturing "saloon, store, bank, office, and drug store fixtures and show cases."[2] His wife Amy, and his daughter Laura, kept the books and did some work in the office. Kruschke moved to 322 9th Avenue West in 1899. Some difficulties may have arisen between the partners, resulting in Kinkel's taking over the business in 1899 and forcing Kruschke to look for other employment. In 1901, Kruschke became a laborer, doing various kinds of work.[3]

There is no record of Kruschke's engaging in figure carving and it can be assumed that the Sitting Bull carving, a creditable figure, was the only one he made.

PROVIDENCE

Charles Dowler (1841–1931)

Charles Parker Dowler came to the United States from England as a gunsmith to make arms for the North during the Civil War. Directly after the war he engaged in wood carving and sculpture and opened his first carving shop in 1869 at 84 Orange Street in Providence, Rhode Island, while residing at Hardenberg in North Providence. Dowler listed himself as an "Ornamental Designer."[1]

Dowler was born in Birmingham, England in 1841, one of a family of fourteen children. He arrived in America in 1863. The following year he married Eliza Norton of Birmingham, a childhood sweetheart also born in 1841. Eliza Dowler was a talented dressmaker who carried on her professional career while her husband was engaged in sculpture and wood carving.

In 1870, Charles Dowler moved to 52 Pine Street at the corner of Peck and the following year moved again to 56 Peck. His advertisement read, "Charles Dowler, Carver and Ornamental Designer—all kinds of carving for furniture & houses in the latest style of the art."[2]

In the mid-1870s, Dowler moved his shop to 49 Peck Street, purchasing a house at 581 Smith Street where he lived for the rest of his life. This wooden structure could have served as his sample for "houses in the latest style of the art," as he added masses of well-designed scroll carvings to the eaves, the porch, and the fences surrounding the dwelling. By 1881, Dowler was well-established as a carver and sculptor. That year he took an advertisement in the Providence city directory which read:

Charles Dowler, Carver, Modeler and Ornamental Designer. Carving for architectural and furn. Decorations, models of fruit, flowers, and statuary, etc. for sale & made to order. Casts taken from the living and dead. No. 49 Peck Street, Providence.[3]

Fig. 135. Racetrack Tout. *Carved by Charles Dowler in 1890. Front of the V. Aidala Tobacco Store at 351 Atwell Avenue, Providence. Height 48 inches. Photograph: courtesy Index of American Design.*

In 1896 Dowler moved his shop to 33 Eddy and 47 Washington, Room 39, and engaged in making patterns for jewelers and bronze work and models for monumental works. About this time he designed the Collyer Monument in Pawtucket as well as the John Sparks Monument at Bristol.[4] Among the figures he was called upon to carve were some show figures for merchants and tobacconists. One of his figures stood in front of the V. Aidala Tobacco Store at 351 Atwell Avenue in Providence until the mid-1930s. According to the owner, the figure was made in 1890, represented a racing tout, and once had a whip in his hand. The figure stood forty-eight inches high on a stand with rollers (Fig. 135).[5] Another racetrack tout is in the Abby Aldrich Rockefeller Folk Art Collection (Col. Fig. 20).

In 1919, after fifty-five years of active work, Dowler retired. Then, although more than seventy-five years of age, he took up painting and became proficient as an artist. He traveled extensively in Europe, photographing points of interest which he used as slides in lectures he gave upon his return. On January 24, 1931, Dowler died in Providence, Rhode Island.[6]

GLOUCESTER

David R. Proctor (Dates Unknown)

The Essex Institute at Salem, Massachusetts, owns a tobacconist's figure of an Indian which stood in front of Mancell's Cigar Store in Gloucester, Massachusetts, until 1910 (Fig. 136). It was said to have been made in 1855 by David R. Proctor. In 1856, Proctor was listed in the directory at Belfast, Maine, as a "shipcarver."[7] The figure, fifty-four inches high, has a silver-painted pelt, red shoes, and a headdress of silver with a blue band. No other figure by Proctor is known.

Fig. 136. Cigar-Store Indian. Carved by David H. Proctor, c. 1855. Height approximately 54 inches. Stood in front of the Mancell's Cigar Store, Gloucester, Massachusetts, until 1910. Essex Institute, Salem, Mass. Photograph: courtesy Index of American Design.

CANADA

Louis Jobin [signature]

Louis Jobin (1845–1928)

Fig. 137. Louis Jobin as a young man. Photograph: courtesy Mlle. Charlotte Perron.

Louis Jobin was born in St. Raymond in the province of Quebec, on October 26, 1845. His father was Jean-Baptiste Jobin and his mother was the former Luce Dion. Jobin spent his boyhood at Point Aux Trembles, above Quebec City. In his youth he took to carving quite naturally. In reply to a question, during his advanced years, if he whittled as a youngster, his answer was, "Oh oui, I cut all the firewood into something. There was a great deal of wood in all my figures then. Their bodies were what you call—clumsy—clumsy, yes."[1]

At nineteen years of age, Jobin attended the Normal School in Quebec for six months. His ambition was to be a photographer but his grammar instructor, Napoleon LaCasse, urged him to study sculpture, and was influential in Jobin's decision to study with Berlinguet. LaCasse provided Jobin with employment as a janitor until he was ready to enter into an apprenticeship. At the age of twenty, Jobin entered the studio of François-Xavier Berlinguet, a civil engineer contractor, and also a good sculptor, as apprentice-sculptor for three years (Fig. 137). This studio was at 21 St. John Street in Quebec. Berlinguet was the son of Bonhomme Berlinguet, a sculptor, one in a long line of master sculptors in Canada, whose art was derived from that of the sculptors of medieval France with traditions formulated in the thirteenth century. In 1657, under the patronage of Ste Anne, the brotherhood of master woodworkers and sculptors was introduced in Canada, by Jean Le Vasseur and his companions.[2]

Jobin considered his master Berlinguet and Berlinguet's brother, Thomas, not as fine carvers as their father. Jobin's apprentice contract stipulated that the master would board him free of charge, without salary for the first year, and that he would give him one piastre per month the second year, and two piastres the third year. Jobin's first assignment was to carve a fox for a merchant of Saint Roch. When the opportunity permitted, he worked on statues. The master gave him a block of wood to work on his own, showing him how to take the measurements and the points. In this studio were other apprentices; August Richard, Pite Allard, Narcisse Bertrand, and Ouellet.[3]

The work increased, and Berlinguet was absent, being busy with the construction of a railroad. We turned to the master's assistants and to the foreman of the shop to obtain advice, or to books. The books they lent were Vignole, on the five orders of Architecture, Roret on painting, also, another on sculpture.[4]

The Berlinguet shop was kept busy with all kinds of orders for wood carvings. ". . . some religious figures, but in those days it was mostly figureheads with the big wooden ships everywhere."[5]

Near the completion of his three years' apprenticeship, Jobin had the assignment of creating a work of distinguished merit in order to earn him the title of "journeyman." For this assignment, Jobin made a detailed and delicate carving of *Le Bon Pasteur* (The Good Shepherd), which he always considered his masterpiece. This carving is now in the National Gallery of Canada. Upon completion of his apprenticeship in 1868, he left for New York where he continued his training in the "studio of an English sculptor, John Bolton, located at St. John Street, Battery Place . . . it was all downtown in those days, Battery Place and Castle Garden."[6] Jobin was given the job of roughing in the figures and carving images for tobacconists' shops. After a year with Bolton, Jobin went to work with some German carvers, possibly Simon Strauss, who, "had a good hand for finishing work but not for laying it out."[7]

In 1870, Jobin returned to Canada, settling in Montreal. In 1871, Jobin's shop was at 58 Notre Dame. He was kept busy carving lambs for altars, and also, a figure of a lawyer for a gentleman of the legal profession, which stood opposite the Court House on Rue Notre Dame. Especially remembered was a figurehead for Captain MacNeil for the *Chief Angus*.

Above all I made signs: this was the period when shopkeepers set up as merchants. Thus I produced a hanging sheep for a tailor, Indian women announcing tobacco, various models of Indians, even little Negroes. One fine day, farewell to savages! Closing shop, I sold the house and once more took the road to Quebec.[8]

In Quebec, Jobin set up shop in Faubourg St. Jean on Rue d'Aiguillon. Work began pouring in. This studio and his records were burned in the great fire of 1878. He created some of his largest works in his second studio, on Rue La Tourelle. In 1880, he carved the figure of the *Blessed Virgin on Cape Trinity*, which measures 300 inches in height and whose head is circled by twelve stars. It was carved for a man whose life was miraculously saved after a carriage in which he was riding tumbled down a steep cliff. On this cliff he placed his thanksgiving statue. In 1888, Jobin carved the figure of *Neptune* for the old sailors' hotel of that name at the foot of the Côte de la Montagne, opened by P. Lonnergan on December 11, 1809 (Fig. 138).[9] Stripped of its original paint, this ninety-six-inch inn sign is in fine condition except for the front of the feet, lost in dismantling. It is now in the Musée du Quebéc.

About this time, a figure of General Wolfe was stolen and carried off to the West Indies, then to Portsmouth, and eventually returned to Quebec. Jobin carved a figure to replace the original (now in the library of the Quebec Historical Society) and had it sheathed in copper to preserve it against the elements. Jobin's figure of Wolfe used to mount guard at the corner of Rue St. Jean and the Côte du Palais.[10] It is now in the Musée de la Citadelle in Quebec. In the 1888 record of accounts and deliberations of the Vestry Board at Ste Anne de Beaupré is entered "Crèche et statues —$175." The name of the maker of the crèche is not mentioned, but it is believed that the work was done by Jobin.[11] A large equestrian group, "St. George Slaying the Dragon," was carved by Jobin in wood. When deterioration set in some years later, he sheathed it in copper, after making repairs to the figure. It now stands in front of the Church of Saint-George de Beauce (Fig. 139).

Jobin has been called the father of ice sculpture. For the famous Winter Carnival of 1894 in Quebec, Jobin was asked to carve huge figures from blocks of ice cut from the frozen St. Lawrence River. Winter carnivals had been a feature of the large Canadian cities since 1882–1883 when Montreal constructed a palatial building from blocks of ice.[12] Jobin carved, or rather chopped, patriotic statues of Samuel de Champlain, Monsignor de Laval, le Comte de Frontenac, le Père de Brebeuf, and many other his-

FIG. 138

Fig. 138. Sign for the Neptune Inn, Quebec. *Carved by Louis Jobin in 1880. Height 96 inches. Courtesy Musée du Quebéc.*

Fig. 139. St. George and the Dragon. *Carved by Louis Jobin. Wood sheathed in copper. Front of the Church of Saint-George de Beauce. Photograph: Père Laurent Proulx.*

FIG. 139

Fig. 140. Tobacconist's Indian. *Carved by Louis Jobin, c. 1885. Height 72 inches. Courtesy Musée du Québéc.*

torical personages. "These transparent statues were a whole revelation. They resembled crystals and shone with a thousand fires in the light."[13] Jobin also created sculpture in colored snow, which attracted equal attention and were declared a great success.

In 1898, when his Rue La Tourelle studio burned with his possessions and records, Jobin moved twenty miles to the northeast to Ste Anne de Beaupré, famous for its shrine. Ste Anne was known as the patron saint of mariners —*beaupré* means the bowsprit and its shrine has many old offerings of the men of the sea. Jobin bought a piece of land on the west side of the basilica where he had a workshop built by Edmond Balduc, a resident of Ste Anne. Around the shop was a platform or porch twenty-five feet long, on which Jobin roughed out his figures in good weather. This was done by marking out, on a log, the dimensions and a rough outline of the figure. The figure was then formed by chopping away the wood with an axe until the shape was approximated, the same as the system used by the New York shipcarvers. For this chore Jobin employed his nephew, Edouard Marcotte. The figures were then carved by Jobin and stored until they were sent to their destinations.[14]

Jobin had married a Miss McClean who was born in New York and was an artist specializing in wax figures. His nephew, Edouard Marcotte, besides roughing out the figures, had the task of applying gold leaf to them. Work kept them busy from early morning until late at night but Jobin's prices were so low that he had to keep working to make ends meet. He continued making figureheads and shop signs but the larger part of his work was making religious figures for shrines. One of his tobacconist's figures, an Indian Chief seventy-two inches high, was acquired and is exhibited by the Musée du Quebéc (Fig. 140). The carving shows Jobin's skill in the execution of the figure, the garments, the facial features, and especially the hands. The dignity of his religious figures is revealed in the simple but splendid shop sign.

A trim tobacconist's Indian by Jobin, is now in the Virginia Museum of Fine Arts. The figure, slightly over seventy-two inches on an eleven-inch base, was once part of the Haffenreffer collection (Fig. 141). Another Jobin Indian, nearly identical, is in the shop of a New York antiques dealer. The known Jobin figures of Indians are nearly all similar in height and pose, which would suggest that he used paper patterns for shaping out his figures (Fig. 142). A heavier-set Indian, with a different style headdress, has the typical Jobin pose, the left arm at chest level holding up a robe while the right hand holds a bundle of cigars (Fig. 143). The location of this figure is unknown.

Outside Jobin's shop, which stood on a hill overlooking the St. Lawrence River, were many figures, large stands for figures to be placed upon at roadside shrines, and logs to be cut into figures (Fig. 144). A Gabriel blowing his horn was on top of the building, several religious figures were under the eaves, and over his doorway at one time stood a figurehead

FIG. 142

FIG. 141

Fig. 141. Tobacconist's Indian. Carved by Louis Jobin, c. 1880. Height 73 inches, base 11 inches. Courtesy Virginia Museum of Fine Arts, Richmond.

Fig. 142. Tobacconist's Indian. Carved by Louis Jobin, c. 1875. Height 48 inches. Courtesy Index of American Design.

of Napoleon which has since been placed in the Musée du Quebéc. On the wall inside the shop was a wooden thumb carved to hold a hat; there were patterns, cherubs' heads, angels' wings, and bits of carvings. On his bench was a trumpet for some Gabriel, his carving tools, and an unfinished figure. Also in the shop were a wood stove, a chair, and a carpenter's horse.

About 1901, among other altars and sculptures, Jobin carved the altar of Ste Anne at St. Louis, Ile aux Coudres in county Charlevoix, P. Q., as well as the Calvary of the cemetery and the statue of St. Louis which dominates the church. Needing assistance, Jobin engaged Regis Perron, a native of Ile aux Coudres. Upon termination of the work, Perron was brought back to Ste Anne where he built Jobin a residence at 9790 Royale, Ste Anne de Beaupré, attached to the studio. For the next fifteen years, Jobin continued to employ Perron in a secondary capacity including covering the carvings with copper. As work increased, Jobn took on two apprentices, Télésphore Lacasse and Oscard Dupont.[15]

Jobin made hundreds of religious figures. For the church at Saint Henri he carved as many as thirty-two figures. For the church at Rivière du Loup, he carved seventeen. Many of Jobin's figures were to be found in wayside shrines and many others were made for churches throughout the northeastern United States. In the cemetery of the little church at Cape Rouge is one of Jobin's signed figures. "I did that, put my name to them when I was young . . . a beginner, but I've long got past all that."[16] Several figures for a church in Lake Wales, Florida, were purchased by a Mr. Pelletier. Another American bought a figure of a Chinese holding a laundry board, to be used as a bench for his lawn (See Fig. 144).

Records of Jobin's work are virtually nonexistent. Two fires destroyed his early account books, and the only ones remaining are those of the end of his life, making it impossible to reconstruct a complete inventory of his works. The ledgers that exist from 1914 show that twenty figures were made that year; thirty in 1916; seventeen in 1919; and twenty-three in 1920. He did a statue of Sarouek and his dog on the facade of the ancient church of Sarouek at Quebec; a monumental *Sacred Heart* at the church at St. John Baptiste; a one hundred and forty-four inch *Sacred Heart* at the College of Longeau; exterior statues of the church of St. Foir; a large statue in the seminary of the Angel of Resurrection and many other statues in Canada and the United States. His *Saint Jean,* seventy-eight

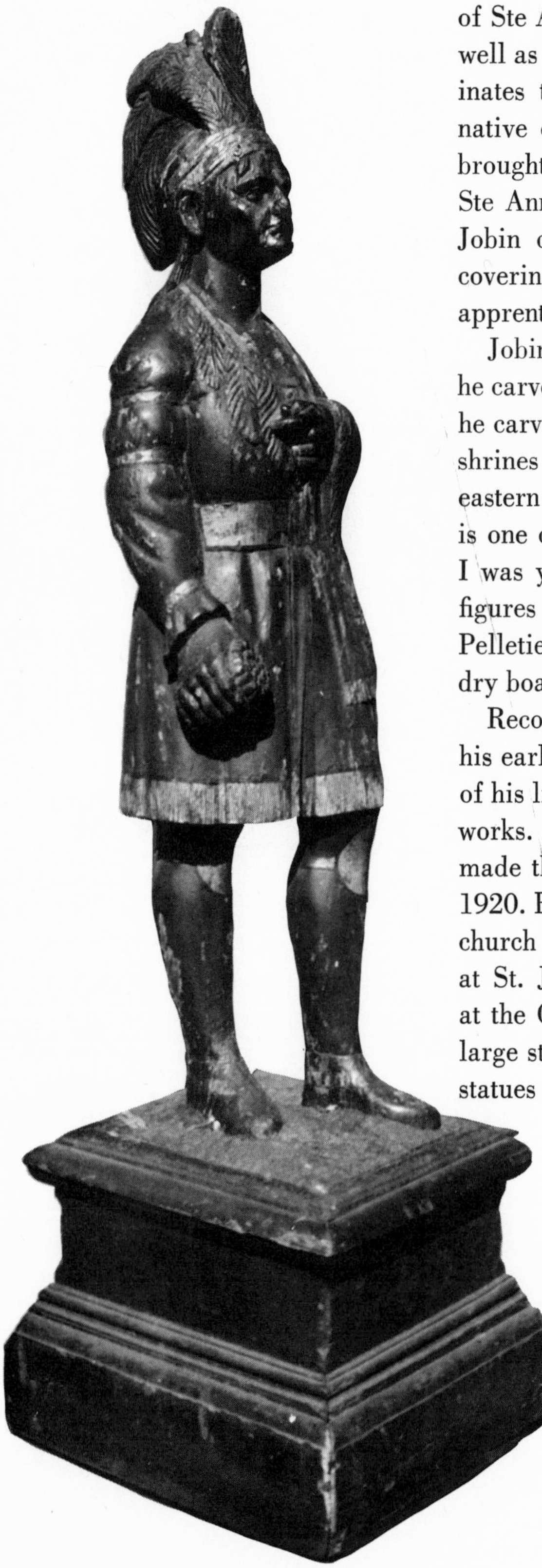

Fig. 143. Tobacconist's Indian. *Carved by Louis Jobin, c. 1875. Height 71 inches. Courtesy Index of American Design.*

Fig. 144. Ste. Anne de Beaupré. Studio and home of Louis Jobin. To his right is his nephew, Edouard Marcotte, with his two children. To the left are pedestals for shrine figures. The St. Lawrence River is seen in the background. A Chinese show figure, a Gabriel perched above the roof, and other religious figures adorn the studio exterior. Photograph: courtesy Mlle. Charlotte Perron.

inches high, covered with white paint to simulate marble, was carved about 1880 for the shrine at the cemetery at Montmagny. It is now in the Musée du Quebéc (Fig. 145). In 1873, in Montreal, Jobin made a sailor and an Indian for a tobacconist who used both in front of his shop. Another Indian, made in 1912 for Maurice Bistien of La Jeune-Lorette, had a huge peace pipe and was painted in the most vivid colors.[17]

Jobin never achieved fame during his lifetime and today might be unknown if he had not been visited in 1918 by Victoria Hayward, a journalist, who discovered him by chance. She became fascinated by the man and his carvings and, in December of 1922, had an article published in the *Canadian Magazine*, and later, in a book, *Romantic Canada*. A photograph taken for this article by Edith Watson, who accompanied the author, showed Jobin at his bench carving the head of an angel. The photograph and article caught the eye of the art historian, Marius Bar-

Fig. 145. Saint Jean. *Carved by Louis Jobin for the cemetery of Montmagny, c. 1880. Height 90 inches. Courtesy Musée du Quebéc.*

beau, who went to visit Jobin, taking with him A. Y. Jackson and Arthur Lismer, two leading painters. Barbeau was astonished at Jobin's workmanship and purchased many carvings for the National Museum and National Gallery of Canada, including figures of *St. Mark* and *St. John*, which had stood on the front gable on Jobin's roof. Jobin was eighty years old at the time of the visit and had stopped working a few years before.[18] He was a humble man, very religious, and charitable toward everyone. He died on March 11, 1928.

Jean-Baptiste Côté (1834–1907)

Jean-Baptiste Côté was born in the year 1834 in Saint Roch near the dockyards of the St. Charles River, in the suburbs of Quebec in Canada. His parents were Jean-Baptiste Côté and Hélène Grenier. After completing his basic education at the Seminary of Quebec Côté entered the studio of François-Xavier Berlinguet, as an apprentice architect. He was taught the basic information of his profession, and no doubt gave much attention to the art of wood carving.

During his association with Berlinguet, he helped in the preparation of plans for a church at Beauport, since burned. After a short and unsuccessful career in architecture, handicapped by his disdain for the work, which he did not consider a pure art, he turned to wood carving. Côté opened a shop at 132 St. Valier Street in Saint Roch, listing himself as a "carver." In 1862 at 130 St. Valier Street, he listed himself as a "sculptor."[19] In addition to his work as a sculptor, Côté participated in the struggle against the confederation of Canadian provinces—an issue still debated. He published a satirical journal, *La Scie* (The Saw), writing the material himself as well as engraving the caricatures and illustrations. As the readers of *La Scie* were partly English speaking, this quarterly appeared in two languages. At the head of Volume 1, Number 1, was "Quebec, Tuesday, 29th Oct. 1863, Editor in Chief. . . ? Proprietor: C. C. Boar." On Volume 1, Number 2, this was replaced by "Editor-proprietor: C. C. Lescieur," which means the sawyer or reaper.

The caricatures were original in conception, biting in sarcasm and remarkable for the subtlety of their humor. *La Scie* lampooned people in high places, attacked mediocrity in government and tore dirty politics to shreds. Côté put a caricature of himself in the issue of February 23, 1865, and it is the only known representation of his features. Côté created many enemies with his writing and woodcuts, and one day he was accosted by the police who had orders for his arrest. In 1865, *La Scie* stopped appearing even after an attempt was made to change its identity by changing its format and ownership. In 1868 it was succeeded by *La Lime* (The File), whose slogan was "He saws well who saws last." In 1868, Côté moved to 32 Crown Street in Saint Roch. During the middle of the nineteenth century, Quebec became a center for Canadian shipbuilding, and the scarcity and need for shipcarvers gave Côté ready employment. "A shipbuilder asked him to come to work for him, he was a man who was needed."[20] This builder may have been his mother's brother, Narcisse Rosa, as Côté's father was a ship's carpenter and foreman at Rosa's shipbuilding yard.

While employed there, Jean-Baptiste Côté married Mlle. Auger, sister of Elzéar Auger, a shipbuilder. After many years, Côté was once again a native of the dockyards of the St. Charles River, carving figureheads,

stern carvings, and all the decorative work; the kind he had observed during his youth on the prows of ships. After 1870, his shop or studio was on the ground floor of his house at 125 Rue de la Couronne (the numbers have been changed since). Here he made figureheads, effigies, signs, tobacconists' Indians and Black Boys, animals for Christmas mangers, and furniture of all sorts. Côté tried to study for a higher level profession, but, found the pressure of incoming work and the need to support a family required most of his time, he despaired of such ambitions and fell into his daily routine with deep resignation.

After the big fire of 1880 in the suburbs of Saint Roch and Saint Jean, Côté built for himself a two-story house with a workshop on Rue Richardson near Rue de la Couronne, where he remained with his family for the rest of his life. The studio-workshop was on the ground floor and the living quarters on the second story. Above the door of his shop he placed a large sign carved and painted by himself, entitled *Progress*, now preserved in the Musée du Quebéc (Fig. 146). This sculpture in low relief represents the goddess Ceres pouring out her horn of plenty; a medallion of a sailing vessel on the seas; a farmer behind his horses pulling a plow; and a train steaming along bearing the initials, C. P. R. (Canadian Pacific Railway).[21]

Côté's assistants were his brother Claude, also a sculptor, and his son, Claude, a very fine wood-carver. Côté also had a daughter Laure, who remembered her father as a sensitive individual, devoted to his work with little concern for money. "My father was a handsome man, original—he had distinguished manners, and a good circle of friends. His repartee was sharp and biting."[22]

Monsignor Adjustor Faucher, who in 1930 was with the General Hospital of Quebec, recalled:

When I was a little boy, I stopped often to watch him [Côté] at work in his workshop on the corner of Rue de la Reine and de la Couronne—the entrance was to the west, on Rue Richardson. This house still exists. He sculptured statues and nymphs for ships, he was located near the shipyards. With age he had become frail. Of medium height, he had already the appearance of an old man. The poor man never made his fortune.[23]

His friends called him "Johnny" Côté, a name that stuck with him all his life.

About 1880, Montreal became the most important industrial city in Canada, taking the lead from Quebec. Shipbuilding came to a halt in Quebec and Côté found himself without work. Declaring, "I'm a finished man, I'm lost!"[24] Côté thought that he had arrived at the end of his career. His brother Claude left for Chicago to help in the rebuilding after the fire. Thomas V. Brooks of New York was also attracted to Chicago at just about this time.[25]

But somehow, there was work to be found in Quebec, mostly in church and religious figure carving, which brought out Côté's most sensitive feelings. He found that he was deeply moved in working with religious themes. According to his daughter Laure, Côté found it difficult to carve *The Last Supper* now in the Musée de Quebéc. She reports his saying, "How can I even represent so much holiness?" and adds that "he worked at full speed with inspiration. However, many times he did not finish all that he started, with so much fire. When he carved the *Holy Family,* he wept—the Christ made him suffer."[26] His friend, Pierre Goulet of St. Pierre, Isle d' Orleans, spoke of him in words of great praise, "His profession was sculpture and he worked well. Everywhere he looked for images for instruction. He carved from them, as for example, his *Our Lady of Pity.*"[27]

After the death of his first wife, when Côté was already middle-aged, he remarried. While continuing his religious carvings, Côté carved a great number of animal figures which earned him the name of animal specialist. However, Côté never attached any importance to these works. Among them were: great elks, cows browsing or ruminating, dogs on the track of game, lions and griffins, horses and horses' heads, cranes, guinea fowl and partridges, and sheep in the manger. Côté worked until about 1903 when he became paralyzed. "My father was ill for four years—not capable of budging—before that he always had his nose to his work—as soon as his meal was finished he would return to his work where I always saw him toward the end, and a good old man, never going out," recalled his son, Claude.[28]

Jean Baptiste Côté died in 1907 leaving behind a large amount of wood carvings. Much of his work, his figureheads, show figures, signs, and religious carvings, have been claimed by the elements. Fortunately, others have survived and have been catalogued. Côté worked in more than one style but always in the same character; most of his sculpture is fresh and extremely ahead of his time in the simplification of forms, the smoothness of the finish, and the attitude of the figures. Some of his best works are

Fig. 147. Gutenberg. *Carved by Jean Baptiste Côté in 1880. Height 78½ inches. Musée du Quebéc. Photograph: Luc Chartier.*

in the Musée du Quebéc. Quite modern in their form and conception are five large statues carved toward the end of 1890, representing *St. Joseph,* the *Holy Virgin, St. Joachim* (carrying a dove in a nest as an offering to the temple), *Ste. Anne,* and an adolescent child *Jesus.* These large figures have been stripped of their paint and one has the feeling of seeing them as they were in the sculptor's studio.

Also in the Musée du Quebéc are two carvings of Gutenberg, inventor of movable type (Fig. 147). One is small, the other is seventy-four inches in height. There are also *Winter* and *Summer*, a small and moving bas-relief of *The Last Supper*, Côté's shop sign, several other sacred and secular carvings, and a tobacconist's Indian which is signed by his son, Claude Côté (Fig. 148). This last work may, however, be by Côté's brother, also Claude, who in 1883 was a foreman of a carving shop in Chicago, located at West 22nd Street corner of Fisk. He lived at 110 Brown and worked in statuary, perhaps for the churches in and around Chicago and the places surrounding it. For one year, 1895, he was employed as an engraver on wood. From his home at 2245 North Sawyer, Claude Côté worked as a carver until 1912. No figures known to have been carved by him have been identified.

Other Canadian Carvings

In Canada, the carving of tobacconists' figures was not always the work of trained sculptors and figures cannot be attributed. On either side of

FIG. 148

FIG. 149

Fig. 148. Tobacconist's Indian. Signed Cote. Carved by Claude Côté, c. 1890. Height 60 inches. Courtesy Musée du Quebéc. Photograph: Luc Chartier.

Fig. 149. Tobacconist's Indian. From the Quebec area, c. 1875. Height approximately 30 inches. Courtesy Musée du Quebéc.

the entrance to his tobacco shop at 1709 St. Catherine Street, Montreal, G. Stremenski had a pair of crudely carved Black Boys. G. Hanner of Barrie, Ontario, had a very primitive Indian carved in a stark pose to the side of his window which featured the Bombay cigar. H. Lloyd of Irillia, Ontario, had a very fine figure of a boy dressed in a drum major's costume in the center of his window, which featured on one side Sandow, the strongman, holding a pack of cigarillos and on the other side, a drum majorette advertising Sweet Caporal cigarettes. An unidentified tobacconist's Indian slightly under thirty-six inches high, with an intense gaze and unnatural proportions, is in the collection at the Musée du Quebéc (Fig. 149). A very beautiful carved squaw stood in front of C. S. Honsinger's Mazeppa Cigar Store in Owen Sound, Ontario, at the turn of the century (Figure 150).[29]

Fig. 150. Squaw. *Front of the Mazeppa Cigar Store of C. S. Honsinger, Owen Sound, Ontario, c. 1901.*

NEW YORK

New York did not become a center for shipcarving until long after Massachusetts was so established and some years after Philadelphia had been supplied by a number of craftsmen, some recently arrived from England and some of native origin and training. In 1729, George Warburton set up his shop in the New York port and engaged in his craft as a shipcarver.[1] On June 30, 1755, Henry Hardcastle advertised in the New-York *Mercury*, "HENRY HARDCASTLE—Run away from Henry Hardcastle, of the city of New York, carver, an apprentice lad. . ." A more industrious and durable apprentice of Henry Hardcastle's, Stephen Dwight, inserted an advertisement in the New-York *Mercury*, July 21, 1755:

STEPHEN DWIGHT, late an apprentice to Henry Hardcastle, carver has set up his business, between the Ferry Stairs and Burlington Slip, where he carves all sorts of ship and house work; also tables, chairs, picture and looking glass frames, and all kinds of work for cabinetmakers, in the best manner and all reasonable terms.

Dwight also did "Portrait and History Painting . . . and will teach drawing in Crayon, black and white chalk, Indian Ink and black Lead Pencil, in the quickest and best Manner." In 1774, he was in partnership as Dwight & Davis, doing carving and gilding and supplying ladies and gentlemen with girandoles, looking glasses, and picture frames.[2]

A few tobacconists also advertised, and as early as 1735 a maker of tobacco pipes inserted his advertisement in The New-York *Gazette* of March 24 and March 31:

Tobacco Pipes.—A very good dwelling house with a Kitchin and store House a good Stable, a pleasant Garden with an Orchard and about Twenty Acres of Clay ground fit for making Tobacco Pipes, with two Negro slaves, utensils and other conveniences to carry on that business. It lyes opposite to Froggs Point at White Stone in the Township of Flushing, in Queens County.

Another, in 1773 acquainted the

. . . publick in general, that he has removed his tobacco manufactory from horse and cart street, towards the lower end of Wall-street, at the sign of the bladder of snuff and roll tobacco, where he intends to carry on the business as usual, and has for sale best inspected leaf tobacco by the hhd [hogshead] or barrel fit for shipping &c. superfine pigtail, common do. hogtail and cut tobacco, scotch and rappee snuff . . .[3]

On July 4, 1776, the Declaration of Independence was signed amidst great patriotic celebrations. Five days later when it was read to a rebellious citizenry, they pulled down from its pedestal the gilded lead statue of King George III in Bowling Green. Some years later, in its place, was mounted a wooden statue of the Father of our Country, George Washington. The figure was one hundred and eight inches high and weighed over eight hundred pounds, the work of William Sullivan. The figure is said to have been carved in 1794. In 1843, when the Battery was made into a park, the figure was sold at auction and purchased by a Mr. Jacques of South Norwalk, Connecticut for $250. When he died in 1860, it was sold again at auction to Mr. A. Decovato of New York for $300, who in turn sold it to Fred H. Theobold, a tobacconist, at 273 West 125th Street, who put it into service as a tobacconist's figure. In 1886, Mr. Theobold offered it for sale, and in 1889, it was on top of the Arch at Washington Square, a temporary wooden structure designed by Stanford White as part of the centennial celebration of Washington's inauguration. Years later, it was discovered by Senator Coleman Dupont in front of another tobacconist's shop. It was purchased and donated to the Historical Society at Wilmington. More recently, it was sent back to New York for a short time to be exhibited at the Museum of American Folk Art on West 53rd Street.[4]

Philadelphia's William Rush had an apprentice who came to New York, receiving good publicity in the New-York *Gazette and General Advertiser* of May 23, 1799:

Mr. Daniel N. Train, a young gentleman of genius and abilities, late a pupil of Rush, the famous carver of Philadelphia, some time since arrived in this City, has lately completed the ornaments of the Ship Adams', soon to be launched at the Walabought, Long Island.

The following is a sketch of these ornaments: On the head of the ship is a figure of the President, represented in the attitude of addressing both Houses of Congress. In his left hand is a scroll, supposed to be his address—his right is raised in a spirited positon, as if in the act of bidding defiance to the enemies of America. At his side, is a branch of oak, springing from a rock, emblematic of his firmness and patriotic virtues, in support of the rights of his country. On the stern, in the center of the Taffrail, are the Arms of the United States, supported by Sybele and Neptune —the latter with his left hand resting on his Trident, and his right extended over our "Infant Navy" with some attributes of Commerce. The former reclining on a sheaf of wheat, with a Scepter in her right hand—in the left is the Key of the Earth and supporting a Cornucopia. At her side is a Youth with the Emblems of Agriculture, offering its productions for the support of the United States.

The Ornamental part of this vessel exhibits a striking proof of Mr. Train's abilities. We wish him success in the Carvings for the "44," now building at Corlears Hook which we are told, he is engaged to execute.[5]

The young carver followed up this free publicity, by placing an advertisement in the same publication two days later:

DANIEL N TRAIN, Carver, No. 144 Cherry-street, near the Ship Yards, offers his professional services to the citizens of New-York and others, particularly owners and builders of ships. Having studied Naval Sculpture under Wm. Rush, of Philadelphia, whose talents are extensively known, he hopes, from this advantage and his future exertion, to merit the patronage he now solicits. Heads and other ornamental parts of ships will be excepted or prepared with neatness and dispatch.[6]

The prows of ships being built in the New York harbor carried interesting carvings, especially one built by Henry Eckford near the Brooklyn Navy Yard in 1801 for the ship of 350 tons, the *Samuel Elam*. Its figurehead represented a man on horseback, and its bowsprit was high enough to clear the man's head.[7]

Down the street from Train's shop at 119 Cherry Street was the shop of the brothers Simeon and Samuel Skillin, shipcarvers. Their father, Samuel, was the son of the distinguished Boston carver, Simeon Skillin. The New York Skillins were listed at the same address until 1830 when the directory shows that a Simeon D. Skillin, at 106 Cherry street was in the crockery business, ending forty-one years of carving practice in New York.[8]

When Joseph Mangin and John McComb were designing New York's City Hall, they did not select a shipcarver to create the figure of Justice to grace the cupola, but instead picked John Dixey, an Irish sculptor who had come to America in 1789, after completing his studies at the Royal Academy in London. Dixey's shop was at 118 William Street, where he met a genteel class of patrons who could obtain there "a new and fashionable assortment of Looking-Glasses, Picture Frames, Brackets and Borders . . . Ornaments and Figures, in basso relieve, or otherwise, for buildings &c and generally Carving and Gilding . . ."[9] Dixey designed the one hundred and eight inch figure of Justice for which he was paid $310. "Rising from the middle of the roof, is a Cupola, on which is placed a colossal figure of Justice, holding in her right hand, which rests on her forehead, a balance and in her left a sword pointing to the ground. Justice is not blindfolded as she is represented in Europe."[10]

The original sketches, along with McComb's drawings for City Hall, are preserved in the Print Room at the New-York Historical Society. Another Justice was made for the State House in Albany. Dixey was a popular and prominent member of New York and Philadelphia art circles. He was one of the founders of the American Academy and was at one time vice-president of the Pennsylvania Academy. He exhibited his sculpture in New York and Philadelphia, maintaining his shop with his son, George, who was his apprentice and later his assistant. In 1817, Dixey drew up his will, appointing his friends George Ireland and Anthony Steenbach as executors. Three years later Dixey died, leaving "to my son George all my Working Tools used in carving and gilding, also my drawings, Sketches &c that relates to the said business. I also give to my son George in order to promote him in business the Sum of Five hundred dollars.[11]

Charles J. Dodge (1806–1886)

Charles J. Dodge was born in 1806 in New York City on Bedlow Street (now Madison Street) between Catherine and Montgomery Streets. His father, Jeremiah Dodge, had been a shipwright before turning to shipcarving, establishing his own carving shop at 75 Columbia Street in 1828, and later at 84 Columbia Street where he remained for many years. Jeremiah Dodge was the great-great-grandson of Tristram Dodge, who was one of the original settlers of Block Island and whose name appeared in the public records for the first time in 1660.[12]

Jeremiah Dodge had been in partnership with Simeon Skillin for a short period from 1804 to 1806 and with Cornelius N. Sharpe on Lewis Street from 1815 to 1821. In 1820, Dodge and Sharpe carved the figurehead for the USS *Ohio*—a large bust of Hercules with a lion's pelt draped over one shoulder and the waist terminating in a scroll. The USS *Ohio* was launched from the New York Navy Yard on May 30, 1820. The Hercules figurehead is now at the Suffolk Museum and Carriage House at Stony Brook, Long Island. In 1828, Charles J. Dodge started out as a shipcarver at 77 Columbia Street, and in 1833, he joined his father in partnership as Jeremiah Dodge & Son, Shipcarvers, at 75 Columbia Street. Charles lived with his parents at 264 Rivington Street near the shipyards.

On Monday, March 16, 1835, a small notice appeared in the New-York *Daily Advertiser:* "On Saturday forenoon the head carved by Messers Dodge & Son of this city, was placed on the trunk representing President Jackson, on the bow of the frigate *Constitution.*"[13] However, the Dodges had carved only part of the head of Andrew Jackson. The original figurehead had been carved the year before by Laban S. Beecher of Boston for the frigate *Constitution*. President Jackson's popularity was not honored by many people and threats of damage to the head were received.[14] Beecher had been offered a large sum of money to permit the head to be stolen but instead promptly notified the Commodore of the Boston Navy Yard, Jesse D. Elliott, of the dangers. Beecher completed the head within the security of the Navy Yard, and it was placed in position on the ship. Security measures were taken and sentries posted. During the night of July 2, 1834, in the midst of violent thunderstorms, a young man, Samuel W. Dewey of Falmouth, Massachusetts, reached the ship by rowboat and, undetected, sawed off the head just below the nose. This episode was the cause of much newspaper coverage, providing work for the illustrators and for writers of prose of all kinds. One Boston writer (source unknown) put it tersely in two lines:

For Old Hickory there is no rest-itution
For damage to his Constitution.

The damaged remains of the figurehead were covered with canvas and the following year, the ship proceeded to the New York harbor where a new part of the head was carved and fitted to the figurehead by the firm of Jeremiah Dodge & Son.[15] The huge figurehead of Jackson with the Dodge addition is now in the Museum of the City of New York.

In 1835, Charles was married and, with his wife Mary, moved to 272 Third Street where the following year, a daughter, Rebecca, was born.

Fig. 151. Jeremiah Dodge. *Carved by Charles J. Dodge, c. 1845. Painted wood, life size. Courtesy New-York Historical Society.*

He began taking an active part in community affairs and an interest in politics. In 1842, he moved his shop to South Street and Market Slip. Jeremiah Dodge who was no longer in partnership with his son had taken on some duties in the Custom House. In 1845, Charles was elected an Alderman from the Eleventh Ward which took in a large area north of the east side of Manhattan. His duties may have interfered with his work, for in 1846 he went into partnership with Jacob S. Anderson, another ship-carver, as Dodge & Anderson, at 236 South Street. The partnership was dissolved the following year. Charles J. Dodge continued carving at the shop on South Street. Correspondence shows that he was very much in want of funds.

Mess. Fernald & Pettigrew
  Greet.
    I send you today by the Brig Victorine the taffrail and eagle for stern of your ship which I hope will be satisfactory to you. I will send the Head by next opportunity. I regret that I could not send it by the present, being very much in want of funds. I called on Mess. Kingsland & Co to advance me Two Hundred Dollars, they desired me write you for an order on them for the amount will you have the goodness to do so and very much oblige.

Yours Respectfully
Charles J. Dodge.[16]

An undated letter carries a proposal:

I agree to carve Figure Head, Trailboards and Chocks, Taffrail & Eagle for Stern, 12 Feet Spread, & paint & gild it—except the Trailboards, including the gilding of Taffrail Four Hundred & thirty five Dollars.

(signed) Charles J. Dodge[17]

He finished the work and sent it by ship on January 27, 1849. Four days later he sent another letter with a sketch of the head, and excused his delay because of a "continued illness of more than five weeks." The head was seven feet three and one-half inches in length.[18]

In 1855, Dodge took a job as an assessor at No. 4 Hall of Records, and in 1864, he became the Deputy Tax Commissioner at 32 Chambers Street, moving up to commissioner in 1867. Jeremiah Dodge died in 1860 and Charles took over the shop and business. He also became a school trustee, a colonel of the tenth regiment of militia, and a thirty-third degree Mason.[19]

Perhaps while his father was still alive, Charles J. Dodge carved a bust of Jeremiah Dodge which, in imitation of white marble, is painted a flat white over the pine wood (Fig. 151). The carving shows the fine talents of Charles J. Dodge, as expressed in the strong determined character, sensitive mouth, intelligent and inquisitive eyes, and high forehead. Dodge achieved fine composition and carving in a difficult medium. The bust was donated to the New-York Historical Society by his granddaughter Fannie

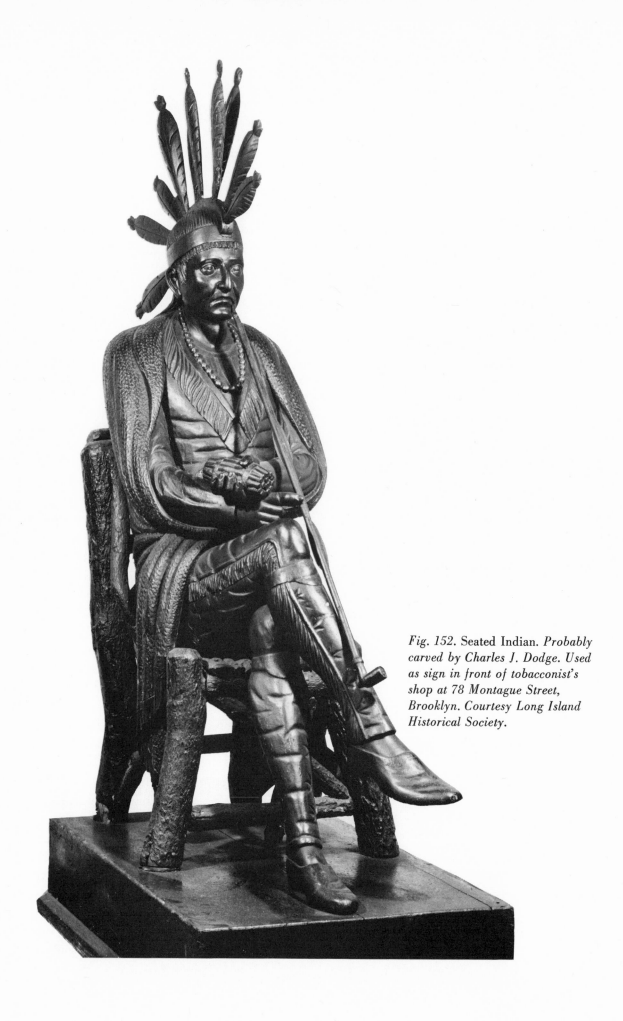

Fig. 152. Seated Indian. Probably carved by Charles J. Dodge. Used as sign in front of tobacconist's shop at 78 Montague Street, Brooklyn. Courtesy Long Island Historical Society.

E. Marquand, in 1952. Another work probably by Dodge is the figure of Jim Crow, possibly a portrait of T. D. Rice in character, and now in the Shelburne Museum in Vermont (*See* Fig. 17).

Tobacconists' figures of seated Indians are extremely rare. One, seated on a log chair smoking a long calumet and holding a bundle of cigars, was formerly at the tobacconist's shop at 78 Montague Street in Brooklyn (Fig. 152). This also may be the work of Charles J. Dodge. The figure has not moved very far—it is now in the Long Island Historical Society in Brooklyn, a short distance from the original site of the tobacconist's shop.

Having given up his carving shop in 1870, Dodge moved to South Second Street near his fellow carvers. In 1874, he built a stone house on four plots of land at 146 Keap Street in Brooklyn, fifty-three feet above tide-water.[20] He lived here for twelve years where, but a short distance from his home, he could watch the ships sailing in and out of the harbor, some still, no doubt, with his figureheads on the bows. Charles J. Dodge died in 1886.

Thomas Millard, Jr. (1803–1870)

"It appears that the first man to introduce carved figures as tobacconists' signs was a certain Chichester. They were carved by one Tom Millard," wrote Frank W. Weitenkampf, a cub reporter for *The New York Times*, on August 3, 1890. He had gathered this information from Samuel A. Robb, with whom he had an interview at Robb's shop on Centre Street in Manhattan. While Robb had a personal knowledge of the history of the art, it is doubtful that his knowledge was complete or entirely accurate. However, in the opinion of the carvers themselves, Millard was the pioneer in the art of carving tobacconists' figures in New York. Thomas Millard, Jr., was born in 1803 in Connecticut, to Catherine J. and Thomas Millard, Sr. Millard, Sr., may have been working in Philadelphia in 1795 as a Thomas Millard was listed in the city directory. There is no record of the youthful activities of his son but it is likely that he may be the same Millard who was described by another shipcarver as "a clever workman named Millard, who was an apprentice under William Rush . . ."[21] At twenty-four years of age, Thomas Millard, Jr., opened his own shop at 191 Cherry Street; his father's carving shop was at 6 Pelham Street. For the next few years, Millard, Jr.'s business must have been successful, as he was able to buy land from James De Braun, ship chandler—a corner piece on Lombard and Walnut Street in the Seventh Ward for $3,800. Then, on the following day, he bought another section and sold that to his father.[22]

In 1845, Millard moved to 204 Centre Street, so named because the city surveyors had found that it was the geographical center between the East and North rivers. His home, a short distance from his shop, was at 376 Monroe Street. Millard's father may have died in 1847 for Millard dropped the junior after his name and left it out of future directories.

In 1849–1850, Millard formed a partnership with Thomas V. Brooks.[23] Their shop was at 260 South Street at the intersection of Rutgers Slip. The partnership lasted for one year. Millard kept the shop and later Brooks moved two or three doors down the street.

About 1852 or 1853, Millard began producing tobacconists' figures for James M. Chichester at 51 Bowery, who had started to supply tobacconists with wooden Indians and other show figures. Unfortunately there exists no visual record of Millard's carvings and since none is known to have been signed, his work goes unrecognized. In 1855, Millard moved his residence to Brooklyn and started a molding mill at 59 Mangin Street in Manhattan. Except for the year 1861, when Millard was at 104 Centre Street, he did not maintain his own carving shop again, working mostly from his house on Lafayette Avenue in Brooklyn or as a free-lance or journeyman carver.[24] His wife, Louisa C. Millard, died about this time, leaving him the care of five children. Thomas Millard kept active at his work until 1870 and on November 23 of that year, he died in New York. His five children were "all of full age except Louisa C., a minor, aged 17 years."[25] Unfortunately, neither of his two sons followed their father's profession.

John L. Cromwell (1805–1873)

John L. Cromwell was born in Massachusetts in 1805, the same year as Laban S. Beecher, who like Cromwell became an excellent shipcarver. Massachusetts already had a number of fine shipcarvers at the time these young men were ready to start their apprenticeship, foremost among them were Samuel Skillin and Isaac Fowle. Cromwell may have been engaged to one of these carvers for the period of his apprenticeship.

At the age of twenty-six, Cromwell was in New York and opened his shop at 179 Cherry Street, some doors down the street from Millard's shop, near Mechanics Alley, now the site of the Brooklyn Bridge approach, where once the mechanics trod on the short route to the shipbuilding yards. Here, too, were the warehouses, the sail lofts, spar yards, and ship chandler shops, not to mention the groggeries, cheap lodgings for sailors, and places of entertainment for Jack Tar who had been at sea for nearly a year. It was here, the shipbuilder or ship's owner would come to order a figurehead and other carvings for his new vessel.[26]

In 1836, Cromwell moved to 260 Division Street and in 1839 to 419 Water Street using the Division Street location as his home. In 1841 or thereabouts, he took into his shop a talented apprentice named Thomas V. Brooks whose training in Cromwell's shop developed him into an excellent carver of ship and tobacconists' figures. In Cromwell's shop, where orders for Indian figureheads were on hand, Brooks learned his trade well. In 1846, Cromwell had an order to carve a figurehead for Fernald & Pettigrew of Portsmouth, New Hampshire, who were building a ship for Richard H. Tucker of Wiscasset, Maine. Tucker wrote Cromwell on December 1, 1846:

Dear Sir:

I've a letter some time since from Mess. Fernald & Pettigrew of Portsmouth, N.H. Master Ship builders who are building me a Ship, saying they had, or were going to get the Bust head, taffrail or Stern moulding it done by you, and asked if I had any particular directions to give. Will you have the goodness to give me a sketch of the stern moulding & design to correspond with her name, altho the design of the bust as regard costume & head dress that I may suggest an alteration if necessary. The name I wish kept *confidential* so that no one else shall assume it before I do. The flourish at each end of the name on boards, I wish dispensed with altogether and made plain something after this model or plan. [Here, two rough outlines are sketched, one noting "Black ground, Gilt letters."] The above is something hear what I should like for the quarters, though for the Head boards, the ends will want to be beveled to conform with the rake, which you better understand than I do, and depend more upon your judgement than any description I can give. Please let me hear from you as early as convenient.[27]

Cromwell's reply or sketch is not in the file but we learn that the name of the vessel was *Samoset* named for the Indian Chief of the Pemaquid tribe on that part of the Maine seacoast.[28] For another Indian, or possibly the same, Cromwell sent to Fernald & Pettigrew his contract for carving:

This may certify that the under signed has agreed with Capt Herman Eldredge to do the Following named carved work for a Ship about 550 tons gross, Mess. Fernald & Pettigrew Portsmouth NH, viz to find a stock & carve a mail Indian Bust. Head. also to furnish stock & carve a Tafferal. the Trail Boards & chocks (to be got out by Fernald & Petigrew, and sent on) to be carved by the under signed. Allso to be painted gilded & collered in good stile. Tafferal to be carved to correspond with the head. to be compleated by the first of April 1847 to be Boxed up & safely delivered on Board one of the Portsmouth Packets. cash on Deliver in full for the above named carved work Compleat one Hundred Dollars.

John L. Cromwell[29]

In 1847, Cromwell, his wife Frances, and their family of five children moved to 2 South Sixth Street in Williamsburgh, a good row across the strong currents of the East River unless they took the Grand Street Ferry or one of the other ferries nearby. Cromwell had as an apprentice his son, Ludwick, who was fifteen years of age at that time.

John Stephenson, a former Irish immigrant, made street and stage coaches at his shop on the north side of 27th Street between what are now Madison and Fourth Avenues. He later made omnibuses and horsecars and, still later, trolley and cable cars and also made the first circus band chariot. The Van Amburgh Triumphal Car, which was made to hold a small brass band, was elaborately carved. The main feature was an elevated rear section terminating in a dome upheld by two dolphins, with an eagle for a finial. The front end was dominated by a pair of carved lions' heads. Cromwell is credited with doing the carving.[30] While no documenta-

tion can be found to justify this claim, another circus band chariot, made by John Stephenson for the Welch, Delevan & Nathan National Circus about 1846 or 1847 is accredited to Cromwell with more validity.

In 1850, Cromwell moved his shop to 222 South Street at the intersection of Market Slip. He shared a floor with James Wilkins Liquors. Here he remained during the 1850s, and it was here that he, like other ship-carvers, switched from ship figures to show figures, with Indians predominating. Cromwell created a life-sized figure of a Mohawk warrior with a roach or scalplock on his shaved head. His raised right hand held a tomahawk and the left hand clutched a catamount robe or a bearskin pelt slung over the shoulder. A stylized headdress of feathers was added,

Fig. 153. Tobacconist's Figure.
*One of the prototypes designed and
carved by John L. Cromwell,
c. 1856. Photograph: Peter Hujar.
Herbert W. Hemphill, Jr.,
Collection.*

and the figure standing with the right foot forward was placed on a small platform with wheels (Fig. 153; Col. Fig. 21). This became the prototype for the models of most of the other show-figure carvers.[31]

About 1856, Cromwell started turning work over to Brooks, spending more time at his home in Williamsburgh. Toward the end of the 1860s, Cromwell took on very little work. In 1873, he died in his home on South Sixth Street.

Thomas J. White (1825–1902)

Thomas J. White was born in New York and at fourteen years of age was apprenticed to John L. Cromwell to learn the art and trade of ship-carving. White was a youth with an unusual amount of talent for carving and drawing, and under the direction of his master, he made rapid progress in the busy shop.[32]

In 1847, when Thomas V. Brooks had one more year to complete his apprenticeship to Cromwell, White left Cromwell to go on his own. White may have gone to work as a journeyman in the various shops along South Street, as no shop is listed in his own name. About 1852, White married a Massachusetts girl and for the next two years he and his wife Harriet made their home in Westchester, New York, where a son Edwin was born. In 1856, when the effects of the depression were being felt in the shipbuilding yards, White and his family moved to Boston. At 223 Commercial Street, he opened a shipcarving business as Thomas J. White & Co., with W. H. Rumney as a full partner. White rented a house in Malden and in 1863 moved his family into a house in Chelsea. With Rumney, White kept busy, shortly moving to a larger shop at 233 Commercial Street, near the waterfront between the Philadelphia Packet and the Eastern Packet Piers.[33]

About 1866 or earlier, White returned to New York, leaving W. H. Rumney in charge of his Boston shop. White took up residence at 85 South Fourth Street in Williamsburgh. In 1871, White, who now lived but a block away from Brooks, joined him in partnership as Brooks & White at 90 Pike Slip, several blocks below the numerous shipbuilding yards at and above Corlears Hook. The partnership was dissolved the following year, but Brooks maintained the shop at the address until 1875. White still did some work for Brooks, but was engaged mainly by William Demuth & Co. until 1876 when he joined Samuel A. Robb, who had opened his shop at 195 Canal Street, just across the street from what is now Chinatown in Manhattan. A long and happy association began. White worked for Robb, off and on, for more than twenty years.[34]

White was quite content in this shop, a very busy one, making tobacconists' figures, eagles, steamboat and ship carvings, dentists' signs, carved letters, circus-wagon carvings, and every conceivable type of wood carving —even artificial hands, "Which upon having a spring inserted can make any movement of the natural human kind."[35] White sometimes took carving jobs at two of the other shops in the area and sometimes took work to his home. In 1890, in a visit to the Robb shop at 114 Centre Street, Manhattan, Frank W. Weitenkampf, noted in an article for *The New York Times*, "White even went into ideal statuary to such an extent as to produce a 'Greek Slave' and 'Adam and Eve' in wood." White also assisted Robb in many of the tableau carvings made for Adam Forepaugh and the Barnum & London circus wagons.

Toward the middle of the 1890s, White may have been employed by the Charles W. F. Dare New York Carousel Company in the execution of some of the carousel figures. On February 28, 1902, Thomas J. White dropped dead of a heart attack on the corner of Broadway near Kent Avenue in Brooklyn, not too far from his home and only a block away from the carousel factory.[36]

Thomas V. Brooks (1828–1895)

In 1870, the carving shop at 240 South Street, at the corner of Pike Slip, about 200 or so feet from the pier on the East River, could well have been mistaken for a corridor leading to a ballroom where a fancy costume ball was in progress. There were Turks, Sultanas, Punches, Scotsmen in kilts and tall bearskins hats, Columbias, English officers with small fatigue caps, Uncle Sams, Walter Raleighs, Dolly Vardens, and Indians of all ranks and tribes with their squaws. The figures were nose to nose and back to back as though discussing the events or local scandals of the day. The shop of Thomas V. Brooks must have been confusing and awe-inspiring because no other carver at this time could boast of such a large stock on hand (Fig. 154). After twenty-four years in the business of figure carving, Brooks could easily accumulate one hundred figures in half a year's time.[37]

Thomas V. Brooks was born in New York in 1828 and in the year 1840,

T. V. BROOKS,

(Established 1848),

Show Figure and Ornamental Carver,

No. 240 South Street, N. Y.

From 75 to 100 Figures always on hand.

Fig. 154. Advertisement in Trow's New York Directory, 1872–1873.

Fig. 155. Leaning Indian. *Carved by Thomas V. Brooks. Bought from Edward Hen in 1861 by Philip Poss of Fremont, Ohio. Photograph: courtesy Rutherford B. Hayes Library.*

entered the shop of John L. Cromwell at 419 Water Street, as an apprentice shipcarver. In 1848, Brooks established his own shop at 260 South Street, and the following year he entered into a partnership with the older, more experienced carver, Thomas Millard. While the partnership did not last more than a year, each continued using the same facilities at 260 South Street. In 1853, Brooks moved to 258 South Street. About 1855, Brooks was approached by Edward Hen, who knew him through Millard and Chichester, to supply Hen with carved tobacconists' figures. At this time, work in the shipbuilding yards was falling off and the depression that was to bring shipbuilding to a standstill was only two years off. Brooks undertook this work and was kept busy filling the orders received by Hen from all parts of the country. A very shrewd businessman and investor, Hen advised Brooks on his investments, including property in Williamsburgh. Brooks bought a house and moved to 85 South Third Street, near Cromwell and White. The Peck Street ferry, which went across the East River to the slip at South Seventh Street, made the trip from shop to home a short and rapid one.[38]

One figure of an Indian, which Brooks supplied to Hen in 1861, was in the leaner series, so called because the figure was leaning on a log stump (Fig. 155). It stood for over ninety years in Fremont, Ohio. The Indian was originally owned by Phillip Poss whose tobacco shop was on South Front Street. In 1877, Poss sold his store and Indian to Charles Barth, who sold it in 1883 to J. Youngman, with whom it remained until the 1950s when it was sold to Jack Hoffman.[39] About 1864, during the Civil War, Brooks took into his shop a young apprentice who, before his apprenticeship was over, was to become a competitor of Brooks and the leading carver of tobacconists' figures in America. His name was Samuel Anderson Robb.[40]

Brooks moved to 240 South Street right after the Civil War and prospered. By 1870 he had real estate valued at $45,000 and a personal estate of $3,000. Two years earlier he had married, and Laura his wife, sixteen years younger, gave birth in 1869 to a son, James A. Brooks. In 1871, Brooks joined Thomas J. White in partnership. The firm, known as Brooks & White, was located at 90 Pike Slip. With White taking over some of the carving responsibilities, Brooks was able to indulge in the various business and real estate ventures in which he was engaged.[41]

Sometime before this White had encouraged the apprentice, Sam Robb, to study the fine arts in order to develop his aptitude and talents. Robb left Brooks and was engaged by William Demuth as a carver of tobacconists' figures. Demuth also encouraged Robb to follow his natural talents.

The partnership with White was dissolved in 1872. White remained with Brooks as a journeyman for a short while, but did most of his carving at Demuth's. Brooks's shop was kept busy; it has been estimated that a carving shop with a staff such as his could produce about two hundred figures a

FIG. 156

Fig. 156. Indian with Eagle-feathered Headdress. *Carved by Thomas V. Brooks, c. 1865. Tomahawk is missing from right hand, cigars or tobacco from left. Courtesy Shelburne Museum. Photograph: Einars J. Mengis.*

Fig. 157. Negro Tobacconist's Figure. *Probably carved by Thomas V. Brooks, c. 1860. Courtesy New-York Historical Society.*

Fig. 158. Leaning Tobacconist's Figure. *Carved by Thomas V. Brooks. Height 75 inches. Extensive repairs and replacements were made on the face, arms, legs, feet, and pedestal. Photograph: Taylor & Dull.*

FIG. 157

FIG. 158

year.[42] Some of the carvings made in Brooks's shop are still in existence, though most have disappeared. A Brooks Indian (Fig. 156) is in the collection of the Shelburne Museum. The feathered headdress gives it great height. The tomahawk is missing from the right hand and the left probably held cigars, a knife, or a spear. The figure was cut from a single spar; the arm was carved separately and joined afterward. A fine leaning figure holding out cigars in the left hand is now in the Van Alstyne Folk Art Collection at the Smithsonian Institution. The feathers in its headdress are bent to the right, giving action and direction to the figure, as though the wind were blowing in that direction. A quite similar figure is in the collection of the Maryland Historical Society. Another leaner, a small Negro figure with the right leg crossed over wears a beehive type hat and holds out a bundle of cigars with his right hand. Mounted on a stand, it is in the collection of the New-York Historical Society (Fig. 157). Over the years, some figures lost hands, headdress, feet, legs, and other parts due to exposure, lack of paint, and vandalism. The bases, with the feet and legs, usually were the first to go. One Brooks figure has extensive replacements —a new base, feet, hand, and part of a face (Fig. 158). A fine Brooks squaw, seventy-two inches high on a seven and one-half inch stand, is in the collection of Dr. Louis C. Jones at Cooperstown, New York (Fig. 159). An Indian scout, seventy inches high on a sixteen-inch pedestal, is represented in a studio photograph from the Robb file, has the name "Brooks" penciled on the back of the photograph (Fig. 160), and shows some retouching. Noted as No. 23, it may have been used for sales promotion. A rare figure of Jack Tar, probably carved by T. V. Brooks is in the New-York Historical Society (Fig. 161).

Brooks was affectionately called "Daddy Brooks" by his apprentices, former apprentices, journeymen, and others who worked or had worked with him in his shop.[43] His former apprentice Samuel A. Robb, set up shop in 1876 and before long was a strong competitor of Brooks. On August 25, 1876, the first loop of cable was strung across the East River from the Brooklyn to the Manhattan side of the towers for the new Brooklyn Bridge. From his shop at 240 South Street, Brooks could watch the progress. However, he did not wait to see the bridge completed. After moving his shop to 211 Hudson Street, closer to the North River, he sold his real estate and made plans to relocate in Chicago, as the competition in New York was getting too strong for him. Furthermore, the Chicago fire on October 8, 1871, had nearly wiped out all the tobacconists' shops and their signs, offering an unrivaled opportunity for this work. Brooks had decided on the move after a visit to Chicago sometime in the 1870s. In 1879 and 1880, Brooks moved to Chicago with his wife, his ten-year-old son James, and three carvers, one of whom was Isaac Lewin[44] and another probably Nicholas E. Collins.

Brooks opened a shop at 51 West Van Buren, making his home a few doors away at 47 West Van Buren. In 1881—the following year—he moved, and in 1882 was well established. In that year his advertisement read:

New York   Chicago

CARVING CO.

110 W. Van Buren St.   Chicago, Ill.

SHOW FIGURES

For signs, Stores, etc. 75 to 100 always on hand,
Church, Circus, Menagerie, Ship, Steamboat, House,
Sign and Architectural Carving, Scroll Sawing
Turning, etc.

T. V. Brooks,
Resident Manager.[45]

When Brooks came to Chicago in 1879, he found that there were Indians and other tobacconists' figures already there; some were recently made, some were survivors of the fire, and in unaffected areas some were quite

Fig. 159. Squaw. *Carved by Thomas V. Brooks, c. 1875. Height 72 inches. Photograph: Taylor & Dull.*

Fig. 160. Indian Scout. *Photograph from Robb's file has "Brooks" penciled on reverse side.*

Fig. 161. Jack Tar. *Tobacconist's figure probably carved by Thomas V. Brooks, c. 1850–1860. Rim of hat is tin. Courtesy New-York Historical Society.*

FIG. 159

FIG. 160

FIG. 161

old (Fig. 162). In front of Zinngrabe's tobacco shop at 3825 South Halsted was a recent Demuth metal *Captain Jack;* at 989 West Madison Street was a crudely carved figure of an Indian; in front of J. Derudder's Stationery and Cigar Store at 396 South Halsted was a primitive-type Indian (Fig. 163). Some of the older type carvings were quite crude (Fig. 164) and seemed out of character with a growing metropolis. Probably reinforced with photographs of his work, Brooks was able to obtain a large number of orders in advance before deciding on the move to Chicago. He may have worked with Metzler, Rothschild & Co., importers and manufacturers of tobacconists' supplies and smokers' articles at 62 Lake Street at the corner of State Street, who issued a forty-two page illustrated and colored catalogue. A cut on the cover shows their building, in front of which is a monumental tobacconist's figure. One page shows three Indians, two in wood and one in metal (Fig. 165). The two wood figures are in the Brooks style, the metal figure, probably a new design created for the Chicago firm by Brooks, may have been cast in the foundry of Henry Dibblee Iron Works of Chicago. The pedestal is similar to those used by Demuth for expensive metal figures.[46]

A fine figure of a squaw, with a bundle of cigars in one hand and a spear in the other and with legs crossed, stood in front of Otto C. Larsen's tobacconist's shop and shaving parlor in the early 1880s. The figure, by Brooks,

FIG. 162

FIG. 163

Fig. 162. Early type of tobacconist's figure in Chicago, location unidentified. Photographs taken about 1860–1870. Courtesy Chicago Historical Society.

Fig. 163. Early type of tobacconist's figure in front of J. Derudder's Stationery and Cigar Store at 396 South Halsted Street, Chicago. Photograph taken about 1880–1885. Courtesy Chicago Historical Society.

Fig. 164. Early type of tobacconist's figure, probably from Chicago before 1880. Compare with figure in front of J. Derudder's shop (Figure 163). Photograph: courtesy Index of American Design.

FIG. 164

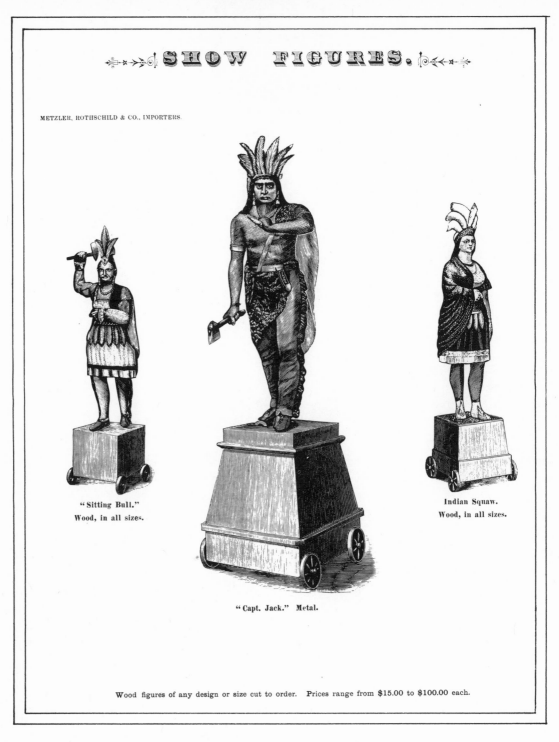

Fig. 165. Three figures from a page of the catalogue issued by Metzler, Rothschild & Co. at 62 Lake Street, Chicago, in 1879. The two smaller figures are of wood in the Brooks style. The center figure was of cast zinc and made in the foundry of Henry Dibblee of Chicago, probably from an original carving in wood by Thomas V. Brooks.

is quite similar to many of those made in the shop of Robb in New York (Fig. 166). One of Brooks's Indians made in the 1890s was still standing on Clarke Street in Chicago, at least until 1930 when a photograph taken of it showed it to be in excellent condition (Fig. 167). It held cigars in one hand and a musket in the other.

Brooks not only supplied tobacconists' and other show figures to buyers in Chicago but also to those in many of the other cities, towns, and villages of the expanding western United States. On occasions when the shopkeepers would come to Chicago to order their merchandise from the large supply houses, Brooks's shop would be a point of call to order to figure for the shop. In 1880, Charley Manley came in from Livingston, Montana, ordered a large Indian from Brooks and paid him $350 plus another $100 for packing and freight to Livingston. In 1888, Manley moved to Tacoma, Washington, taking with him his Indian, which he called "Skookum," and set up a cigar factory and store at Ninth and Pacific. Seventeen years later, he moved with "Skookum" across the street. Here the Indian stood until Manley retired, when it was sold to the Washington State Press Club of Seattle, an event which stirred the Tacoma press to note.

A group of men from the northern city, straightening their hand-painted ties and trimming fingernails on the crease in their trousers, walked into Charley Manley's cigar store at 9th and Pacific last week. . . . The Chief turned pale beneath his tan as he heard the telltale riffle of banknotes in their hip pockets when they walked in the door and counted off $900 without even wetting a thumb [Fig. 168].[47]

The sight of a New York policeman in the streets of Chicago must have attracted attention, especially when he was made of wood and stood in front of a tobacconist's shop. This was attested to by Robb in an interview:

"Don't you create anything yourself?"
"Oh, yes, I once created a policeman, but had him loafin' around here for a long time before I could get him off my hands. One day a man comes here from Chicago, and sees him. He was so took with him that he thought a New York policeman would be a fine thing in Chicago, an' I let him go for $40."

Fig. 166. Squaw. Carved by Thomas V. Brooks. Front of Otto C. Larsen's tobacconist shop at 503 South Jefferson Street, Chicago, about 1880–1885. Photograph: courtesy Chicago Historical Society.

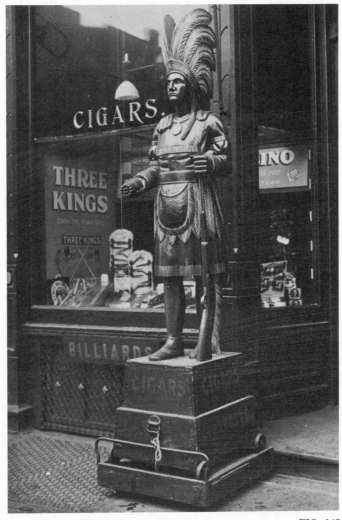

FIG. 167

FIG. 168

Fig. 167. Indian. Carved by Thomas V. Brooks. Front of the tobacconist's shop on Clarke Street, Chicago. Photograph taken in 1930. Courtesy Chicago Historical Society.

Fig. 168. Chief "Skookum." Ordered from Thomas V. Brooks's Chicago shop in 1880 by Charley Manley of Livingston, Montana. Photograph: Seattle Historical Society.

The New York policeman was quite a rage in Chicago for some time and Brooks had quite a run on him. . . .[48]

In 1887, Brooks moved his shop to 205½ South Desplaines and in 1889 moved again to 408 West Madison, taking his son into the business as Thomas V. Brooks & Son. James A. Brooks, like many another apprentice starting out in his own business, listed himself as "sculptor." In 1890, Brooks & Son moved to 318–320 West Van Buren. James took a large advertisement in the Chicago Business Directory under "Show Figures." Brooks, Sr., was not in the best of health, and when preparations were being made for the Columbian Exposition of 1893 in Chicago, Brooks did not get much of the work. At this exposition, Demuth exhibited a fine display with a huge central figure of *Gambrinus*, flanked by the *Scout*, the *Egyptian Princess*, *Puck* and *Captain Jack*, all in metal. Demuth also exhibited a huge pipe depicting Columbus's discovery of America. However, another Brooks, Caroline S. Brooks, seems to have stolen the show:

No one thing exhibited at the Centennial attracted more general attention, or was more distinctly remembered than the *Sleeping Iolante*, in butter, by Mrs. Caroline S. Brooks. Since that wonderful success the artist has done several notable bits in a characteristic vein, the best-known being *Lady Godiva*, a bas-relief which was also in butter.[49]

During the 1890s, due to failing health, Thomas V. Brooks left more of the duties to Isaac Lewin, who changed his name to Lewis. Brooks died in 1895 in Chicago and the business was bought by Lewis. James A. Brooks returned to New York, taking up residence at 144 South Third Street in the Greenpoint-Williamsburgh area of Brooklyn. He carved and sold his Indians and show figures under the firm name of Standard Show Figure Company until 1905. He specialized in small outdoor figures and indoor counter figures. Brooks went into the painting and contracting business, moving around a good deal, and in the 1920s, with his wife Belle R. Brooks, moved to Tampa, Florida, where he continued to paint. During the depression of the 1930s, Brooks died in Tampa.[50]

Samuel Anderson Robb (1851–1928)

In 1848, Peter Robb, shipwright of Scotland, found conditions there intolerable; famine had struck a large part of the British Isles and the labor situation was unpredictable. On Lewis Street in New York, Robb had relatives who were ship joiners and sawyers, and his wife, the former Elizabeth Wales Anderson, was related to Jacob S. Anderson on South Street. The New York port was the busiest shipbuilding center in the world and workmen were scarce. Peter Robb, age thirty-two, and his twenty-one-year-old wife left Scotland for the United States in 1849.

Robb may have lived with his relatives on Lewis Street for a year or two but after the birth of his son, Samuel Anderson Robb, on December 16, 1851, he moved to 238 Seventh Street, not far from the shipbuilding yards of William H. Webb and Westervelt & Mackay, which stretched from Fifth to Seventh Streets and from Seventh to Eighth Streets, along the western bank of the East River. On the opposite side, the "Williamsburgh shore, with its modest cottages, gardens and orchards, was the favorite fruit market of the calkers and ship-carpenters; they used to row across the river in small boats, and steal the apples that complemented their mid-day meals."[1]

In 1855, another son was born, named Charles, and Peter Robb moved with his family to Fourth Street. Due to the impending depression of 1857, the shipyards were beginning to feel a great letdown in work and many men were being laid off. Robb listed himself as a carpenter, yet how he managed to get through this period is not known. Sometime after the Civil War, Robb apprenticed his son, Samuel, to Thomas V. Brooks to learn the trade of shipcarving. Jacob S. Anderson, who was a relative of Robb's wife, had been a very talented shipcarver, but he had died in 1855. Had he lived, Samuel might have become his apprentice. However, Brooks had an excellent reputation, his shop was usually very busy, and a young, intelligent apprentice could learn a great deal. Robb had a talent for carving and drawing which developed quite rapidly and received a great deal of encouragement from the men in the shop, especially from Tom White, who later became a partner of Brooks.[2]

In 1865, Brooks's shop was at 240 South Street north of Market Slip where Pike intersects.

North of Market Street the surroundings are entirely maritime. The houses are full of ship-chandlery—great cables, blocks, anchors and wheels; the signs of sail-lofts flap from upper stories; boats run their bows out-of-doors; spar-yards are full of men hewing great timbers; and shipsmith shops glow with forges and echo with blows on the anvil. Here and there a window is full of quadrants, compasses, Chronometers and other navigating instruments.[3]

After five years in Brooks's shop, Sam Robb went to work for William Demuth, carving tobacconists' figures at 403 Broadway. In 1869, Demuth's exhibition of show figures at the American Institute won a medal and thus gave a great impetus to the show-figure carvers, especially the young art student Samuel Robb. Perhaps his was one of the figures exhibited by Demuth. Under the influence of Demuth, Robb entered the National Academy of Design, taking Mr. E. Wilmarth's course in "Drawing from Life."

In 1869, the National Academy of Design was at Fourth Avenue and 23rd Street, then the center of Manhattan. It occupied a splendid building known as the "Doge's Palace" because of its vague resemblance to the palace of the Piazza San Marco in Venice. The National Academy of Design and its school had been founded in 1825 by Samuel Finley Breese Morse, portrait painter and inventor of the telegraph. The school had opened with a class of twenty students on November 15, 1826, in a room of the Philosophical Society of New York, located in the Old Alms House in City Hall Park. It was the first art school in New York. Before 1865, the school moved several times but then, together with the Academy, it opened in an impressive structure on 23rd Street, on the site of the Metropolitan Life Insurance Company. In 1870, Robb took the Antique Drawing Class, instructed by Wilmarth. The students had their choice of plaster masks or scaled-down models of statues from antiquity from which to draw. Their easels were set in front of the model, and they would sketch in charcoal.[4]

During this time, Robb also applied and was accepted in the "Free Night School of Science and Art" in the Cooper Union at Cooper Square in New York. He took the course in Perspective Drawing, given by Professor Constantine Herzberg, A. B. The records of the School of Art show that Robb placed sixth in a graduating class of thirty-six.[5] In 1873, Robb completed his studies in drawing from life and from the casts at the National Academy of Design and received his certificate.[6] While Robb was working hard during the day as a carver and attending the art schools at night, he lived with his parents at 54 Greenwich Avenue and found time to sing as a soloist in the Jane Street Presbyterian Church.

After his graduation from art school, Robb gave thought to opening his own carving shop. The next year, he met Emma Jane Pelham and on June 14, 1876, they were married. Emma's father, Thomas M. Pelham, who had died a few years earlier, had been an inventor of a patent steamdriven elevator, which was said to have been displayed at the Philadelphia Centennial the year they were married. On the marriage certificate in reply to question No. 5, occupation, Robb filled in "Artist in Wood."[7] The young artist in wood and his bride moved in with his parents at 406 West 13th Street, in Manhattan. Sometime later that year, Robb opened his carving shop at 195 Canal Street in a two-story wooden building owned by Solomon Stone. It was seventy-five feet deep and twenty-five feet wide and had once been the property of George Lorillard, the tobacco merchant and manufacturer. Behind the building was the Chichester & Derby chair factory, while from the corner to Mott Street was the upholstery factory of P. Schneider & Sons. Across the street to the east, the St. Nicholas buildings extended to Elizabeth Street and the Fifth Regiment Armory was around the corner on Hester Street.[8] The Bowery was but a block and a half away, and the area today is the approach to the Manhattan Bridge. The street floor of Robb's shop consisted of a long room, part of which had a dirt floor. Near the front of the shop was a small office. A stairway led to the upper floor, which had an opening in the rear over the dirt floor area. From the rafters hung a pulley by which the carvings could be raised or lowered. Here, tobacconists' figures by the dozens were turned out each month.[9] A description of the shop was given by a *Mail & Express* reporter some years later:

In the cockloft above two able bodied men were making chips and Indians as fast as they knew how. Both brandished long, thin bladed chisels, and were whacking away, apparently without the slightest regard for consequences. Three savages ready to graduate to the painting department were standing in one corner, and showed that the chopping by the two men was not so reckless as it seemed. The nose of a young buck grew out of the block before the other wood sculptor while the reporter looked on.[10]

In 1877, Alexander C. Robb, Samuel's youngest brother, died. The following year, Emma Jane Robb gave birth to a boy, who was named Clarence. Six months later, Emma died and was buried in Woodlawn Cemetery in the Bronx. Robb designed a monument with the symbol of the four major religions carved on each of its sides and, on the front, a rose complete with leaves and thorns. The monument is inscribed, "The Memory of the Just is Blessed." Following the inscription, Robb carved tobacconists' squaws holding roses, with cigar boxes and packages of snuff under their arms.

Robb felt the loss very deeply but kept hard at work. In 1881, he inserted a half-page advertisement in Lain's Brooklyn Directory directed toward the tobacconists of that borough (Fig. 169). The linecut shows a Sir Walter Raleigh type, sword at side, smoking a cigarillo. Besides tobacconists' signs, he also did "ship and steamboat carving, eagles, heads [figureheads], block letters, shoe, dentist, and druggist signs."

Thomas J. White had come to work in the Robb shop shortly after it was opened and remained there, off and on, for many years. With Robb he carved many of the tobacconists' figures, signs, heads, eagles, and other

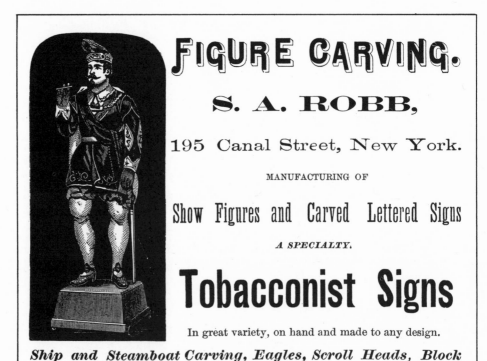

Fig. 169. Advertisement of Samuel A. Robb in Lain's Brooklyn Directory, 1881.

Fig. 170. The carving shop of Samuel A. Robb at 195 Canal Street, Manhattan, about 1879. Posed in the paint department are: Right, Samuel A. Robb; Center, Thomas J. White; the man at left is unidentified. Behind Robb is an unpainted figure of a baseball player; the figure on pedestal to left is a Sir Walter Raleigh type. Paper patterns hang from wall behind White.

work which were sold throughout the country and locally not only through Demuth, but also from Robb's shop. Through one of the rarest of photographs, which came from Robb's files, we can tell what part of the shop looked like, as well as the carvers who worked there (Fig. 170). Samuel Robb stands to the right; to his right is Thomas J. White; while the man on the left is unidentified. The figure on the pedestal is a completed Sir Walter Raleigh, similar to the linecut in Robb's advertisement; behind Robb are three squaws and an unpainted baseball player. Behind White

Fig. 171. Squaw. Signed, "S.A. Robb. Carver. 195 Canal Street, N.Y.," c. 1881. Courtesy New-York Historical Society.

are three Indians; over White's left shoulder is a Brooks-type Indian, right hand holding a tomahawk. Around the room are some paper patterns and to the left are some discarded pedestal wheels, identical to those used on freight weighing scales. In the foreground is the trimming part of the paint department and the broadaxe used to shape the log after the pattern had been traced. The shop had been making carvings for circus wagons, religious figures for the increasing number of Italian churches in the neighborhood, and probably dragons for the Chinese in the area known as "Chinatown."

During this period, Robb signed his carvings. Not all of the figures he carved were signed but only those he had made and completed by himself, perhaps as samples for a new line, or as demonstrations of the quality of work that should bear his name. As far as is known, except for Jobin and some of the other Canadians, Robb was one of the only carvers who signed not only his name but also the address of his shop and the city. Melchers had incised script initials in the medals of his Indians; Cromwell had some kind of stamped mark,[11] and Crongeyer had added a small metal plate bearing his name and address. Robb incised his name on top of the front board enclosing the base. In the New-York Historical Society there is an Indian squaw in a fine state of preservation, signed at the base "S. A. Robb, Carver, 195 Canal Street, N.Y." (Fig. 171). The face is not Indian and may even have some of the features of his deceased wife, Emma Jane. A figure of a fireman is signed "S. A. Robb, 195 Canal Street" (Fig. 172). It stands twenty-nine inches from the toe to the top of the extended arm, on a two and three-quarter-inch-high base. The numeral 14 on the belt buckle was the symbol of the Columbian Hose Company No. 14, for which it was made. The right hand once held a trumpet, now missing. It is doubtful if the figure was ever used out of doors. It is now in the collection of the H. V. Smith Museum of The Home Insurance Company in New York. Several other signed figures exist from a later period. Many of the sideboard stands would rot from years of exposure and, when they were replaced, the incised Robb signature was discarded.

On March 3, 1879, Robb enlisted in the New York State National Guard and was assigned to Company I, First Division, First Brigade of the Twenty-second Regiment, under Captain Wheelington. The command was under Colonel Joseph Porter.[12] Robb cut a neat figure in his uniform, and legend has it that Tom White cut a neater figure of Robb, immortalizing him in wood, in a figure now known as *Captain Jinks* (Figs. 173 and 174).[13] The character was taken from a popular song during the Civil War, called "Captain Jinks of the Horse Marines." It was published by Metzler & Company in London in 1862 and reprinted by the New England News Company in Boston in 1868 with a picture of an officer, sword under arm, wearing a tall bearskin hat. The Holbrook & Redman Tobacco Company of Louisville put out a brand with a similar figure on its packages. The

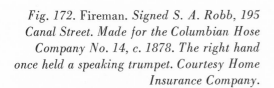

FIG. 172

FIG. 173

FIG. 174

Fig. 172. Fireman. *Signed S. A. Robb, 195 Canal Street. Made for the Columbian Hose Company No. 14, c. 1878. The right hand once held a speaking trumpet. Courtesy Home Insurance Company.*

Fig. 173. Captain Jinks. *Tobacconist's figure probably created by Thomas J. White as a caricature of Samuel A. Robb in his military uniform. Courtesy Shelburne Museum. Photograph: Einars J. Mengis.*

Fig. 174. Captain Jinks. *Side view of figure in the Smithsonian Institution.*

song was very popular and was a jibe at officers and their fancy uniforms. There are innumerable verses. The version taken from the American edition follows:

> *I am Captain Jinks of the Horse Marines,*
> *I often live beyond my means,*
> *I sport young ladies in their teens,*
> *To cut a swell in the Army.*
>
> *I teach the la—dies how to dance,*
> *How to dance, how to dance,*
> *For I'm their pet in the Army.*

[Spoken] *Ha! ha! ha!*

Chorus *I'm Captain Jinks of the Horse Marines,*
> *I give my horse good corn and beans,*
> *Of course, it's quite beyond my means,*
> *Tho' a captain in the ar—my.*
>
> *I joined my corps when twenty-one,*
> *Of course I thought it capital fun*
> *When the enemy came then off I run,*
> *I wasn't cut out for the army.*
>
> *When I left home mama she cried,*
> *Mama she cried, mama she cried,*
> *When I left home mama she cried,*
> *"He aint cut out for the army."*

[Spoken] *No, she thought I was too young, but then I said*
> *Oh! Mama.*

Chorus *I'm Captain Jinks of the Horse Marines etc.*
>
> *The first day I went out to drill,*
> *The bugle sound made me quite ill,*
> *At the Balance step my hat it fell,*
> *And that wouldn't do for the army.*
>
> *The officers they all did shout.*
> *They all cried out, they all did shout,*
> *The officers they all did shout,*
> *"Oh that's the curse of the army."*

[Spoken] *Of course my hat did fall off, but oh! nevertheless,*

Chorus *I'm Captain Jinks of the Horse Marines etc.*
>
> *My tailor's bills came in so fast*
> *Forced me one day to leave at last,*
> *And ladies no more did cast,*
> *Sheep's eyes at me in the army.*
>
> *My creditors at me did shout,*
> *At me did shout, at me did shout,*
> *My creditors at me did shout*
> *"Why kick him out of the army."*

[Spoken] *I said, Oh! gentlemen Oh! Kick me out of the army? Perhaps you are not aware*

Chorus *I'm Captain Jinks of the Horse Marines
I give my horse good corn and beans,
Of course it's quite beyond my means,
Tho' a captain in the ar—my.*

In the September 1879, issue of *Scribner's Monthly*, "Captain Jinks" was used to describe a carved figure in an article, "Signs and Symbols," by Frank B. Mayer.[14] In 1902, Clyde Fitch adapted the song as a play, "Captain Jinks of the Horse Marines," given at the Garrick Theatre, featuring Elizabeth Kennedy as Mme. Tentoni, and produced under the management of Charles Frohman. This type of carved figure was also called "Dude" or "Swell." The resemblance to Robb is more than coincidental when comparison is made with the studio portrait of him (Fig. 176). The Twenty-second Regiment had a long and colorful history engaging in the Harper's Ferry campaign of 1862; it had several engagements with the Plains Indians and was the relief force that found the last of Custer's last stand. The dress uniform of officers consisted of the white double-breasted frock coat and blue trousers, with black stripe. The crushed cap-kepi, the tunic, and trousers fit no particular regimental costume but is in the style used by many of the militia or volunteer units during and after the Civil War period.[15]

The Robbs had been friendly through the years with the Loudon family, also of Scottish background and members of the Jane Street Presbyterian Church. James Loudon had appeared as Sam's witness in his application for his first marriage certificate. Agnes Loudon, James's sister, was ten years younger than Sam Robb and lived with her parents at 688 Hudson Street, a property owned by her parents. On October 12, 1881, Sam Robb and Agnes Loudon were married by the clergyman, W. M. Gibner. Robb moved into the home of his twenty-year-old bride and her parents, leaving his three-year-old son with his parents (Figs. 175, 176). William Loudon was a strong-willed father and a stronger-willed father-in-law, while the young

FIG. 175

FIG. 176

Figs. 175, 176. Wedding photographs of Agnes Loudon Robb and Samuel A. Robb, October 12, 1881.

FIG. 177

FIG. 178

wife had her own ideas on how to be supported. She had been the only daughter in a family with two children, and her father, who doted on her, had the means to keep her in fine clothing, good schooling, and lavish vacations. The hardworking artist in wood found less than complete happiness in his new surroundings.[16]

Robb's entry into the business of producing tobacconists' figures had taken much of the business away from Thomas V. Brooks, his former master with whom he always maintained a good relationship. Brooks moved to Chicago and Robb got the major part of the show-figure business in New York City, as well as most of the circus carving from Adam Fore-

Fig. 177. Highlander. Holding a mull and offering a pinch of snuff. Carved in the Robb shop, c. 1878. Height 75 inches. Courtesy Shelburne Museum. Photograph: Einars J. Mengis.

Fig. 178. Grenadier. Tobacconist's figure carved in the Robb shop, c. 1884. Height 77 inches, base 8½ inches. Photograph: Taylor & Dull.

Fig. 179. Religious Group. Made in Robb's Canal Street shop, c. 1882, for a local Italian organization.

Fig. 180. Elephant. Made in Robb's Canal Street shop before 1888, for a Tenth Avenue saloonkeeper.

Fig. 181. Santa Claus. Made in Robb's shop, c. 1880, for a Broadway toy dealer. Courtesy the Van Alstyne Collection, Smithsonian Institution.

paugh and Barnum & London. Robb produced various new figures and many standard figures such as the *Scottish Highlander* (Fig. 177), the *Grenadier* with the Dundreary type of beard and military outfit (Fig. 178), and also some religious figures. In a religious grouping of three figures carved and painted for the local Societa Unione Del Sannio, he could not resist his circus carving training and the base decorations are more fitting for a circus wagon tableau than for an ecclesiastic setting (Fig. 179). Among other types of carvings were an elephant for a saloon keeper (Fig. 180), and a *Santa Claus* for a toy shop (Fig. 181), now in the Van Alstyne Folk Art Collection.[17]

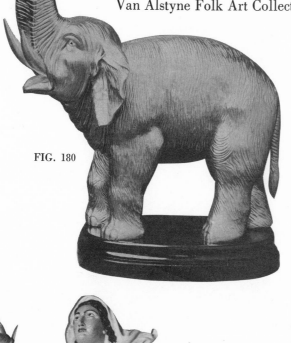

FIG. 180

FIG. 181

FIG. 179

A DEVOZIONE LA SOCIETÀ UNIONE DEL SANNIO.

The wagon sides and carvings for the tableau for Forepaugh's St. George and the Dragon circus wagon were made in Robb's shop on Canal Street (Figs. 182, 183). The four corner figures seem to have been altered slightly from Robb's inventory of tobacconists' figures. The two page boys (Fig. 184) are almost identical to those cast in zinc for William Demuth, except that the raised right hand holding cigars was now at the side holding a sword (See Fig. 33). Like the pages, the court jester to the left rear was used by Robb as a tobacconist's figure on at least one occasion before 1875, and with a few changes in the costume could well be the figure used by Robb in his advertisement (See Fig. 169).[18]

The carvings of lions, lionesses, half-nude female figures, and a large amount of scroll carvings with irregular mirrors were in high relief, eight inches deep. The driver's seat and footrest were supported by a spread-winged eagle. The wagon was twenty-three feet long and ten feet high and weighed six tons without the tableau. The St. George and the Dragon

Fig. 182. The St. George and the Dragon Tableau. *A street parade. Courtesy Richard E. Conover.*

Tableau was used until 1890 when it was acquired by the Ringling Bros. Circus. At that time the tableau was removed and placed upon a wagon to be drawn by ponies, while the wagon itself was converted into a band-wagon, becoming known as the Lion and Mirror Bandwagon No. 1 (Col. Fig. 9). It was eventually acquired by Carson, Pirie Scott & Co., of Chicago and donated to the Circus World Museum in Baraboo, Wisconsin.

Robb's shop supplied the carvings for additional cage wagons or Tableaux Dens for the Barnum, Bailey & Hutchinson interests. He supplied four huge apes for what in later years was known as cage wagon No. 63, and

Fig. 183. St. George and the Dragon Wagon. *Converted to Bandwagon No. 1.*
without the tableau. Constructed by Jacob Sebastian of New York for Adam
Forepaugh. Now at the Circus World Museum in Baraboo, Wisconsin. Photograph:
Clarence J. Laughlin.

page boys (Fig. 185) quite similar to those on the St. George and the Dragon Tableau and to his tobacconists' figures. These page figures as well as those removed from wagons in later years are now in the collection of the Shelburne Museum; also a group of figures from similar wagons that were part of the Ringling Bros. and Barnum & Bailey Circus (Fig. 186).

Sometime during the carving of the large group of figures for the cage wagons, he carved a portrait in relief of his wife, Agnes, and somewhere found room to attach this to a wagon. During the 1930s, when Ringling Bros. and Barnum & Bailey Circus wagons were abandoned at Bridgeport, the landlord, in lieu of payment of rent, had the gold leaf scraped off the wagons by schoolboys, and sold the carving and gold leaf separately. The portrait of Agnes was bought by William L. Warren, along with several other carvings and corner figures that are still in his collection (Fig. 187).

In addition to Tom White, Robb was assisted by his brother Charles, by his father Peter, and, when very busy, by some of the older carvers who were employed in the other shops. In 1882, the Loudons bought a house at 329 West 21st Street, and that year Samuel Loudon Robb was born, just one block from the street where his mother had been born twenty-one years earlier. During the winter of 1881–1882, Robb had completed a large order of corner figures for the Barnum & London cage wagons, keeping the shop working full time. In January, 1884, Martha Dunlop Robb was born and in March, Robb's service in the National Guard was terminated. With

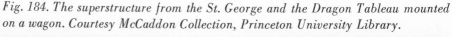

Fig. 184. The superstructure from the St. George and the Dragon Tableau mounted on a wagon. Courtesy McCaddon Collection, Princeton University Library.

a growing family, the Loudon residence was getting too small and, in February of 1886 when Alexander Loudon Robb was born, Robb and his family moved into a house owned by his father-in-law at 155 Madison Street in Brooklyn. Signs of tension were building up between the sensitive artist in wood and the tough, old stone contractor who had supplied the facings for the huge Dakota Apartments at 72nd Street and Eighth Avenue (now Central Park West), and later had the contract for raising the obelisk in Central Park.

The year 1888 was one of hard work, great sorrow, and hard feelings between Samuel Robb and his father-in-law. The Madison Street house was needed by Loudon, so Robb and his family moved into another property owned by Loudon at 249 Halsey Street, but a short time after the same

Fig. 187. Carved wood relief of Agnes Loudon Robb, wife of the carver. Removed from one of the tableaux dens. Courtesy R. Warren Collection.

thing happened and they moved to still another family house at 119 Quincy Street. When Loudon needed this property as well, Robb gathered his belongings and, standing by the front door, gave his wife Agnes the choice of him or her father. Pregnant with another child, spoiled by her father, and accustomed to the niceties furnished by an indulgent Victorian parent, Agnes answered that she must stay with her family. Robb walked out the front door and did not see Agnes again nor the child she was bearing, for seventeen years.[19] Shortly afterward, Elizabeth Wilson Robb was born.

Later that year Robb made another break and moved his carving shop to 114 Centre Street just a few blocks to the southwest, near the Tombs and on the site where a beautiful lake was once situated, known as the Kalchhook Pond or Collect. The name translated from the Dutch means, "Lime shell point." This was once Manhattan Island's largest natural fresh water pond; from its side rose short sheer cliffs and hills covered with hickory and chestnut trees. It was fed by large springs bubbling from its great depths and two streams carried off its waters, one into the East River and the other into the marshes to the north and west. Indian hunters sought this spot in search of shellfish, and wigwams were built on its shores. Huge shell deposits found on the lake's western promontory indicate it was a favorite camping place. The water was so pure that water for tea was

Fig. 186. Group of figures from the abandoned tableaux dens of the Ringling Bros., Barnum & Bailey Circus. Courtesy William W. Warren Collection.

sought from one of its fountains, called the Teawater, located at Roosevelt and Chatham Streets. By 1811, most of Collect Pond was filled in. By 1816, the paving of Collect (Centre Street) began, and modest houses were built on its site.[20]

The arrangement was almost the same as in the Canal Street shop, and it is possible that Robb may also have used the Centre Street shop as his living quarters for some time. Perhaps because Robb had legal difficulties with William Loudon,[21] he placed the business under the name of his father, Peter Robb, listing himself as "Manager." In March, 1889, Martha Dunlop Robb, age five years, died. Robb did not attend the funeral. On July 1, 1889, his brother Charles married Marie Kissinger and moved into his father Peter's house at 303 West 20th Street.

The shop was extremely busy. Sam Robb kept occupied running the business, carving, painting, seeing clients, and keeping some of his accounts well supplied. Demuth was still sending orders and Robb was filling them with all kinds of figures. Tom White was still working in the shop producing some new figures. Robb had created a new style of Indian carrying a shield with hanging feathers on which a brand name of tobacco could be painted. The Indian wore a stunning headdress with an eagle head and wings, a tassled sash around his waist, knee feathers, and long earbobs. In the right hand he held a huge pipe or a bundle of cigars. Robb had the figure engraved on his new business card (Fig. 188). One of the finest examples of this figure, minus shield with hanging feathers, is in the Van Alstyne Folk Art Collection (Col. Fig. 22). Another, with cigars, is at the Shelburne Museum, which also has a bust of this figure (Col. Fig. 23). A head alone is in the author's collection (Fig. 189).

Robb received a visit from a *New York Times* reporter, Frank W. Weitenkampf, whose story appeared on August 3, 1890, under the heading "Lo, The Wooden Indian." Robb had been interviewed several times before by reporters from *The Sun, Mail & Express,* and *Tobacco,* and by an anonymous publication whose story was used by Henry Collins Brown for his *Valentine's Manual* of 1927. *Harper's Weekly* had also interviewed Robb at the Canal Street address. The subtitle of *The New York Times* story read, "The Art of Making Cigar-Shop Signs—Sculptors in Wood

FIG. 188

Who Began by Making Figureheads of Ships—How the Work is Done." A partial inventory of the work of Robb's shop follows in a section of the report:

. . . some dealers, with discriminating tastes or peculiar hobbies and with the money to indulge them, have special figures made to order.

One old gentleman on Third Avenue, near Ninth Street, had himself cut out in wood, in the uniform of some military company to which he belonged. Another gentleman, on Broadway, put up a figure of Edwin Forrest, in Roman garb, redundant of muscle, in front of his store. This figure has since gone to Philadelphia. Still another, up town, on Tenth Avenue, ordered the counterfeit presentment of Boston's shining light, John L. Sullivan, in his baseball suit. Another Tenth Avenue man had an elephant and the golden calf made for his two saloons [see Fig 180]. One Western man ordered figures of the Goddess of Liberty and of Bartholdi's statue, somewhat altered from the original. The carver naturally is glad to get out of the rut of wearisome conventionality sometimes, and puts his best foot foremost when filling such orders.

But the tobacconist is not by any means the only customer that the sculptor in wood has to supply. Chiropodists want large white or gilt feet to display before their doors, glove sellers hang up wooden gloved hands as signs of their calling, and livery-stable owners call for heads of horses. More than that, our artist in wood is at times called upon to exercise his cunning in manufacturing wooden hands for such persons as have had the misfortune to lose one of those that nature provided them with. A down-town firm puts springs into these, so that they can be used to some extent by the wearer.

P. T. Barnum has been supplied with a number of wooden figures which appear in his parades. They are all life size or larger, and include Bluebeard, Cinderella, Mother Goose, Sinbad the Sailor, Little Red Riding Hood, and the Old Woman who Lived in a Shoe. Forepaugh has an equestrian figure of St. George and the Dragon. The figures on Barnum's vans are also carved in wood.

One firm that deals in woolen rags had a figure of a ragman, 9 feet high, placed on top of its building on Franklin Street, near Centre. When it moved to its present quarters, on West Street, near Canal, a similar figure was put for it, so that there are two of them now. Another well-known figure is the cow that is milked daily on Coney Island. At Narrangansett Pier there is a huge dragon 23 feet long, which curls around a column on the water tower in Earl's Court. Again, William Demuth has had carvings executed on his yacht at Lake George, and similar work has been produced for others. Nearly all of these figures came from Robb's shop, and many of them are Thomas White's handiwork. White even went into ideal statuary to such an extent as to produce a "Greek Slave" and "Adam and Eve" in wood. There are

FIG. 189

Fig. 188. Trade card of Samuel A. and Charles Robb at 114 Centre Street between 1898 and 1900. The inked-in address, 223 E. 43 St., was that of the Sebastian Wagon Company, and used by Samuel Robb during his work there.

Fig. 189. Indian Prototype. Similar to one used on Robb's trade card, c. 1890. Courtesy Shelburne Museum. Photograph: Einars J. Mengis.

Fig. 190. The Inexhaustible Cow. Carved wood. At Coney Island in 1881. Made at 195 Canal Street by Samuel A. Robb.

Milk on Draught

probably but two or three men in the city who engage in the business. S. A. Robb, who has been at it for twenty-six years, is full of reminiscences concerning the history of the art.

The *Inexhaustible Cow* at Coney Island was a larger than life-sized wooden cow with a hollow interior into which was placed cans of milk on ice. Spigots fitted into the wooden udder poured milk for a nickel a glass (Fig. 190).[22] Robb made many baseball players; one, bearing the incised signature, "Robb, MANU'F'R. 114 CENTRE ST. N.Y." (Fig. 191). While the figure is out of proportion, with a very short torso, it presents a good silhouette as though one were looking at the batter from the bleachers. The figure is in the collection of Carl W. Haffenreffer at Little Compton, Rhode Island (Col. Fig. 24). Another baseball player, of earlier and unknown origin, minus the bat, is in the collection of the Hopkins Center Art Galleries at Dartmouth College (Fig. 192). Still another baseball figure, bat at side, legs crossed, is in the collection of the Baseball Hall of Fame at Cooperstown, New York (Fig. 193). Another signed figure is an Indian Chief carved in wood. This figure, seventy-nine inches high, has a pedestal twenty-three inches high. William Demuth was awarded a medal for a facsimile in metal, which was exhibited at the Centennial Exhibition in Philadelphia in 1876 in the Tobacco Exhibit in Agriculture Hall.[23] The wood figure (Fig. 194a), which is in the Van Alstyne Folk Art Collection, Smithsonian Institution, wears a necklace of bearclaws, a sign of bravery, but the bow in the right hand and the arrow in the left is missing. Under

FIG. 191

FIG. 192

FIG. 193

Fig. 191. Baseball Player. *Incised on base:* Robb, MANU'F'R. *114* CENTRE ST. N.Y., *c. 1890–1900. Height 51 inches, base 23 inches. Courtesy Carl W. Haffenreffer. Photograph: Ernst Beadle.*

Fig. 192. Baseball Player. *Carved in the style of Thomas V. Brooks. Height 70 inches. Left hand may have rested on baseball bat. "Briggs" painted on chest may have represented name of sporting goods establishment. Uniform from the 1880s or earlier. Courtesy Dartmouth College Collection.*

Fig. 193. Joe Wood. *Used as a sporting goods figure in Rochester, New York. Said to have been made in 1867. Courtesy Baseball Hall of Fame, Cooperstown, New York.*

*Figs. 194a, 194b. Indian Chief. Similar to
Demuth catalogue figure No. 53, c. 1889.
Carved wood. Height 79 inches. On the stump
(Fig. 194b) under the left foot is
doubly-incised, "Robb* MANU'F'R. *114* CENTRE *St. N.Y."
Courtesy Smithsonian Institution.*

the foot is the incised name, "Robb MANU'F'R. 114 CENTRE St. N.Y." Two
signatures appear, one over the other (Fig. 194b).

On May 2, 1892, Robb's mother died. In the Robb shop, Charles did
much of the shaping, some carving and painting, and performed some of
the other duties such as purchasing the spar ends, attending to deliveries,
and some office work. Samuel's son, Clarence, helped out after school and
picked up enough experience over the next several years to later list him-

Fig. 195. Sign made for cutlery shop of Henry J. Westpfal in Robb's Centre Street shop, c. 1889.

self as a carver. White and another carver, called Henry, were also part of the staff. The business did well, work came in from several directions, Demuth continued to be supplied, and many orders went out to various parts of the country.[24]

As the city spread out, all kinds of businesses were established. New York was becoming a forest of signs, which jutted out into the streets over the heads of pedestrians like the bowsprits of clippers over South Street in former days. The multilingual groups arriving each day from foreign ports could easily find the service or product needed, guided by the visual symbol or the sign lettered in almost every language. The sign painter and the carver were kept working, making new images, giving new directions, and depicting the tremendous variety of trades and crafts to be found in the great metropolis.

Two years after his Wooden Indian article, Frank W. Weitenkampf, walked the streets of New York, noting the variety of signs:

The mortar and pestle of the druggist, the gilt boots and hats of the shoemaker and the hatter, the dummy clocks and real ones in front of jewelry stores, and the giant eyeglasses of the opticians are as familiar to our eye and as readily indicative and suggestive of the various trades they represent as are the three gilt balls of the pawnbroker shops, the cigar-store Indian, and the quite historic barber pole.

Similarly, dealers in sporting goods indicate their calling by mammoth guns, (to which a Murray Street dealer adds a huge cartridge,) and locksmiths hang out keys and saws. Huge cigars, pens, pipes and horseshoes pendant over doors also leave no doubt as to what can be had inside, while single umbrellas or perpendicular strings thereof remind us that we must be prepared for a rainy day. Many of these carved figures are gilt. Some chiropodists place big sawed-off white feet before their doors, just as a large gloved hand shows us where to get gloves.

The conventional mortar of the druggist is occasionally varied by the addition of an eagle, or even of a cupid-like imp, and Gaull & Lembke add to the usual opticians' spectacles an enormous pair of opera glasses. Huge gilt molars are still found pendant before some dentist's offices. William Demuth indicates his business by a huge meerschaum pipe, and more than one wine dealer set up a sugar post for thirsty humanity in the shape of an immense demijohn. A large pair of scissors indicates the business of some cutlery shops [Fig. 195], and a wooden red-striped stocking emphasizes the lettered sign in front of a German knitting establishment on Sixth Street, while a Bowery sausagemaker lures in the Teuton gourmand by a fine gilt wurst, and a gilt wheel steers you to the store of a Fourth Avenue firm dealing in yachting uniforms and furnishings. A pallette is a not unfamiliar sign over artist material stores, while the little pyramid of painted barrels is quite extensively used by dealers in painters' materials. Some photographers, like Falk, set up a dummy camera as a sign; Fisher, the music dealer, blows his own large trumpet to attract bandmasters, and a manufacturer of musical instruments on Twenty-third Street, near Third Avenue, has long used a huge and weatherbeaten French horn. Similarly, Gemünder hangs up a gold "Strad," to make sure that you do not mistake your man, and a gold "cello" may be seen on Third Avenue, near Fifty-ninth Street. A gilt faucet is used by a Sixteenth Street firm that deals in plumbers' supplies, and a down-town goldbeater has hung out a large gilt arm, grasping a hammer. The large lantern that hangs out over the "L," not far from Franklin Square, leaves no doubt as to what is manufactured in that building, and many probably remember the huge teapot that used to decorate the establishment of a well-known dealer in hardware. A large illuminated "T," by the way, has been quite extensively used by some of the tea companies, and a similarly illuminated keg may be seen over the door of a few beer saloons in this city. One saloon on Seventh Street has a swinging sign, into an open space of which is set the carved representation of a foaming glass of beer. An enormous bamboo cane which stretches up along the front of the building, indicates the business of a firm of cane manufacturers on East Fourth Street.

We occasionally come across old figures marked out on boards, cut out and painted on both sides. Such flat figures are found in front of some old shooting galleries, and a Fourth Street carpenter glories in an "equestrian statue" of Washington made in this way.

Stuffed bears hang on to poles in front of many a furrier's establishment and dealers in carriages and harness are supplied from Paris with life-sized presentments of fiery dapple-gray steeds to set up in their windows or before their doors. Down in Warren Street there is one that seems to be walking out of the solid wall, and has only got half through, while another one near by has only succeeded in poking its head through the stones.

Some of these down-town streets, by the way, are particularly rich in figure signs. Warren, Murray, Frankfort, and other streets in that vicinity are filled with gilt coffee pots, saddles, guns, pipes, and many other objects. One Warren Street dealer in cutlery has set up a huge knife and fork over his door on one side and an equally large razor on the other, while on Frankfort Street a rocket of enormous dimensions conjures up visions of the "glorious Fourth." The well-known safe manufacturers at Broadway and Murray attract attention to their place by a gilt eagle, which bears no relation to their business, however, and seems to have no special purpose but to hold up a disc with the inscription: "Seven world's fair medals." A figure of Peter Stuyvesant is set up by one insurance company, a phoenix rising from the flames symbolizes another, while a third is well-represented by a globe half sunk in a lettered signboard.

The gilt figure of an ostrich proclaims to the public the business carried on at the northeast corner of Sixth Avenue and Seventeenth Street, and it was B. Fitch of Fourth Avenue, I think, who for years advertised his business in feather beds by a stuffed goose reposing on a bed of down. Some undertakers still affect the wooden tombstone, a few dealers in leather and findings indicate their business by a large awl, and the significant beehive is occasionally found over the doors of savings banks.

. . . the fireman on the Bowery near Grand Street and the Gambrinus, at Thirty-fifth Street and Broadway, now somewhat dilapidated, are both old and familiar figures. Schirmer has set up a bust of Beethoven, possibly to show that he wishes to keep music up to a classical standard, and another firm, near Steinway's has decorated the front of its house with a number of busts of musicians. A large symbolical figure of a female with sunglass stands over the entrance of Kurtz's Galleries. A One Hundred and Twenty-Fifth Street cigar store is graced by a wooden statue of Washington 11 feet in height. It is said to have once stood on Bowling Green, and to be the first statue of Washington made in this city, although these statements may be taken with a mental reservation.[25]

During the entire time of Robb's separation from his wife and children, he had no communication with them, did not see them nor attempt to do so, even when the urge must have been near unbearable. Agnes Robb referred to herself as a widow, and despite having no man in the house,

Fig. 196. Samuel A. Robb, top row second from right; Charles Robb, top row right; Clarence Robb, 2nd row center. Tintype, about 1897.

managed her affairs quite well. She had an income from her father's properties which she helped to administer. The children were well dressed, knew no hardships and went on numerous vacations, visiting relatives with summer villas.[26]

By 1896, Samuel Loudon Robb was fourteen years of age and by tradition should have entered his father's shop to learn the trade of the carver. Instead, he went into the secondary schools, showing a fine talent for the arts. Robb's third son Alexander Loudon Robb, was ten years old, and Elizabeth Wilson Robb, his daughter, whom he had never seen, was eight. Later this year, his father Peter Robb died at the age of seventy-nine.[27]

In 1897, Clarence was engaged to be married to Charlotte Hartman. To celebrate the occasion, an outing and party were held, the group posing for a tintype photograph (Fig. 196). As a joke, Clarence gave a ring, carved in wood, topped with a small wooden diamond. When Charlotte showed surprise and disappointment, another was produced, the same as the first but with a larger wooden diamond. Again, she showed disappointment. A third was produced with a diamond in wood, as large as an orange. Again she was disappointed but Samuel urged her to push the edges down. When she did, wooden doors opened up and there was a small velvet box with a small but real diamond.[28]

In 1897–1898 the carving business was transferred to Charles Robb, at least in name, with Samuel actually in charge. In 1898, the Barnum & Bailey circus departed for their tour of Europe, carrying with them many of the wagons with sides and figures carved by the Robb shop. Samuel Robb had a nationwide reputation among the circus impresarios as the finest wood-carver in the country and the most dependable as well. The European tour of Barnum & Bailey was a financial success, except for the loss of one week in Germany due to the death of Empress Frederica, mother of Wilhelm II. About 1900, plans were being made for a triumphal return to the United States and in the usual circus manner, they were on a grandiose scale. The following year the plans became more definite and late in 1901, James A. Bailey came back to America to explore the sources for his plans and discuss with them their capabilities and schedule. The minutes of Barnum & Bailey, Ltd., record his final arrangements:

That on the 14th of January 1902 Mr. Bailey on behalf of the Company had entered into a Contract with the Sebastian Wagon Company of New York City for the construction of 4 Tableaux Cars, 6 Racing Chariots and 8 additional Tableaux Cars; the work to be completed and ready for delivery to the Company about the Month of December 1902.

Robb was engaged to do the carvings.[29]

Samuel A. Robb, with his brother Charles, and his son Clarence, and one or two assistants were handling various carving jobs at the Centre

Street shop. While the carving shop was adequately large for tobacconists' Indians, show figures, signs, restorations, eagles, and an occasional figure-head, it would be too great a distance from the East 43rd Street Sebastian Wagon Company and too small to handle the carvings that would require frequent fitting on the wagons. Robb also had an apartment and shop at 10 West 13th Street as well as a telephone as the General Address Book of Barnum & Bailey, Ltd., shows.[30] It was decided that Charles Robb would handle the business and shop on Centre Street, while Samuel A. Robb and his son Clarence, with one or two of the carvers, would move into the eastern part of the wagon factory at 223 East 43rd Street between Third and Second Avenues. This was done after March 1, 1902. The Budweiser brewery had a building on the southeast corner of 44th Street and Third Avenue, next door to one of Sebastian's properties at 202 East 44th Street. The wagon factory occupied five lots, twenty-five feet wide by one hundred feet, five inches long. The middle lot extended to and in-cluded 224 East 44th Street with a wide alley running alongside to both streets. The carving shop occupied the ground floor with a stairway leading to the upper floor. Here, Robb and his carvers started working on the largest order of circus wagons ever to be undertaken at one time.[31]

At first the pace was leisurely, with some small pieces assigned to the Centre Street shop. Robb, himself, undertook some of the ambitious pieces, under the approving eye of Charles A. Stadler, president of the Sebastian Wagon Company and the American Malting Company and a director in various banking and business houses. Stadler, who was born in Germersheim, Germany, on July 15, 1848, was a New York State senator from 1888 to 1892, as well as a delegate to the State Constitu-tional Convention and a member of the Democratic Party's State Execu-tive Committee.[32] As time went on Robb had to hire additional carvers to keep abreast of his schedule to complete the thirteen wagon carvings according to contract. The group of thirteen wagons comprised:

1. The Triumphal Car of Balkis (Balkis, the Mohammedan name for the Queen of Sheba)
2. Phoenician Galley at the Court of Balkis
3. Throne Tableau Car of the Illustrious Queen
4. Imperial Chariot (of King Solomon) En Route to Welcome the Queen
5. Asia Tableau
6. Africa Tableau
7. Europe Tableau
8. America Tableau (See Frontis)
9. Two Hemispheres Band Wagon
10. The Golden Age of Chivalry (Col. Fig. 17)

11. Our Country
12. Funny Folks
13. Fairy Tales

In a set of probably the rarest photographs of circus wagons, recently discovered with the Robb papers, is shown the interior of Robb's carving shop in the Sebastian Wagon Company with his carvers at work creating masterpieces of circus art (Fig. 197). By early spring of 1902 Robb had finished the Phoenician Galley and had some of the figures of the Europe, Africa, and Asia tableaux. The America tableau was done in sections and may have been completed in the Centre Street shop. Robb is shown with chisel in hand posed with the nearly completed Phoenician Galley with Stadler standing nearby. In front are two of the corner figures of the Europe group with Europa and the Bull, back to camera alongside the wall. On the floor are the seats for the Africa wagon and on a shelf to the left is a center section of the America wagon. The techniques of the tobacconists' figure-carver and shipcarver are shown in the figures in the center and left. An iron pipe extends from the center of the head for easy handling by more than one person when turned on the carving bench. One figure is ready to have an arm fitted and fastened, and the leaning figure, pipe on woodblock in the roughened stage, is ready for finer tools and already prepared to be fitted to a group. Wagon hubs served as footrests, stools, and braces for the larger pieces. In this photograph, Robb looks unworried, having six months to go before delivery time.

In another photograph (Fig. 198), Clarence Robb and another worker are posed in front of the nearly completed Europe group showing *Europa* mounted on the bull, while grouped around her are the allegorical figures of *Commerce, Justice, Philosophy,* and *The Arts,* so named by the publicity department of Barnum & Bailey, Ltd. The photograph also shows the two center sections of the America wagon—on the shelf are some of the carvings fitted to the wheels, parts of spars in a pile to the left, and part of a large spar entering the photograph on the right.

In still another photograph (Fig. 199), Robb and an unidentified carver are putting the finishing touches on the centerpiece of the Africa wagon. One of its corner figures stands in the right foreground. Robb (collarless) seems more haggard, probably beginning to feel the pressure of work and time.

More hands have been employed. One picture (Fig. 200) shows Clarence, left, and four unidentified assistants applying gold leaf to the centerpiece of the Asia wagon. The gesso has been applied, over which gold leaf will be placed to cover the figures completely. A head from a figure of the America group is on a block to the right and is already gold leafed.

With time closing in, all the available wood-carvers were called in to complete the work. Two floors were used for the carving and production

FIG. 198

FIG. 199

FIG. 200

Fig. 198. Assembled group posed before the Europe Tableau. Part of the America Tableau is on shelf at left. Helper at left is unidentified. Clarence Robb is seated at the right.

Fig. 199. Robb, left, and an unidentified carver, right, putting the finishing touches to the Africa Tableau center figure. The Scribe, one of the corner figures, is at the right, completed but for the gold leaf.

Fig. 200. Applying gold leaf to the centerpiece of the Asia Tableau. A head from the America Tableau is at the right. Clarence Robb is on the left; all others are unidentified.

continued into the fall of 1902, just a few months away from the promised delivery. Of all the carvers (Fig. 201), Robb, extreme right, has been the only one identified. No doubt this was the largest assembly of America's best wood-carvers to pose for a photograph and to work as a group on one project. A tired, worried, and haggard Robb is bent over the drawing and blueprints, none of which have survived. In the center foreground is one of the two figures at the foot of the throne Tableau Car of the Illustrious Queen. The carver, fifth from right, is posed with the center head of the Africa wagon. To the left of center is a corner figure from the Africa wagon; in the background is seen part of the Phoenician galley.

Robb completed the contract for the Barnum and Bailey wagons in late February or early March 1903. The press was invited to Bridgeport to see the wagons before the paint was dry, on March 2, 1903. Pictures of the wagons, some shown at the Bridgeport, Connecticut quarters and others on parade reveal the positions of the carved tableaux figures, the portraits representing the countries in each of the continents, the positions of the living figures, and the proportionate sizes.

With the circus wagons delivered, Robb's "Mammoth Atelier" in the Sebastian factory was quiet (Fig. 202). The sound of the carver's mallet and of the broadaxe shaping the rough spars had been stilled.

Fig. 201. The Robb carving shop in the Sebastian Wagon Company, late fall, 1902. Robb, right, appears tired and haggard. On the table are drawings and blueprints. Parts of the various circus wagons are being worked on by the unidentified carvers.

Fig. 202. Clarence Robb painting a tobacconist's Indian in the late spring of 1903.

The Centre Street shop was given up. The Indians and show figures as well as the tools moved to 10 West 13th Street, near Fifth Avenue. Charles Robb became seriously ill and the 13th Street shop had to close, too. Some of the work moved into the Sebastian shop on East 43rd Street where it was finished. When the Pawnee Bill carvings were completed, Robb moved out and with Clarence set up a shop at 329 West 24th Street. After an illness of several months Charles Robb died on March 13, 1904, and was buried in Greenwood Cemetery in the Kissinger plot. Samuel Robb felt the loss deeply and was further depressed when his nineteen-year-old son Alex died February 22, 1905.

One day, shortly after, Robb, head down, was walking toward his shop, when he looked up and saw coming toward him, without prearranged plan, his wife, Agnes, whom he had not seen or heard from in seventeen years. They walked toward each other slowly, stared at each other for a long time, and without a word fell into each other's arms.[33]

At this time Robb's shop was at 329 West 24th Street, three blocks north of the house owned and occupied by his wife and children. Shortly after the unplanned meeting in the street a reconciliation was effected. Robb moved into their house at 329 West 21st Street in the Chelsea area of Manhattan. Elizabeth was now sixteen, and a son, Samuel P., then six years old was now twenty-two. The young man was cordial to his father and the carver was just as pleased to be reunited with his family. Elizabeth, who had never seen her father and regarded him as a deserter, planned to ignore him completely and never speak to him. But before the day was over, a complete reunion had taken place and old grievances had been forgotten.

In March 1905, Samuel A. Robb received a communication from Arthur Curtiss James, a yachtsman, also one of the nation's richest men, indicating that he wanted some panels carved for his townhouse, the sketches to be supplied by his architect.

Robb built a small workshop in the 21st Street house and carved some of the panels for James in this workshop; the young people watched their father with great interest while he charmed them with stories of the missing years.[34] The panels were of historic scenes and figures from episodes in the American Revolution. However, Robb still maintained his shop at 339 West 24th Street, from which Clarence, the son from his first wife, and possibly some assistants, supplied the trade with show and tobacconists' figures.

Sidewalk space was becoming valuable; new restrictions and city ordinances, forbidding the crowding of sidewalks and declaring these protuberances unlawful, had their effect on the show-figure carving business. Also, new electric signs began to replace the carved figures. The demand for new figures fell sharply and the chief source of income came from repairing old figures, making patterns, molds, signs, and small figures of Indians for the counters of tobacconists' shops. Many tobacconists kept their figures with the same affection mariners had for their figureheads; others—practical, unsentimental, and businesslike—sent their Indians off to the city dumps or to be used as firewood. Other figures, gladly contributed or involuntarily, found their way to the Election Day and the Fourth of July bonfires, which were kindled by the gangs in the cities.[35]

In June, 1905, when Elizabeth won an award in the New York City History Competition conducted by *The New York Times*, a large celebration was held in the Robb home, and father, mother, and daughter posed for a photograph, their first together (Fig. 203).

In 1907, the James McCutcheon & Co. linens and dry goods store moved from 64 West 23rd Street to their new building on Fifth Avenue and 34th Street. Their trademark, even in the days prior to 1864 when the business was known as Milliken & Co., then located at 748 Broadway, was a spinning wheel. Robb was engaged to design and carve the symbol in wood. His carving was then used as a pattern for a casting in bronze, which remained over the entrance to the Fifth Avenue Store, for many years one of the famous trademarks on the Avenue.[36]

Fig. 203. Samuel, Agnes, and Elizabeth Wilson Robb reunited, June, 1905.

*Fig. 204. Admiral George Dewey.
A tobacconist's sign on Third
Avenue, New York, c. 1911.
Photograph: Kate Sanborn.*

*Fig. 205. The same tobacconist's
sign, with base and legs
amputated, converted into a ship's
figurehead by an enterprising
antiques dealer. Photograph:
Taylor & Dull.*

After the victory of Manila Bay in the Spanish-American War on May 1, 1898, Admiral George Dewey was given a hero's treatment and his image found its way into stone carvings of keystones and plaques for new buildings going up around the country, especially in New York on the west side of Manhattan and in the lower Bronx. Tobacco brands with his name became popular, and Robb carved at least one tobacconist's figure of him for a Third Avenue merchant (Fig. 204). In later years, when the base and feet had rotted away, an enterprising antiques dealer, finding that figureheads were bringing considerably higher prices than partly decayed tobacconists' figures, had the lower part of the legs cut away, mounted the remaining figure on a scroll, then on a base, and received $3,300 for it at auction (Fig. 205).[37]

FIG. 206

FIG. 208

Fig. 206. Baseball player. *A tobacconist's figure on Third Avenue in New York City, c. 1910. Probably from the shop of Samuel A. Robb, New York. Photograph: Culver Pictures, Inc.*

Fig. 207. New York Policeman. *A tobacconist's figure in front of shop on West 42nd Street between Eighth and Ninth Avenues, c. 1902. Photograph: Culver Pictures, Inc.*

Fig. 208. Sir Walter Raleigh. *A tobacconist's figure on Third Avenue, New York, c. 1910. Signed "Robb, 339 W. 24th St." on pedestal near top. Compare with illustration on Robb's 1881 advertisement. Photograph: Culver Pictures, Inc.*

FIG. 207

FIG. 210

FIG. 209

Figs. 209, 210. Tobacconists' figures on the sidewalks of New York, c. 1910. Photographs: Culver Pictures, Inc.

Teddy Roosevelt's Rough Riders were not unheralded, and at least one figure of a Rough Rider was carved, perhaps by Robb. Until the 1920s, it stood in front of a downtown tobacconist's shop and helped advertise the pool and billiard parlor, which sometimes occupied the rear part of a tobacconist's shop. Baseball players (Fig. 206), policemen (Fig. 207), Sir Walter Raleigh (Fig. 208), jockeys, Turks, West Point cadets, George Washington, Rip Van Winkle, dudes, Dundrearys, Sultanas, Scottish Highlanders, and many others (Figs. 209, 210, 211, 212, 213), violating the law but still advertising the various tobacco brands, were to be found on Second, Third, Sixth, and Ninth Avenues in New York through the 1920s. In New York and other cities there were oriental figures advertising tea (Figs. 214, 215), dressmakers' shops with stylish figures, one dressmaker shop with a figure from an era no longer fashionable (Figs. 216, 217, 218), Moors, Turks and Sultanas advertising their brands of tobacco (Figs. 219, 220), and of course, most popular of all—the Indians (Figs. 221, 222, 223, 224). Other cities and small towns had their show figures, some produced by the experienced carvers and others by local sign makers

FIG. 211   FIG. 212

Figs. 211, 212, 213. Tobacconists'
figures on the sidewalks of New
York, c. 1910. Photographs:
Culver Pictures, Inc.

FIG. 213

FIG. 214

Fig. 214. Oriental Tea Shop
Figure. *Height 36 inches. Present
whereabouts unknown. Courtesy
Index of American Design.*

Fig. 215. Tea Shop Figure. *Early
type, compare with Fig. 214.
Probably from Chicago before
1880. Photograph: courtesy Index
of American Design.*

FIG. 215

FIG. 216

FIG. 217

Fig. 216. Dressmaker's or Milliner's
Figure. *Height 62½ inches, base 2½
inches. Courtesy the Van Alstyne
Collection, Smithsonian Institution.*

Fig. 217. Tailor's figure, Dude or Racetrack Tout. *Height 68 inches, base 7½
inches. Courtesy Virginia Museum of
Fine Arts.*

(Fig. 225). A gun-shop figure from San Jose, California (Fig. 226), is one example. Cape May, New Jersey, had a distinctive sign in front of the tobacco shop owned by Frank Hebenthal, placed there well before 1895. In a mortgage of the property, the figure referred to as *one Pompey* hung from the wall at the right side of the entrance (Fig. 227).[38] The backboard is a separate part of the log from which the figure was carved. This is the only such figure known; in all probability, it was copied from a more sophisticated work and simplified to the carver's ability. It is now in the collection of Harvey Kahn of New York.

In 1908, Robb took space in the carving shop of Charles Brown at 11 Summit Street in Brooklyn near the wharves of Buttermilk Channel. Here he made small show and tobacconists' figures, which he sold through J. Reeber & Co. at 529 Flushing Avenue in Brooklyn. He also did some architectural work, patterns, signs and similar work.

The Hudson–Fulton Celebration Commission had been established to plan and carry out the many aspects of the 300th anniversary of the discovery of the Hudson River by Henry Hudson in 1609 and the 100th anniversary of the first successful application of steam to navigation upon the river by Robert Fulton in 1807. One aspect of the celebration was a carnival parade of fifty floats. The idea was borrowed from old carnivals which had allegorical, mythological, and historical scenes represented upon moving vehicles. The historical pageant was to have fifty-four floats with tableaux of events in American history. The carnival pageant was to illustrate Old World folklore. Robb applied to the parades committee with the thought of creating another series of tableaux like the 1902 Barnum & Bailey set. His disappointment was great when he learned that most of the work on the floats was to be voluntary, with much of the material gratuitously supplied. Even the chairman, Herman Ridder, was to work without compensation. Instead of carved wood, papier-mâché, canvas, wire and stucco, were used. The carnival pageant was overweighed with Germanic themes, especially scenes from Wagner's operas. In some respects, many of the tableaux did resemble those from the Barnum & Bailey set. The parade of 104 floats was a huge success in spite of the threatening weather, which caused a two-hour delay and a great mix-up in the intended order of parade. The one piece of wood carving was on the replica of Hudson's ship, the *Half-Moon*, and that was done in Amsterdam, across the Atlantic. At the base of the foremast on the upper deck was a deck block for the foresail, carved into a bust of a Dutch sailor.[39]

Fig. 218. Dude or Lord Dundreary.
Tobacconist's figure. Height 61½
inches, base 5½ inches. Photograph:
Taylor & Dull.

FIG. 219

FIG. 220

FIG. 221

FIG. 222

*Fig. 219. Sultan. Tobacconist's figure. Height 64½
inches, base 8¾ inches. Courtesy Virginia Museum of
Fine Arts.*

*Fig. 220. Sultana. Tobacconist's figure. Usually
advertised turkish tobacco. Courtesy Shelburne Museum.
Photograph: Einars J. Mengis.*

*Fig. 221. New York tobacconist's shop with two figures.
One on left, inside the window, is a cast zinc figure by
Wm. Demuth, c. 1886. The Indian scout was probably
from the shop of Samuel A. Robb. Photograph: Culver
Pictures, Inc.*

*Fig. 222. Tobacconist's shop in Brooklyn between 1869
and 1877. Tobacconist's Indian probably carved by
Thomas V. Brooks. Photograph: Culver Pictures, Inc.*

FIG. 223

Fig. 223. Cigar-Store Indian. *Height 68 inches, c. 1875. Found in Springfield, Mass. Courtesy Index of American Design.*

Fig. 224. Tobacconist's Indian from Springfield, Massachusetts. *Height 68 inches. Courtesy Index of American Design.*

FIG. 224

FIG. 225

Fig. 225. Tobacconist's figure known as a Bowery Girl, in Long Branch, New Jersey, c. 1902. Photograph: Culver Pictures, Inc.

Fig. 226. Gun Shop Figure. From San Jose, California. Height 69 inches, base 22 inches. Carved and painted redwood. Courtesy Smithsonian Institution.

FIG. 226

FIG. 227

Late in 1909 or early 1910, Arthur Curtiss James had a barkantine yacht built at the Fore River Shipbuilding yard at Quincy, Massachusetts. The figurehead was a portrait of the last queen of the Hawaiian Islands, Queen Liliuokalani, who was deposed in 1893. There is uncertainty over who carved the figurehead. Robb had done some work for James, for his New York town house, his mansion in Newport, Rhode Island, and for the interior of one or more of the yachts built for James in the 1890s. Robb was also one of the last of the shipcarvers, and so may have carved the figurehead of the *Aloha*. The records of the period do not show any invoice or note about this item.[40] When the ship was scrapped in 1937, her engines and the figurehead were removed and all else junked. The figurehead is now in the collection of the Newport Historical Society.

In 1910, Robb and his family moved to 516 West 156th Street in Manhattan. He gave up his part of the carving shop in Brooklyn. Moving his bench, tools, patterns for show figures, drawings, blueprints, and files to the apartment on 156th Street, he continued working by himself, and for the first time, without shop, staff or assistance, taking whatever work he could manage in that restricted space. Among the items he carved here were ventriloquists' dummies, molds for castings, nameplates, some carved lettered signs, dentists' tooth signs, and especially eagles, which he enjoyed carving. A small eagle, exquisitely carved (Col. Fig. 25), was in the Robb household for many years and was later acquired by Mrs. Walter Liebling, a relative of the Loudons.[41]

For the next few years, Robb kept active doing only those carvings that did not require carting and could be handled by himself. His shop, on the second floor of a large apartment house and reached by three flights of winding stairs, did not permit work of a large size. He could still push a chisel with vigor but he had lost weight, and at the age of sixty-five his health had begun to fail. Illnesses came more often and lasted longer. In 1917, finding himself unemployed he became despondent, but through his church he learned that the Ford Motor Company in Philadelphia was hiring men of his age and needed coachbuilders. Robb packed his bag and with his chest of tools left for Philadelphia. He found employment and a small room near the factory, where he remained for nearly two years. During this period he became ill and sent for his wife who came with Elizabeth to nurse him back to health. In 1919, he returned to New York. The following year, his son Samuel L. Robb died, and of his original family of five children, only Clarence, the son of his first wife, and Elizabeth, his daughter, survived.[42]

Robb enjoyed visiting Clarence's children and interested them by carving or whittling amusing figures and objects. However, Clarence was always ill at ease when visiting the Robb home.[43] In 1921, the Robbs moved from the 156th Street apartment to 222 Seaman Avenue in upper Manhattan, to be closer to Clarence's home in Riverdale. With great reluctance and misgivings, Robb conceded to his wife's wishes, leaving his patterns, blueprints, large framed photographs of his major works, illustrations, drawings, records, and some of his larger tools and lumber behind. He took only his tools, a small bench, his notebooks, a box of photographs, parts of catalogues, and his personal records. In 1920, the Sebastian Wagon Company filed for a voluntary dissolution of the corporation, which was granted. Anton Sebastian, whom Robb had known for many years had died almost penniless in 1919; the art of show-figure carving was no longer required; and the era of the artist in wood had come to an end.

For Christmas of 1923, Robb had been working quietly and secretly on a small figure which he kept locked in a closet in his workshop. On Christmas morning, Elizabeth found next to the tree a carved and painted Santa Claus. In the hollow pack on his back, filled with candies and small wrapped gifts was a card, "To Elizabeth, Merry Christmas, from Dad." This was the last figure Robb carved (Fig. 228).[44]

FIG. 228

Fig. 227. Tobacconist's Indian once hung on the wall outside of Frank Hebenthal's tobacco shop in Cape May, New Jersey. Indian height 36 inches, painted board 52 inches. Courtesy Harvey Kahn.

Fig. 228. Santa Claus. The last carving made by Samuel A. Robb, as a Christmas gift to his daughter, Elizabeth Wilson Robb. Height 33½ inches, base 2½ inches.

Fig. 229. Show figures ready for the auction block in 1956, at the Parke-Bernet Galleries in New York. Photograph: Taylor & Dull.

For the next three years, Robb, who had become seriously ill, was confined to bed. On May 3, 1928, Charles A. Stadler, the former president of the Sebastian Wagon Company, died at his home in Fort Myers, Florida. Two days later, Samuel Anderson Robb, at the age of seventy-seven was dead. In accordance with his wishes, he was buried in a plot next to his first wife, Emma Jane, in Woodlawn Cemetery in the Bronx. Agnes Robb died in 1945, and Elizabeth, who never married, died in 1967. Both were buried in the Loudon plot in Greenwood Cemetery in Brooklyn.[45]

In a sale at the Parke-Bernet Galleries in 1956, a large number of show figures and tobacconists' Indians were brought together (Fig. 229). Represented in this group were carvings by Cromwell, Brooks, White, Jobin, Yaeger, Sailor, and many others. The largest number of figures were from the shop of Samuel Anderson Robb. Most of these figures were once part of the collection of Anthony J. Pendergast, and in turn became part of the Rudolph Haffenreffer collection. At auction, the figures were sold to museum and private collectors.[46]

William Boulton (Dates Unknown)

About 1860–1861, William Boulton came to the United States from Great Britain and set up his carving shop at 733 Eighth Avenue in New York City. Boulton had been trained in England as a sculptor in stone. In 1864, he moved to 838 Third Avenue, and in 1868 he moved to 106 South Street where he set up his shop just east of the Fulton Market and

Schermerhorn Row. At this address he no longer listed himself as a "sculptor" but as a "carver." He resided on Staten Island.

In 1870 or 1871, Boulton moved to 2 Coenties Slip and specialized in carving wooden figures for tobacconists and other tradesmen. It was about this time that Louis Jobin, the Canadian wood-carver, entered Boulton's shop, where he remained for about a year. Jobin had some experience with religious figures, but mostly with figureheads and shipcarvings, which stood him in good stead in the Boulton shop. In his late years, Jobin recalled his additional training in the "specialty of roughing in the statues, which pleased me well. I also had to cut little figures [figurettes], wooden figures for tobacconist shops."[47] Jobin stayed for one year, then found work with some German carvers, and later returned to Canada. Boulton remained at 2 Coenties Slip through 1874. His business was not well attended to and the shop fell into great disorder, with a journeyman trying to fill the orders. Boulton gave up his shop and moved to 142 First Avenue. All trace of him disappears after this time and it is possible that he returned to England. In an interview with Marius Barbeau in 1924, Jobin recalled that Boulton, ". . . drank like a fish, poor man."[48]

Simon Strauss (?–1897)

Simon Strauss came to America at the end of the Civil War, making his home at 69 Avenue C on the Lower East Side of Manhattan. He received his training as a wood-carver in Bavaria, and no doubt he was already proficient in figure carving when he established his own shop in 1871, after five years of working for others. His shop at 253 South Street was once the carving shop of Charles J. Dodge, in carvers' row, on the two block stretch on South Street which included Pike Slip and Rutgers Slip, now bounded by the Brooklyn and Manhattan Bridges.[49]

Strauss advertised in Trow's Directory of New York City for 1871, listing himself as a "Carver of Figures for Segar Stores." Business must have warranted his remaining at this work, for his advertisement for the year 1873–1874 was quite large listing him as an "Ornamental—Ship—and Figure Carver." In 1876, Strauss, who had wisely invested some capital in tenement real estate, moved to 179 Lewis Street. In addition to his carving activities he undertook the manufacture of cigar boxes, which became equally important to him and probably far more profitable, as he purchased the property in 1878.[50]

Strauss must have been a very active individual, handling his properties, engaging in lawsuits with his tenants, going after trade, overseeing the box manufacturing, obtaining supplies, carving tobacconists' figures, signs, and ship carvings. His wife, Bertha, handled the growing domestic affairs of the family.[51]

The factory at 179 Lewis Street grew and his business expanded, requir-

S. STRAUSS,

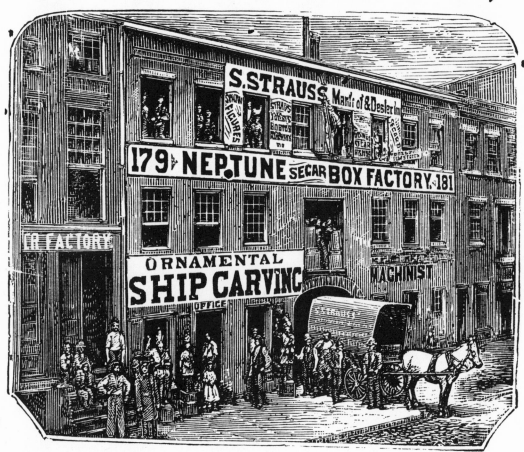

Manufacturer of

Cigar Boxes & Show Figures

Importer of and Dealer in

SPANISH CIGAR RIBBONS.

German Cigar Moulds, Presses, Straps, Cutters, etc.

All kinds of Figures Cut to Order and Repaired in the Best Style.

THE TRADE SUPPLIED.

---

179 & 181 LEWIS STREET

NEW YORK.

ing an addition. Strauss purchased the two structures at 181 Lewis Street, adjoining the original factory. He was a firm believer in advertising and took ads in the trade publications and the Jewish press appealing to the cigar makers and tobacconists (Fig. 230).[52] Strauss had an able book-keeper and general superintendent, Simon Sladkus, who assisted him in his business enterprises, which prospered through the 1880s and into the 1890s. In 1891, Strauss became dissatisfied with his son Joseph, and removed him from his will. When Strauss died in 1897, his probated will showed that by a codicil, he reinstated his son Joseph, who received $10,000. However, his daughter, Minnie May, in a separate codicil was specifically excluded to the loss of $10,000. Each of his three other children, all minors, received the same amount. His father, Solomon Hirsch Strauss, in Herligen Kreutz (Holy Cross) in Bohemia, was willed a bimonthly sum for the rest of his life.[53]

To date, there are no wooden figures which can be identified as being carved by Strauss. No doubt, he did little carving himself after 1880, but had assistants who may have worked in other shops when there was work to be had. With minor changes in costume and in coloring, the figures may not have been distinguished enough from those they did in the shops of other carvers.

John W. Anderson (1834–1904)

The tradition in many families of shipcarvers and shipwrights, as in many other trades during the middle of the nineteenth century, was for the son to carry on the father's trade and to hand it down to his son. The Anderson family was no exception to that rule, but in this case, when the father Jacob S. Anderson died in 1855, his son John W. was only twenty-one years of age and his mother, Jane S. Anderson, took over the business and handled it successfully for over twenty-three years with John's help. In 1878–1879 the city directory of New York listed her as a "carver"![54]

Jacob S. Anderson was born in New York in 1810 and at the age of twenty-one opened his own carving shop, Jacob Anderson & Co., for a short time. In 1834, two years after his marriage, John W. was born. In 1846, he went into partnership with Charles J. Dodge as Dodge & Anderson at 236 South Street, New York. Actually, Anderson handled the business while Dodge went into politics. He ran for the office of Alderman and was elected. In 1847, the partnership was dissolved. In 1853, Greenman & Co. of Mystic, Connecticut, were building a clipper ship, the *David Crockett*, and Anderson cut the figurehead. This fine carving is now in the San Francisco Maritime Museum. Another figure which has been preserved, and is presumed to have been made by Anderson, is of a sailor, one foot upon a keg, holding a binnacle. Made for the clipper ship, the *N. B. Palmer*, it served for just one round trip to China and was then

Fig. 230. Advertisement of Simon Strauss from the Cigar and Tobacco Manufacturers Directory 1882–1883. Courtesy Betty W. Walters.

removed as the helmsmen claimed that they saw the eyes move on the night watch. On the figure's hat is the warning, "Mind Your Helm." After it was removed, the figure served as a shop sign for its owners T. S. & J. D. Negus (now M. Low, 69 Pearl Street). Later it was donated to the Museum of the City of New York.[55]

Anderson died in 1855 at the age of forty-five. Besides his wife, he was survived by his sons, John W. and Edward A., and his daughters, Mary Stratton, whom he adopted at birth, and Adeline E. He had owned a brick building at 24 Henry Street where they lived and left some money and a good business at 236 South Street, which his wife decided to keep going. Jane Anderson must have been a strong-willed woman with an unusual personality and a good sense of business to have continued in a field of work dominated exclusively by tough and shrewd males. She left five-year-old Mary Stratton and the tasks of the household with Katherine, her Irish servant, while she herself handled the affairs of a carving shop. Her seventeen-year-old daughter, Adeline E., who was a schoolteacher, was capable of helping at home.[56]

When Jane Anderson took over the business, she moved the shop to 222 South Street. She sold the house on Henry Street and moved the family to 27 Suffolk Street for two years and then to 261 West 24th Street. In 1875, the shop was moved to 226 South Street. About 1880, John W. Anderson took over the business in his own name but Jane was still listed until 1884. About 1868–1869, John W. Anderson carved a figurehead of Admiral David Glasgow Farragut for the medium-size clipper *The Great Admiral,* built in East Boston, Massachusetts, by Robert E. Jackson. The figurehead, one hundred and two inches, was mounted on a billet with a shield and anchor. The figure was in full uniform, the right hand to the right breast holding a spy glass and the left hand on the sword at his side. The figurehead is in the collection of Mystic Seaport, Connecticut.[57]

Like the other shipcarvers, John W. resorted to carving tobacconists' figures. In 1881, he advertised, "Ornamental Figures for Cigar Stores Constantly on Hand." That same year Anderson moved to 355 West 40th Street with his family, keeping the shop at 226 South Street. In 1885, he moved the shop to 233 South Street, taking a loft above the street floor, and, like many other carvers, he set up his residence at 178 South Fourth Street in the Williamsburgh section of Brooklyn. After moving his shop to 240 South Street in 1894, he moved it to 90 Pike Street the following year. In 1900, he resided at Katonah, New York, but still had his shop at 90 Pike Street. One of the last of the East River shipcarvers, he died in 1904.[58]

Nicholas E. Collins (1838–?)

Among the first carvers in New York who made tobacconists' figures exclusively was Nicholas E. Collins. In 1871, his shop was at 222 South

Street which was in the same building as Anderson and which some years earlier had been the shop of John L. Cromwell. From 1871 until 1879, Collins was listed as a shipcarver and, thereafter, as a wood-carver, carpenter, and carver. In 1875, he moved his shop to 204 South Street, back again to 222 the following year, and in 1878 to 211 South Street. The 1877 directory lists Collins & Brown as shipcarvers.

With his wife Marie, who was born in Canada, and his two sons Harry and William E., Collins lived in Brooklyn at 230 Bridge Street and later at 81 Raymond Street, where nearly everyone was Irish and where the Raymond Street jail dominated the landscape.

After moving to 204 Church Street in 1881, Collins gave up his shop and worked for the various figure carvers still in business. He may have gone to Chicago with Brooks, but returned to New York and was still carving in 1890, possibly for Elijah Tryon who was located on Goerck Street not far from Collins's old shop on South Street. After that date no record appears for Nicholas E. Collins.[59]

Charles Brown (1846–1917)

Charles Brown was born in New York City in 1846. When about twenty years of age, he was employed as a ship's carpenter in the construction of medium-sized vessels.[60] About 1870, Brown listed himself as a "shipcarver." In 1872 to 1878, he was in partnership with Nicholas E. Collins, first at 222 South Street and then in a three-story building at 204 South Street, where they made various types of shipcarvings, steamboat eagles, tobacconists' and other show figures, trade signs, and mold for castings (Fig. 231). The partnership may have lasted longer than six years, but Collins retained ownership of the business. Brown had various connections with shipbuilders, custom agents, and later the Coast Guard, and as a result various commissions from these sources came to his shop.[61] Two stylized eagles made for the U.S. Coast Guard are in the collection of the Shelburne Museum and both are signed, "C. Brown, 11 Summit." The USCG forming an overlapping inscribed monogram is on the front of one base and on the side of the other.

From 1885 to 1889, Brown was listed to 20 James Slip as a shipcarver. An existing photograph of the interior of his shop shows, among other carvings, one of his stylized eagles for a pilot house (Fig. 232). Brown had moved to 4 North Pier Atlantic Dock in Brooklyn, and during the 1890s and later, he engaged in doing yacht work on special order. In addition to his carving department, he had an iron and blacksmith shop. Orders came from important clients, and a carved figurehead for one of the Vanderbilt yachts is attributed to Charles Brown.[62]

About this time, Brown made a tobacconist's Indian which was given to a relative and remained in the family until recently. When layers of paint

FIG. 231

were removed, a sharply cut figure in full war bonnet was revealed (Fig. 233). About 1900 or earlier, Brown opened a studio-workshop at 11 Summit Street, Brooklyn, near the wharves fronting on Buttermilk Channel and opposite Governor's Island. He kept this shop until 1914, at times leasing it or part of the premises to other carvers. In 1908, the shop was shared with Samuel Anderson Robb.[63]

Brown, who never married, belonged to several fraternal organizations and would often be seen in parades dressed in his ceremonial uniform. He

FIG. 232

FIG. 233

Fig. 231. Shipcarving shop of Collins & Brown at 204 South Street in 1887. Charles Brown is at left, next to sign; Nicholas E. Collins is in the center; person on right is unidentified. In open window at upper left is a tobacconist's figure of John Bull, a part of a shipcarving, and a pilothouse eagle. Underneath is an old weathered sign, "Collins & Brown," and in the right window is another eagle and a carved billethead.

Fig. 232. Interior of carving shop of Charles Brown. Brown is on the right; carver on the left is unidentified. One of Brown's stylized eagles is in the center; patterns, and other carvings are hanging on the walls. Probably about 1886.

Fig. 233. Tobacconist's Indian. Carved by Charles Brown, c. 1890. Height 58 inches, base 4 inches.

was very fond of boats and ships, sailing on many for which he furnished both carvings and ironwork. One of his favorite pastimes was sailing aboard the *Sea Pigeon* on one of Frank Boyle's Fishing Club excursions. Brown lived with his sister, Nellie Stephenson, and a half-sister, Mary Deasy, at 36 Winona Street in the Jamaica section of Brooklyn. He died on May 1, 1917, and is buried in the Evergreen Cemetery in Brooklyn.[64]

Elijah Tryon (1844–?)

One of the last of the shipcarvers in New York, Elijah Tryon came into the business when the shipyards closed down after the Civil War. Born in New York in 1844, Tryon was only four years old when Thomas V. Brooks opened his carving shop. His apprenticeship must have terminated after the Emancipation Proclamation was signed, because he did not list himself as a carver until 1872–1873. Having no shop of his own, he worked, from his home at 68 Broome Street. In 1874, he lived at No. 1 Hester Street, near Clinton, an area later known as the Lower East Side, where, in ten years time, hundreds of thousands of immigrants from Russia and Poland would be settling. By 1879, Tryon was at 310 Stanton Street near the waterfront at the opposite end of which was the small building known as the Stanton Street Jail.[65]

Not until 1881 did Elijah Tryon establish his own shop which produced "Indian Show Figures for Cigar Stores," at 132 Goerck Street, a few blocks from the waterfront. Tryon remained here for nearly twenty years, moving to 134 and later to 131 Goerck Street. He lived in the rear of the shop, where his wife Caroline and his two daughters Jane and Mary must have been able to smell the cut and shaved pine all year. Tryon's advertisement in 1885 read, "Tobacconists' Signs A Specialty—134 Goerck Street." At this time, the two other shops that specialized in tobacconists' figures were across the street from each other on Canal Street; the larger and better-known one was the shop of Samuel A. Robb and the other, which dealt mainly in secondhand figures, was the shop of Justinus North. This was the period when the cigar-store Indian was most popular, and these three shops as well as those in other cities kept a large supply of figures to be shipped anywhere in the United States.[66]

To compete with Justinus North on Canal Street, Tryon took in old figures, which were probably recarved and painted to be sold at reduced prices. His advertisement read, "Indian Figures for Cigar Stores, Old Figures Bought or Exchanged, 35 Goerck."[67] The demand for tobacconists' and show figures decreased and in 1899, Tryon terminated his business.

Fig. 234. Trade card of Justinus Stoll North, c. 1888.

Justinus Stoll North (?–1900)

In 1871, Justinus S. North opened a store at 191 Canal Street selling fixtures to the trade. By 1874, he had increased the variety of his merchandise to include counters, showcases, stools, and furniture. In 1875–1876, Samuel Robb opened a carving shop a few doors away and did a fine business in show figures. In 1880, North moved across the street, selling all types of furniture to the trade. By 1885, North decided to enter the show figure business and listed himself as a "Tobacco Figure Mfr.," and the following year his advertisement read, "North, J. S. Show Figure Manufacturer. Old Figures Repaired & Painted. Figures Bought/Sold & Exchanged. All Work Warrented 188–190 Canal." North may have been a serious competitor to Robb as the customer could walk across the street to see who would make the cheaper figure. In 1888, the year that Robb moved to 114 Centre Street, North listed himself as a "carver," as he also did on his trade card (Fig. 234). The cut of the Indian on this trade card was a stock printer's cut, No. 535, which was sold for fifty cents by the Ernest L. Fantus Co. of Dearborn Street, Chicago. It did not represent an Indian carved in the North shop. North remained in business at 190 Canal Street until 1892, but Robb continued to get the major part of the carved sign business. North died in Brooklyn on March 27, 1900.[69]

Appendixes

NOTES

Chapter 1

1. *Daggett's New York City Directory* for 1851. Listings of occupations, businesses, and professions, by street; *Trow's Directory* for 1849.
2. G. W. Sheldon, "The Old Ship-Builders of New York," *Harper's Magazine,* Vol. 65 (1882), p. 233; John H. Morrison, *History of New York Shipyards,* p. 97.
3. John G. B. Hutchins, *The American Maritime Industries and Public Policy, 1789–1914,* Vol. 6, p. 170.
4. C. Harold Ridge, *Records of the Worshipful Company of Shipwrights,* 1728–1858, Vol. 9; Dennis Chapman, "The New Shipwrights Building Company of Dundee [Scotland], 1826–1831," (article on strike of shipwrights' apprentices); Dundee *Advertiser,* No. 2 (March 9, 1826).
5. Hutchins, *American Maritime Industries,* Vol. 6, p. 171.
6. *Samoset,* Fernald & Pettigrew Papers, Peabody Museum, Salem, Massachusetts; Hon. John McLeod Murphy, *American Ships and Ship Builders* (pamphlet), p. 4.
7. Morrison, *New York Shipyards,* p. 97.
8. Murphy, *American Ships,* p. 4.
9. Morrison, *New York Shipyards,* pp. 153–154.
10. Hutchins, *American Maritime Industries,* Vol. 6, p. 189.
11. *Ibid.*
12. Morrison, *New York Shipyards,* p. 163.
13. Peter Ross, *A History of Long Island,* Vol. 1, pp. 468–469.
14. *Ibid.,* p. 164.

Chapter 2

1. Jacob Larwood and John Camden Hotten, *The History of Signboards,* pp. 56–57.
2. Robert K. Hermann, *Tobacco and Americans,* p. 5.
3. Sir Richard Baker, *A Chronicle of the Kings of England,* p. 65; John Bain, Jr., *Tobacco in Song and Story,* p. 23.
4. Baker, *A Chronicle,* p. 65.
5. Charles G. Shaw, "Black Boys and Their Playfellows," *Antiques,* March 1934, p. 102.
6. Charles G. Shaw, "Speaking of Wooden Indians," *Antiques,* September 1939, p. 133.
7. Ben Jonson, *Bartholomew Fair* (New York: H. Holt and Company, 1904), Act I, Scene 1.
8. Baker, *A Chronicle,* p. 65.

9. Larwood and Hotten, *Signboards*, p. 252.

10. Shaw, "Black Boys," p. 103.

11. Larwood and Hotten, *Signboards*, p. 421.

12. Alice Morse Earle, *Stage-Coach and Tavern Days*, p. 146; Frank B. Mayer, "Signs and Symbols," *Scribner's Monthly*, Vol. 18, No. 5 (September 1879), pp. 105–114.

13. Drake's *History of Boston*.

14. Erwin O. Christensen, *Early American Wood Carving*, p. 38.

15. Baltimore Directory, 1851, pp. 62–63.

16. "The view depicts the corners of Greenwich and Dey Streets, the latter being the street in the foreground. The fine three-story residence at the extreme right of the view was built by Isaac Stoutenburgh. Later it was occupied by the North River Bank, which acquired it May 1, 1829, under foreclosure of mortgage. At the present time the site is occupied by a taxpayer, the corner store being used as an Orangeade stand! The two adjoining houses on Greenwich Street were owned by Robert Campbell and Leonard De Klyn respectively." I. N. Phelps Stokes and Daniel C. Haskell quoted from the back of an original watercolor by Baroness Hyde de Neuville, 1933, in the Stokes Collection, Print Room, New York Public Library.

17. Theodore Bolton and Irwin F. Cortelyou, *Ezra Ames of Albany*, pp. 87, 104; Albany *Gazette & Daily Advertiser*, November 10, 1817, p. 1, col. 4. The carver as well as the artist may have been Ezra Ames.

18. John Gott letterhead, Book 17B, Bella H. Landauer Collection, New-York Historical Society.

19. "An Appreciation," Philadelphia *Evening Telegraph*, n.d. From scrapbook of William Rush Dunton, Jr.

20. *Ibid.*

21. "Cigar Store Indian Becomes a Museum Relic," Baltimore *Evening Sun*, May 14, 1926.

22. Baker, *A Chronicle*, p. 65.

23. Observed by the author in his youth.

24. Maryland, Ca-6, Index of American Design, National Gallery of Art, Washington, D.C.; another formerly in the A. W. Pendergast Collection, present location unknown; one in author's collection.

25. *Charleston Square*, oil on canvas, Abby Aldrich Rockefeller Folk Art Collection, Williamsburg; *Still Life*, Addison Gallery of American Art, Andover, Massachusetts.

26. New York Directories; acquisition records, Museum of the City of New York.

27. Robert P. Nevin, "Stephen C. Foster and Negro Minstrelsy," *Atlantic Monthly*, Vol. 20 (1867), p. 608.

28. Rice was not the originator of the "Jim Crow" song that was known earlier in the century and may have originated after the American Revolution. Jim Crow may have been a real character, and legend or fact dates his beginning to 1754. According to Harry Reynolds in his *Minstrel Memories* (pp. 78–82), his father and mother were South American Indians, brought to New York and sold in the slave market. The young boy and his parents were bought by an American, Squire Crow. The young boy attracted the attention of the Squire who permitted him to receive a rudimentary education from an old slave schoolmaster called Septimus Yamobobannum. When little Jim Crow was nine years of age a new overseer was engaged who treated the slaves with great cruelty, particulary Jim's father and mother who were favored by the squire. The slaves revolted against their oppressor and seizing the overseer fed him into a huge bonfire. Jim's mother and father and the other slaves were executed for the murder. Jim ran away and succeeded in reaching New York, earning a few pennies by singing "De Nigger and De Planter" in the streets, later adding such tunes as "Yankee Doodle," "General Washington," and others. He became popular, adding a fiddle to accompany himself, and in time became a favorite

at dancing houses and places of recreation. When the song "Jim Crow" appeared, he sang it, earning large sums of money at private clubs. By 1787 he had amassed a small farm in Virginia, married a white woman, and settled down to farming. The ex-slave eventually owned several slaves himself. After his death in 1809, the following inscription is said to have been put upon his tombstone:

> Here lies poor Jim, who never more will sing
> His "Jump Jim Crow" or tune the fiddle string
> Unless above, he chance to shake a toe,
> And please his friends by jumping Jim Crow.

29. Reynolds, *Minstrel Memories*, pp. 72–78.
30. "Wood-Carving," *Harper's Weekly*, January 6, 1883, p. 13.

Chapter 3

1. Alexander Pope, *An Essay on Man*, Epistle I-III, lines 99–113.
2. New York Directories; Frank W. Weitenkampf, "Lo, the Wooden Indian: The Art of Making Cigar-shop Signs" (Interview with Samuel A. Robb), *The New York Times*, August 3, 1890, p. 13, col. 1.
3. "First Wooden Indians Close to Wigwam on 14th Street" (Letter to *The New York Times* by Charles A. Flammer), *The New York Times*, May 3, 1927.
4. Invoices, Books 17, 17D, Bella H. Landauer Collection; Warshaw Collection, Smithsonian Institution.
5. "The Last of Edward Hen's Business," *Tobacco*, August 5, 1887; New York Directories.
6. "Poor Lo Still Active" (James A. Brooks letter to J. H. Morrison), *Scribner's Magazine*, January 1929, pp. 40–41.
7. Advertisement, *Trow's Directory* for 1856, p. 380.
8. James A. Brooks.
9. Real Estate Records, Kings County, New York, Registrar's Office, Clerks Minutes, Liber 20, Index, 1873, p. 519; Liber 78, p. 218; Report of Sale, Liber 96, 1868-1879, p. 106.
10. "Old Man Hen Is Dead," New York *Herald*, reprinted in *Tobacco*, August 5, 1887; Edward Hen's Will, May 9, 1887, Probate Dept., Surrogates Court, New York; "E. Hen's Will," *Tobacco*, May 13, 1887, p. 3.
11. "Old Man Hen Is Dead," reprinted in *Tobacco*, August 5, 1887.
12. "Pioneer Pipe Man Passes Away, *Tobacco*, June 29, 1911; New York Directories.
13. "Wood-Carving," *Harper's Weekly*, January 6, 1883, p. 13.
14. S. M. Frank & Co. records; Dr. Edwin Demuth.
15. *Annual Report*, American Institute of the City of New York, 1869–1870, Vol. 12, p. 211; Vol. 28, pp. 477–481 (pamphlets). The first known exhibition of signs, signboards, carved sign figures, etc., was the Grand Exhibition, also known as Bonnell Thornton's Signboard Exhibition, held in Bow Street, Covent Garden, London, April 27, 1762. As such, it may have been the first exhibition of "Pop Art." (St. James's *Chronicle* [London], March 23, 1762.) This exhibition satirized an Exhibition of the Polite Arts, given by the society artists, and held concurrently. Many of the caricaturists and social realists participated in the signboard exhibition, thinly disguising their names, most obvious of which was William Hogarth who signed "Hagerty" to his works. The exhibtiion created a storm in the press, ruffling the "polite" artists and their friends who saw in it a "persifflage" of their exhibition at the Strand. The catalogue of the Signboard Exhibition, which noted "original paintings, Busts, Carved figures, &c.," was documented with the most amusing titles for paintings and sculpture, including one very contemporary title, *Black on All Black*. Others—*Nobody* alias *Somebody*, A Character, by Hagerty; *Absolom Hanging*, a Peruke-

Makers Sign, by Sclater; *Welcome Cuckolds to Horn Fair,* by Hagerty; An Ha! Ha; Under "BUSTS, CARVED FIGURES, &c., &c., &c.," were:

A Blue Boar. By Lester; Two Indian Kings. By Taverner; A Bunch of Grapes from Portugal. By Pendred; Take Time By The Forelock. By Clark; A Dumb Bell. By the same; A Gold Fish, considerably larger than the Life. By Cook; An exact Representation of the famous RUNNING HORSE. Black on All Black; A Stand of Cheese, with a Bladder of Lard on the Top; A Westphalian Ham. These two by Bricken; and Several Tobacco Rolls, Sugar Loaves, Hat, Wigs, Stockings, Gloves, &c., &c., hung around the Room. By the above-mentioned Artists

The catalogue appears in Larwood and Hotten, *Signboards,* pp. 511–526.

16. John W. Chambers, *A Condensed History of the American Institute of the City of New York and Its Exhibitions* (pamphlet).
17. S. M. Frank & Co. records.
18. Original in files, Growth of the United States, Smithsonian Institution.
19. Southern District Court Copyright Records of 1869, Vol. 106, pp. 238, 240, 266.
20. Commemorative Program, William Demuth, 1905; Mrs. Philip H. Steckler, granddaughter.
21. Copyright Office, file no. 8702 F and 8702, August 23, 1875.
22. Samuel McKechnie, *Popular Entertainments Through the Ages,* pp. 77–78.
23. Maurice Sand, *The History of the Harlequinade,* p. 111.
24. *Ibid.,* pp. 114–115.
25. "M. A. Seyfried of 49 Courtlandt Street has had his famous old figure of Punch redecorated, and given him a flag to wave." *Tobacco,* May 3, 1889, p. 3.
26. John A. Kouwenhoven, *Columbia Historical Portrait of New York,* p. 307 (photograph).
27. Richard E. Conover, *The Telescoping Tableaus,* p. 11.
28. "The Tobacconist's Sign," *Tobacco,* April 8, 1887, p. 2.
29. "Modern Woman," *The Nation,* Vol. 7 (October 22, 1868), pp. 332–334.
30. "The Girl of the Period," *Saturday Review,* March 14, 1868, pp. 339–340.
31. Phineas Garrett, ed., *The Girl of the Period* (Philadelphia: Pennsylvania Publishing Company, 1912), p. 14 (pamphlet). *One Hundred Choice Selections,* No. 25.
32. Haffenreffer Collection of Cigar Store Indians, Parke-Bernet Galleries, Inc., October 10, 1956, No. 60.
33. *Tobacco,* June 13, 1890, p. 10.
34. Also made into a flip reel for the American Mutoscope and Biograph Company and used in the crank-turned "Iron Horse Mutoscope" coin-operated peep show.
35. Clarence L. Barnhart, ed., "Captain Jack," *New Century Cyclopedia of Names* (New York: Appleton Century-Crofts, Inc., 1954), p. 2155.
36. Haffenreffer Collection of Cigar Store Indians, Parke-Bernet Galleries, Inc., April 11, 1956, No. 89 (painted plaster). Sold for $300.
37. *Ibid.,* No. 25 (painted cast iron). Sold for $1,200.
38. "Designed by Whittling Yankees," *Tobacco,* May 14, 1886, p. 6.
39. *Ibid.* "Dudes are on the wane and Pucks, that were so popular a few years ago, are now so much dead wood on your hands."
40. "Les Cires de Pierre Inmans," *Albums de Modèles de Bustes pour Salons de Coiffure* (catalogue), (Paris), p. 61.
41. Mrs. Harriet Steckler, granddaughter of William Demuth; Weitenkampf, "Lo, the Wooden Indian," p. 13; Commemorative Program, Wm. Demuth papers.
42. DeLeeuw, R. M., *Both Sides of Broadway,* p. 236; Elizabeth W. Robb.
43. Guest List, Demuth's 70th birthday, Wm. Demuth papers.
44. "Death of Leopold Demuth Brings to Close Brilliant Chapter in Pipe Industry History," *U. S. Tobacco Journal,* April 24, 1943, p. 7.

45. Henry R. Stiles, *The History of Kings County*, New York, p. 816.
46. *Ibid.*
47. *Ibid.*
48. *Ibid.*, p. 817.
49. Brooklyn Directories.
50. *New York, The World's Metropolis, 1623–1624, 1923–1924* (New York: 1924).
51. New York Directory, 1896.
52. Trade cards and business records of J. W. Fiske.
53. John W. Fiske to Warren R. Fiske, letter dated October 17, 1940, Fiske papers.
54. Haffenreffer Collection of Cigar Store Indians, Parke-Bernet Galleries, Inc., April 11, 1956, No. 67. "Painted cast iron. Medium size. Standing figure leaning on a tree trunk, wearing a plumed headdress, nude to the waist and draped with an animal skin, wearing buckskin trousers and moccasins; with right arm extended. The rectangular base with plaquette inscribed: J. W. FISKE, MANUFACTURER, 26–28 PARK PLACE. Total height 5 feet 1 inch." Sold for $725.
55. Order books, Fiske papers.
56. Centennial leaflet issued by J. W. Fiske Architectural Metals, Inc.; Warren R. Fiske.
57. Miller, Dubrul & Peters Manufacturing Co. catalogue; L. C. Hegarty Papers.
58. A. W. Pendergast and W. Porter Ware, *Cigar Store Figures in American Folk Art*, p. 49.
59. *J. L. Mott Illustrated Catalogue Statuary and Animals* (New York: E. D. Slater Press, 1890).

Chapter 4

1. "Wood-Carving," *Harper's Weekly*, January 6, 1883, p. 13.
2. "Lo Takes a Spring Suit," *Tobacco*, April 12, 1889.
3. "Manufacture of Dummy Indians," *Tobacco*, November 12, 1886.
4. "Lo Takes a Spring Suit," *Tobacco*, April 12, 1889.
5. "Designed by Whittling Yankees," *Tobacco*, May 14, 1886.
6. "Lo Takes a Spring Suit," *Tobacco*, April 12, 1889.
7. Weitenkampf, "Lo, the Wooden Indian," p. 13.
8. "Lo Takes a Spring Suit," *Tobacco*, April 12, 1889.
9. *Ibid.*
10. "Designed by Whittling Yankees," *Tobacco*, May 14, 1886.
11. Elizabeth Robb. In 1921, when Robb moved from his apartment on West 156th Street in Manhattan, he left behind packing cases full of these patterns, which must have been destroyed eventually.
12. "Lo Takes a Spring Suit," *Tobacco*, April 12, 1889.
13. "Wood-Carving," *Harper's Weekly*, January 6, 1883; Weitenkampf, "Lo, the Wooden Indian," p. 13.
14. Brewington, *Shipcarvers of North America*, pp. 68, 69, 73.
15. John Philip Yaeger; Clarence and Charles Robb.
16. "The Tobacconist's Sign," *Tobacco*, April 8, 1887, p. 2.
17. Henry Collins Brown, *Valentine's Manual of Old New York*, p. 122.
18. "Manufacture of Dummy Indians," *Tobacco*, November 12, 1886.
19. Marriage certificate, June 14, 1876, Marriage Bureau Records, Municipal Building, New York.
20. Weitenkampf, "Lo, the Wooden Indian, p. 13.
21. Brintzlinghofer, "A Stogie Display at Newark," *Tobacco*, November 27, 1896, p. 3.
22. "Resolution to Purchase Figure of Washington from William Rush," Philadelphia *Bulletin*, September 9, 1931; copy of letter in Wm. Rush Dunton, Jr. scrapbook.

23. "Lo Takes a Spring Suit," *Tobacco*, April 12, 1889.
24. Brown, *Valentine's Manual*, p. 122; "Designed by Whittling Yankees," *Tobacco*, May 14, 1886.

Chapter 5

1. Arthur Pougin, *Dictionnaire du Théâtre*, pp. 173–174.
2. Henry Morley, *Memoirs of Bartholomew Fair*, pp. 15, 493.
3. John and Alice Durant, *A Pictorial History of the American Circus*, pp. 24, 26.
4. Isaac J. Greenwood, *The Circus: Its Origin and Growth Prior to 1835*, p. 114.
5. Brooks, "Poor Lo Still Active" (letter), p. 40.
6. *Ibid.*, Advertisement, Xenia *Torchlight* (Ohio), June 29, 1848.
7. Advertisement, unidentified newspaper, Springfield, Massachusetts, April 25, 1851.
8. *Ibid.*, June 19, 1851.
9. New York Directories.
10. Bill of the Lee & Bennett Circus, San Francisco, reproduced in the New York *Clipper*, October 10, 1874; advertisement, unidentified newspaper, Wakefield, Rhode Island, May 11, 1859, notes a Fielding Bandchariot on the Nixon & Co. Circus, pulled by a forty-horse hitch.
11. *Trow's Directory* for 1863–1864, p. 11.
12. New York *Clipper*, April 1, 1865; advertisement, unidentified newspaper, Augusta, Maine, September 14, 1866.
13. New York *Clipper*, June 1, 1867.
14. Richard E. Conover; New York *Clipper*, February 24, 1872; New York *Clipper*, January 25, 1873.
15. New York *Clipper*, March 2, 1878; Conover, *Telescoping Tableaus*, p. 11.
16. Bridgeport (Connecticut) *Evening Times*, July 17, 1879.
17. Conover, *The Great Forepaugh Shows*, p. 8.
18. Weitenkampf, "Lo, The Wooden Indian," p. 13.
19. Durant and Durant, *The American Circus*, pp. 74–76; Conover, *The Affairs of James A. Bailey*.
20. Durant and Durant, *The American Circus*, p. 74.
21. "Wood-Carving," *Harper's Weekly*, January 6, 1883, p. 13.
22. New York *Clipper*, December 2, 1882.
23. Records of Wills, March 17, 1882, Surrogates Court, New York, Liber 301, p. 37; New York Directories.
24. *Trow's Directory* for 1866–1867, p. 34.
25. *Ibid.*, for 1878.
26. Certificate of Incorporation, September 29, 1885, Surrogates Court, New York.
27. Conover, "The Diminutive Tableaus," *Bandwagon*, September–October 1960.
28. Weitenkampf, "Lo, The Wooden Indian," p. 13. All the pony-drawn tableaux were made in Robb's shop. The "nearly all" refers to some signs around New York, mentioned in the first part of the article.
29. Brown Box No. 1, McCadden Collection, Princeton University Library.
30. Records of New York Supreme Court, July 12, 1893, Surrogates Court, New York.
31. *The Realm of Marvels*, Vol. 2, No. 5 (1904), p. 1. Issued by Barnum & Bailey.
32. Minutes of Directors, Barnum & Bailey, Ltd., p. 114; McCadden Collection, Princeton University Library.
33. Edward Gleichen, *London's Open Air Statuary* (pamphlet); Sir Walter Besant, *London North of the Thames* (pamphlet).
34. Gleichen, *London's Open Air Statuary*; Prince Albert August Charles Emanuel (1819–1861), son of Duke Ernest of Saxe-Coburg-Gotha.
35. *Realm of Marvels*, March 1903, pp. 76–81.

36. *Ibid.*, p. 77.
37. *Ibid.*, pp. 80, 81.
38. New York *Daily Tribune*, March 3, 1903, p. 4, cols. 2, 3, 4, 5.
39. *Ibid.*
40. *Realm of Marvels*, March 1903, pp. 75–76.
41. Records of C. P. Fox, Circus World Museum, Baraboo, Wisconsin.
42. Conover, *James A. Bailey*, p. 13.

Chapter 6

PHILADELPHIA

1. J. F. Watson, *Annals of Philadelphia and Pennsylvania in the Olden Times*, Vol. 1, p. 575.
2. Genealogy records in the Wm. Rush Dunton, Jr. scrapbook.
3. Watson's *Annals*, p. 575.
4. Page from unidentified origin, scrapbook of Wm. Rush Dunton, Jr.
5. Watson's *Annals*, pp. 575–576.
6. Henri Marceau, *William Rush*, p. 11.
7. *Ibid.*, pp. 14–16.
8. "A Pioneer Sculptor, The Life and Important Works of William Rush, The Philadelphia Wood Carver." Philadelphia *North American*, 1892, n.d.
9. Brewington, *Shipcarvers*, pp. 35–36.
10. "Ship-Carving," clipping, n.d., Wm. Rush Dunton, Jr. scrapbook.
11. E. Leslie Gilliams, "A Philadelphia Sculptor," *Lippincott's*, August 1893.
12. Abraham Ritter, *Philadelphia and Her Merchants*, pp. 103–105.
13. Letter, Miscellaneous letters, proposals, etc., 1819–1820, from Naval Records and Library, Navy Department.
14. Marceau, *William Rush*; Brewington, *Shipcarvers*, pp. 36–37.
15. Clipping, no ident., n.d., Wm. Rush Dunton, Jr. scrapbook.
16. "An Appreciation," Philadelphia *Evening Telegraph*, n.d., Wm. Rush Dunton, Jr. scrapbook.
17. Riggs & Brother's letter to author; Philadelphia Directories; Business card, Burton Collection, Print Room, Metropolitan Museum of Art, New York.
18. Philadelphia Directories.
19. E. Leslie Gilliams, "Cigar Store Indians," Philadelphia *Times*, December 18, 1892, p. 18.
20. *Ibid.*
21. *Ibid.*
22. Morrison, "The Passing of the Wooden Indian," *Scribner's Magazine*, October 1928, p. 403.
23. *Ibid.*, Letter from Frank J. Deker to author; Philadelphia Directories.
24. *Tobacco*, July 26, 1889, p. 2, col. 4.
25. Gilliams, "Cigar Store Indians," p. 18.

BALTIMORE

1. Mayer, "Signs & Symbols," *Scribner's Monthly*, September 1879, p. 709.
2. Edward King, "The Liverpool of America," *Scribner's Monthly*, March 1875, p. 685.
3. Brewington, *Shipcarvers*, pp. 62, 72.
4. King, "The Liverpool of America," p. 685.
5. Morrison, "The Passing of the Wooden Indian," p. 394.
6. I. Myrtle Guethlein, granddaughter of John Philip Yaeger; City Directories.

7. Told by Eva Isabelle Papp to I. Myrtle Guethlein.
8. *Ibid.*, Baltimore Directories.
9. "Lo, Wooden Indian Goes to Historical Tepee." Baltimore *Evening Sun*, October 29, 1952, p. 80. "Lo was carved by an unknown craftsman who lived on Lombard Street near Exeter, Mr. Klein said. . . . Lo took up his vigil at 1,000 East Pratt Street sometime in the mid-1880s, according to Alvin Klein."
10. *Ibid.*
11. I. Myrtle Guethlein.
12. Yaeger family records.
13. Letter in Yaeger scrapbook, I. Myrtle Guethlein collection.
14. Teubner-Braecklein family records, Braecklein Papers; Baltimore Directories.
15. King, "The Liverpool of America," p. 685.
16. Edwin P. S. Newman estate.
17. Harold A. Williams, "Eight Hundred Wooden Indians—And Then There Were Eight," Baltimore *Morning Sun*, February 17, 1947, pp. 23–24; Kate Sanborn, *Hunting Indians in a Taxi-Cab*, interview with Gaspari.
18. Sanborn, *Hunting Indians.*
19. Baltimore Directories.
20. Sanborn, *Hunting Indians.*
21. Baltimore Directories.
22. Edwin P. S. Newman estate.

WASHINGTON, D. C.

1. Washington, D.C., Directories.
2. Eighth United States Census Report, 1860; Washington, D.C., Directories.
3. Carl Williams of New York City owned these sketches, later selling them to the Kennedy Galleries of New York.
4. Washington, D.C., Directories.

DETROIT

1. Ferdinand Zumbusch, Genealogical Material Relating to the Melchers Family, 1905. New York Public Library, Genealogical Division.
2. William Edwin Rudge, *Gari Melchers, Painter.* Foreword by Henriette Lewis-Hind.
3. George B. Catlin, "Old Detroit Artists Found Trade Dull but Market for Wooden Indians Brisk," Detroit *News*, January 4, 1925, p. 17.
4. *Ibid.*
5. J. H. Junkin, "The Wooden Indian is Passing Away," Detroit *News-Tribune*, July 23, 1899, p. 17.
6. Catlin, "Old Detroit Artists," p. 17.
7. *Ibid.*
8. *Ibid.*
9. John Hubert Greusel, "Art's Sake! Sculptor Julius Melchers on Sacrifices," Detroit *News-Tribune*, August 22, 1897, p. 13; Detroit Directories.
10. Detroit Directories.
11. Greusel, "Art's Sake!", p. 13.
12. Detroit Directories.
13. *Ibid.*
14. Greusel, "Art's Sake!", p. 13.
15. Catlin, "Old Detroit Artists," p. 17.
16. "Art's Sake!", p. 13.
17. *Ibid.*
18. *Ibid.*

19. "Julius Melchers Suffers a Stroke." The Detroit *News*, May 30, 1907, p. 1.
20. The reverse side of the photograph contains the data on the price, shipping, date, and provenance. The figure is in the collection of William H. Stroh, grandson of J. T. Melchers and was bought for $12,000, the highest price ever paid for a show figure.
21. Perry A. Armstrong, *The Sauks and the Black Hawk War*, pp. 542–543.
22. *Ibid.*
23. *Ibid.*
24. John Francis McDermott, "Another Coriolanus," *Antiques*, August 1948; Bayard Tuckerman, *The Diary of Philip Hone*, entry for October 26, 1837; "Broadway in the neighborhood of the City Hotel has been crowded for the last two days by curious spectators, watching to obtain an occasional glimpse of a large party of Indians, who, after having made a treaty at Washington by which their 'bread lands' are diminished in quantity by the trifling amount of a million and a quarter acres, are now making a tour of the principal cities, receiving presents, and being stared at for the benefit of theatres, fairs, and lectures. There are two tribes, amounting in all to seventy individuals; the Sauks and Foxes, who constitute the most important part of the deputation, are at the City Hotel, and the Sioux at the National, opposite; for these two tribes are not on a friendly footing, and their white keepers do not think it expedient to get up a real war-fight for the edification of the spectators. . . . Keokuk, the chief of the confederated tribes of Sauks and Foxes, and his favourite squaw were seated on a small carpet separate from the rest. He is a fine-looking elderly man of intelligent countenance and dignified deportment. I have heard General Scott speak of him; he thinks him a great man. . . ."
25. Junkin, "The Wooden Indian is Passing Away," p. 17.
26. Detroit *Free Press*, January 15, 1876.
27. Detroit *Free Press*, September 28, 1871, p. 1, col. 2.
28. Detroit Directories; J. Crongeyer.
29. Detroit Directories.
30. Detroit Directories, 1882, p. 136.
31. Detroit Directories, 1888.
32. Junkin, "The Wooden Indian is Passing Away," p. 17.
33. *Ibid.*

ASHLAND, WISCONSIN

1. "Cigar Store Indian Becomes a Valuable Relic," Washington *Star*, August 21, 1932, Sunday Magazine Section.
2. Ashland Directories.
3. *Ibid.;* Letter from Max Wheltman, author's collection.

PROVIDENCE AND GLOUCESTER

1. Dowler family records; Providence Directories.
2. *Ibid.* Dowler did a vast amount of scroll and architectural decoration for rows of houses, hotels, etc.
3. City Directory, 1881, p. 652.
4. "Charles Dowler, Sculptor, Dead." Providence *Evening Bulletin*, January 25, 1931, p. 25, Obituary.
5. Rhode Island—Ca. 6, Index of American Design, National Gallery.
6. "Charles Dowler, Sculptor, Dead," Obituary.
7. Massachusetts—Ca. 122, Index of American Design, National Gallery; Brewington, *Shipcarvers*, pp. 156, 160.

CANADA

1. Victoria Hayward, "Jobin, the Wood-Carver," *The Canadian Magazine*, December 1922, p. 92.
2. Marius Barbeau, "Louis Jobin, Statuaire," *Le Soleil*, June 10, 1945.
3. *Ibid.*
4. *Ibid.*
5. Hayward, "Jobin, the Wood-Carver," p. 92.
6. At the time of Victoria Hayward's interview with Jobin in 1922, Jobin's memory was not too accurate. John Bolton is actually William Boulton who was at 106 South Street, just east of the Fulton Fish Market and Schermerhorn Row. In 1870, Boulton moved to 2 Coenties Slip where Jobin served his post-apprenticeship. "St. John Street" is John Street, Battery Place, the Battery. Castle Garden was at the bend in the harbor, a few blocks away.
7. Barbeau, "Louis Jobin, Statuarie." The only German firms at that time (1870–1871) were Simon Strauss, Kurz & Co., and Charles Eschenbach.
8. *Ibid.*
9. "William Arrowsmith," *Gazette de Quebec*, December 21, 1809, p. 3; Hayward, "Jobin, the Wood-Carver," p. 92.
10. Hayward, "Jobin, the Wood-Carver," p. 92.
11. Les Livres des Comptes et délibérations de la Fabrique Sté-Anne de Beaupré, p. 186.
12. "The Montreal Ice Carnival," *Harper's Weekly*, February 3, 1883, p. 75.
13. Damase Potvin, "Louis Jobin, A Humble Man of the Soil," *La Presse* (Quebec), November 27, 1926. (Edited in 1928 together with an article by the same author, "Les Ilet-Jeremie," under the title, "La Petite Histoire.")
14. Mme. Regis Perron, 1968. Mme. Perron's house at 9791 Royale is across the road from the former Jobin shop. Many of the Jobin tools and items are owned by members of the Perron family.
15. *Ibid.;* Hayward, "Jobin, the Wood-Carver," p. 92.
16. *Ibid.*
17. Compiled by Perè Laurent Proulx, Les Pères Rédemptoristes, Basilique Sté-Anne.
18. Mme. Regis Perron, 1968; Barbeau, "Louis Jobin, Statuaire."
19. Quebec Directories.
20. Barbeau, "Côté, Sculpteur, *La Canada Français*. Quebec, Vol. 30, No. 2 (October 1942), pp. 96–97; City Directories.
21. *Sculpture Traditionnelle du Quebec* (catalogue) Quebec: (Musée du Quebéc, 1967), pp. 148–149.
22. Barbeau, "Côté, Sculpteur," pp. 96–97.
23. *Ibid.*
24. *Ibid.*
25. *Ibid.*, Chicago Directories.
26. *Ibid.*
27. *Ibid.*
28. *Ibid.*
29. *Canadian Cigar & Tobacco Journal*, 1902, pp. 40–42.

NEW YORK

1. Brewington, *Shipcarvers*, p. 5.
2. The New-York *Gazette and General Advertiser*, April 12, 1762; Rivington's New-York *Gazeteer*, March 10, 1774.
3. Rivington's New-York *Gazeteer*, May 13, 1773.
4. *Tobacco*, September 10, 1886, p. 7; Kouwenhoven, *Portrait of New York*, photograph, p. 410.

5. New-York *Gazette and General Advertiser*, May 23, 1799.

6. New-York *Gazette and General Advertiser*, May 25, 1799.

7. G. W. Sheldon, "The Old Shipbuilders of New York," *Harper's Magazine*, Vol. 65 (1882), p. 228.

8. New York Directories.

9. New York *Evening Post*, April 8, 1803.

10. Blunt, *Stranger's Guide to the City of New York*, p. 46.

11. John Dixey's will, August 3, 1820, Surrogates Court, New York, Liber 56, p. 112.

12. Dodge, *Tristram Dodge and his Descendents in America*.

13. Brewington, *Shipcarvers*, p. 133.

14. *Ibid.*, p. 131; Tuckerman, *Diary of Philip Hone*, entry for June 23, 1834; "We saw the noble ship 'Constitution' plainly from Rockaway yesterday afternoon, under a full spread of canvas, on her way up to the city. She sailed from Havre on the 5th and from Plymouth England, on the 16th ult. I do not think much of her commander, have little respect for the effigy on her bow or the manner of its being placed there, and am not exceedingly proud of the country's representative which she now bears in her bosom; but I love her for her name, and honour her for the share she has had in the preservation of her country's glory. She is still 'Old Ironsides.' "

15. Brewington, *Shipcarvers*, pp. 121–138. An excellent account of the entire episode as well as a history of the *Constitution*'s figureheads.

16. Fernald & Pettigrew Papers, Peabody Museum, Salem, Massachusetts.

17. *Ibid.*

18. *Ibid.*

19. Annual Report, Board of Trustees, 1952, New-York Historical Society; New York Directories.

20. Real Estate Records, Kings County, Surrogates Court, New York.

21. Eighth United States Census Schedule, 1860; "An Appreciation," Philadelphia *Evening Telegraph*, n.d., Wm. Rush Dunton, Jr. scrapbook.

22. "Indentures," February 19, 1893, Real Estate Records, Surrogates Court, New York, Liber 293, p. 99; October 6, 1825, Liber 336, p. 594.

23. Trow's Directory for 1849–1850.

24. Ninth United States Census Schedule, 1870; New York Directories.

25. Letters of Administration, November 29, 1870, Record Room, Kings County, Surrogates Court, New York.

26. Seventh United States Census Schedule, 1850, Brooklyn, Book No. 8; New York Directories, maps; G. W. Sheldon, *The Old Ship-Builders of New York*.

27. *Samoset*. Fernald & Pettigrew Papers, Peabody Museum, Salem, Massachusetts.

28. Brewington, *Shipcarvers*, p. 73.

29. *Cromwell*, Fernald & Pettigrew Papers, Peabody Museum, Salem, Massachusetts.

30. Brooks, "Poor Lo Still Active," pp. 40–41; Isaac J. Greenwood, *The Circus*, p. 114. "Purdy & Welch appear to have been the first to travel with a band of music and have a show parade."

31. Jean Lipman, *American Folk Art, in Wood, Metal and Stone*, p. 74; Robb Papers.

32. Robb Papers.

33. New York and Boston Directories; map of Boston, (Boston: Sampson Davenport & Co., 1860).

34. Robb Papers.

35. Weitenkampf, "Lo, The Wooden Indian," p. 16.

36. Death certificate, March 25, 1902; Letter, 72. Kings County, Surrogates Court, New York.

37. Advertisement, New York Directory, 1861.

38. Brooks, "Poor Lo Still Active" (letter), pp. 40–41; New York Directories.

39. "Tecumseh, the Wooden Indian," Fremont *News-Messenger*, October 24, 1956, p. 23.
40. Robb Papers.
41. Ninth United States Census Schedule, 1870; Finance Division, Real Estate Records, Registrar's Office, Clerk's Minutes, November 22, 1873, Liber 66, April 18, 1878, Liber 78, p. 218.
42. "Lo Takes a Spring Suit," *Tobacco*, April 12, 1889.
43. "Designed by Whittling Yankees," *Tobacco*, May 14, 1886.
44. *Ibid.*; Brooks, "Poor Lo Still Active" (letter), pp. 40–41.
45. Chicago Business Directory, 1882.
46. Henry Dibblee, 276 Wabash Avenue (1879), formerly Gould Bros & Dibblee (1876), Dibblee, Mantels & Grates (1881) 266–268 S. Wabash: records in the Chicago Historical Society.
47. Dave James, "He's No. 1 Indian Chief!"; Tacoma *News-Tribune*, February 13, 1937; Lenny Anderson, "Seattle Pays Big Heap Wampum to Lure Chief Tacoman for 58 years," Tacoma *News-Tribune*, October 9, 1946.
48. Brown, *Valentine's Manual*, p. 123.
49. *Picturesque Chicago and Guide to the World's Fair, 1893*, pp. 257–258.
50. Brooks, "Poor Lo Still Active," (letter), p. 40; Chicago, New York, Tampa, Brooklyn Directories; Chicago, city records.

S. A. ROBB

1. Sheldon, "The Old Ship-Builders of New York," p. 224.
2. Elizabeth Robb; Robb Papers.
3. Charles H. Farnum, "A Day on the Docks," *Scribner's Monthly*, Vol. 18, No. 1 (1879), p. 46.
4. Attendance Records, 1869–1875, National Academy of Design.
5. Annual Report of the Trustees of the Cooper Union, 1871, 1872. In this class with Robb were artists who later became famous. Also, Bayard Tuckerman, editor of *The Diary of Philip Hone*.
6. Records of the National Academy of Design.
7. "Return of a Marriage," June 14, 1876, Bureau of Vital Statistics, Marriage License Bureau, Municipal Building, New York.
8. Real Estate Records, 1875–1885, Kings County, Surrogates Court, New York.
9. Elizabeth Robb.
10. "Manufacture of Dummy Indians," *Mail & Express* (New York), n.d., reproduced in *Tobacco*, November 12, 1886.
11. Lipman, *American Folk Art*, p. 74.
12. Certificate of Membership, National Guard S, New York, March 16, 1879.
13. Elizabeth Robb.
14. Mayer, "Signs & Symbols," p. 105–114.
15. General George W. Wingate, *History of the Twenty-Second Regiment*, New York, pp. 375–385.
16. Elizabeth Robb.
17. Weitenkampf, "Some Signs and Others—Sign Painters and Sign Painting Artists," *The New York Times*, July 3, 1892, p. 25. "One toy dealer trades under the protective presence of that great distributor, Santa Claus."
18. Weitenkampf, "Lo, The Wooden Indian," p. 16. "Forepaugh has an equestrian figure of St. George and the Dragon."
19. Elizabeth Robb.
20. New York Directories; Kenneth H. Dunshee, *As You Pass By*, pp. 176–179.
21. Judgments, Record Room, Surrogates Court, New York.
22. "The Inexhaustible Cow at Coney Island," *Harper's Weekly*, August 6, 1881, p. 540.

23. James D. McCabe, *The Illustrated History of the Centennial Exhibition, 1876,* p. 55.
24. Robb Papers.
25. Weitenkampf, "Some Signs and Others," p. 25.
26. Elizabeth Robb.
27. Records, Department of Health, New York; Elizabeth Robb; Robb Papers.
28. Charles Robb.
29. Minutes of Barnum & Bailey, Ltd., McCadden Collection, Princeton University Library.
30. General Address Book, Barnum & Bailey Ltd., McCadden Collection, Princeton University Library.
31. Real Estate Records, Surrogates Court, New York, 1904, Liber 480, p. 14, lot no. 14.
32. Obituary, *The New York Times,* May 4, 1928, p. 5; Charles A. Stadler, *The New York Red Book* (Albany: Williams Press, 1892).
33. Elizabeth Robb.
34. *Ibid.*
35. Recollections of the author. The Greenpoint and Williamsburgh gangs of Brooklyn would confiscate pushcarts, candy-store benches, signposts, and other combustible fuel for these events, storing some the night before. The author recalls when a wooden Indian wheeled to the fire, brought cheers and imitation war whoops and dances, and as the flames consumed this piece of American sculpture, blood-curdling yells would mingle with the rattle of trolleys and the roaring of the Broadway–Brooklyn elevated train as it went by overhead. Thus ended the saga of the "Sigel Street Savage."
36. Elizabeth Robb; Records of Hammacher Schlemmer, new owners of James McCutcheon & Co.
37. Parke-Bernet Galleries, Inc., Sale No. 1948, February 5–6, 1960, Item No. 287.
38. Mortgage, Book No. 6, October 28, 1895, Chattel Mortgages, 281, Cape May County, New Jersey.
39. Elizabeth Robb; *The Hudson-Fulton Celebration 1909,* Vol. 1, pp. 282, 287, 625, 681; Vol. 2, pp. 1173, 1221; Sir Courtenay Peregrine Ilbert, p. 539, carved figure with deck block.
40. Robb Papers; Elizabeth Robb.
41. Elizabeth Robb.
42. *Ibid.*
43. Charles Robb.
44. Elizabeth Robb.
45. *Ibid.*
46. The Haffenreffer Collection of Cigar Store Indians, Parke-Bernet Galleries Inc., April 11 and October 10, 1956.
47. Hayward, "Jobin, the Wood-Carver," p. 92; New York Directories, 1858–1880.
48. *Ibid.*
49. Ninth United States Census Schedule, 1870; New York Directories.
50. Dept. of Finance and Taxation, New York, Ref. Vol. 1, p. 18; Real Estate Records, 1878, Surrogates Court, New York.
51. Judgment (against Simon Strauss), H. 858, 1878. Surrogates Court, New York.
52. Cigar & Tobacco Manufacturers' Directory, 1882–1883; Advertisement, *Judische Gazetten,* April 6, 1887; Real Estate Records, Surrogates Court, New York.
53. Surrogates Court, Probate Dept. (will), January 8, 1897, Liber 567, p. 105.
54. New York Directories.
55. Brewington, *Shipcarvers,* p. 46; Lipman, *American Folk Art,* p. 25; M. Low.
56. 1855 New York State Census, 7th Ward, First, E.D.; New York Directories.
57. Edouard A. Stackpole, *Figureheads & Ship Carvings,* pp. 6–7; New York Directories.

58. Phillips & Co.'s *New York Business Directory*, 1881–1882; Robb Papers.
59. Tenth United States Census Schedule, 1880; New York and Brooklyn Directories; Weitenkampf, "Lo, The Wooden Indian," p. 16.
60. Family records and photographs, Mrs. Wilbur L. Martin Papers.
61. *Ibid.*
62. *Ibid.*, Letter of Dorothy von Allmen to author.
63. City Directories; Robb papers.
64. Family records and photographs from Mrs. Wilbur L. Martin Papers; Administration, May 12, 1917, Probate Dept., Surrogates Court, Kings County, New York.
65. New York Directories; Ninth United States Census Schedule, 1870, 13th Ward, 9th E. D., p. 49.
66. Weitenkampf, "Lo, the Wooden Indian," p. 16; Brown, *Valentine's Manual*, p. 122–123.
67. *New York Business Directory*, 1899.
68. *Trow's Directory* for 1885.
69. Probate Records, Surrogates Court, Kings County, New York, Liber 32, p. 356.

AMERICAN
SHOW-FIGURE CARVERS

Ashland, Wisconsin

| HERMAN KRUSCHKE | 1888 | 408 Ninth Avenue West |
| (DATES UNKNOWN) | 1899 | 322 Ninth Avenue West |

Baltimore, Maryland

JOHN PHILIP YAEGER (1823–1899)	1849	30 Fell St.
	1853	corner Lombard and Concord Sts.
	1855	106 East Baltimore (home)
	1855	northwest corner Baltimore and Frederick
	1858	5 East Lafayette St.
	1864	1 East Lafayette St.
	1870	39 Albemarle St.
	1871	21 Albemarle St.
	1872	41 Albemarle St.
	1879	51 Aisquith St. (home)
	1880	41 East Lombard St.
	1888	919 East Lombard St.

| WILLIAM TEUBNER (DATES UNKNOWN) | 1855 | German and Sharp Sts. |
| | 1855 | 225 Saratoga St. (home) |

| WILLIAM TEUBNER, JR. (1857–1927) | 1874 | 2 Fayette St. |
| | 1883 | 506 Callendar Alley |

| JAMES CAMPBELL | (*see* New Jersey) |
| (WORKED 1851–1900) | 1851 | Baltimore |

| PIERRE G. GASPARI | | |
| (DATES UNKNOWN) | 1861 | 31 South Calvert St. |

RICHARD CALLANAN	1867	19 Philpot St.
(DATES UNKNOWN)	1883	74 Block St.
	1896–1901	1426 Block St.

Boston, Massachusetts

THOMAS J. WHITE (1825–1902)

(*see* New York)
T. J. White & Co.

1856	233 Commercial St. (with W. H. Rumney)
1865–69	233 Commercial St.

Canada

LOUIS JOBIN (1845–1928)

1871	58 Notre Dame, Montreal
1875–78	Faubourg, St. Jean, Rue d'Aiguillon, Quebec
to 1898	Rue La Tourelle, Quebec
1898–1928	9790 Royale, Ste. Anne de Beaupré

JEAN-BAPTISTE CÔTÉ (1834–1907)

1860–61	132 St. Valier, Saint Roch, Quebec
1862–63	130 St. Valier, Saint Roch, Quebec
1863–64	132 St. Valier, Saint Roch, Quebec
1864–65	130½ St. Valier, Saint Roch, Quebec
1868–69	32 Crown St., Saint Roch, Quebec
1870	125 Rue de la Couronne, St. Roch, Quebec
1880–1907	Rue Richardson, Saint Roch, Quebec

CLAUDE CÔTÉ (DATES UNKNOWN)

(*see* Chicago)

1867–68	130 St. Valier, Saint Roch, Quebec
1868–69	32 Crown St., Saint Roch, Quebec

Chicago, Illinois

THOMAS V. BROOKS (1828–1895)

(*see* New York; James A. Brooks, New York)

1880	51 West Van Buren St.
1881	16 West Van Buren St.

New York-Chicago Carving Co.

1882	110 West Van Buren St.
1886	47 West Van Buren St.
1887	205½ South Desplaines

Thomas V. Brooks & Son

1889	408 West Madison
1890	318–320 West Van Buren St.

ISAAC LEWIN (ISAAC LEWIS)	(see New York)	
	1895	342 Hudson Ave.
	1895–96	40 South Peoria Ave.

CLAUDE CÔTÉ	(see Canada)	
	1883	West 22nd St., corner of Fisk
	1886	110 Brown St.
	1891	41 Bibley St.
	1899	97 Loomis
	1904	222 Loomis
	1912	2245 North Sawyer St.

Detroit, Michigan

JULIUS THEODORE MELCHERS	1855	150 Beaubien St.
(1829–1909)	1857	122 Congress East St.
	1862–1900	83 Randolph St.
		340 Fort St. East
		(home)
	1900–09	73 Seyburn Ave.
		(home)

HENRY A. SIEBERT		
(IN PARTNERSHIP WITH		
MELCHERS)	1890–95	83 Randolph St.

THEODORE CRONGEYER	1872	239 Jefferson St.
(DATES UNKNOWN)	1874	49 Farmer St.
	1890	55 Farmer St.

FERDINAND LAPP (DATES UNKNOWN)	1890	72 Congress St. East

ANTHONY OSEBOLD, JR.		
(DATES UNKNOWN)	1882	366 Division St.

CHARLES GUHLE (DATES UNKNOWN)	1888	207 Champlain St.

Gloucester, Massachusetts

DAVID R. PROCTOR	1854	Belfast, Maine
(DATES UNKNOWN)	1866	Gloucester, Massachusetts

New Jersey

JAMES CAMPBELL	(see Baltimore, Md.)	
(WORKED 1851–1900)	1857	1 Clinton, Third St.,
		East Newark
	1861	28 Crane St., Newark
	1862	Civil-War soldier
	1863	680 High St., Newark

ISAAC LEWIN (ISAAC LEWIS)	(*see* Chicago)	
	1871	20 East St.
DANIEL N. TRAIN (DATES UNKNOWN)	1799	144 Cherry St.
CHARLES J. DODGE (1806–1886)	1828	77 Columbia St.
JEREMIAH DODGE & SON	1833	75 Columbia St.
	1835	272 3rd St. (home)
	1842	South St. and Market Slip
DODGE & ANDERSON	1846	236 South St.
	1860–68	84 Columbia St.
	1870	168 South 2nd St., Brooklyn
THOMAS MILLARD, JR. (1803–1870)	1827	191 Cherry St.
	1845	204 Centre St.
	1847–48	376 Monroe St. (home)
	1849–50	260 South St. (Millard & Brooks)
	1851–52	260 South St.
	1852	no listing
	1853	260 South St.
	1854–55	no listing
	1855	Brooklyn (home)
	1856	59 Mangin St. (Moulding Mill)
	1856–57	Lafayette Ave. near Marcy, Brooklyn
	1857–58	not listed
	1859–60	Lafayette Ave., Brooklyn
JOHN L. CROMWELL (1805–1873)	1831	179 Cherry St.
	1836	260 Divison St.
	1839	419 Water St.
	1847	2 South 6th St., Brooklyn
	1850–55	222 South St.
	1856–69	2 South 6th St., Brooklyn
THOMAS J. WHITE (1825–1902)	(*see* Boston)	
	1852–54	Westchester, New York
BROOKS & WHITE	1871	90 Pike St.
	1874	85 South 4th St., Brooklyn
		Employed by Samuel A. Robb
	1876	195 Canal St.
THOMAS V. BROOKS (1828–1895)	(*see* Chicago)	
	1847–49	260 South St.
	1849–50	260 South St. (Brooks & Millard)
	1850–51	260 South St.
	1852–53	258 South St.

1853–54	259 South St.
1854	257 South St.
1871–72	90 Pike Slip
	(Brooks & White)
1874	240 South St.
1876	240 South St.
1877–78	211 Hudson St.

WILLIAM BOULTON (DATES UNKNOWN)

1860	733 Eighth Ave.
1864	838 Third Ave.
1868	106 South St.
1870	2 Coenties Slip
1875	142 First Ave.

SIMON STRAUSS (? –1897)

1866	69 Ave. C
1871	253 South St.
1876–97	179 Lewis St.

JOHN W. ANDERSON (1834–1904)

1855	222 South St.
1863	223 South St.
	(employed by Jane Anderson)
1875	226 South St.

Business in own name

1881	226 South St.
1885	233 South St.
1894	240 South St.
1895	90 Pike St.
1904	240 South St.

NICHOLAS E. COLLINS (1838– ?)

1872–78	204 and 222 South St.
	(Collins & Brown)
1879–80	81 Raymond St. (home)

CHARLES BROWN (1846–1917)

1872–78	204 and 222 South St.
	(Collins & Brown)
1885–88	20 James Slip
1890–1900	4 N. Pier Atlantic Dock,
	Brooklyn
1901–14	11 Summit St., Brooklyn
1915–17	37 Wyona St., Brooklyn

ELIJAH TRYON (1844– ?)

1872	68 Broome St.
1874	1 Hester St.
1879	310 Stanton St.
1881	132 Goerck St.
1882	134 Goerck St.
1888	87 Goerck St.
1892	131 Goerck St.
1899	35 Goerck St.

JUSTINUS STOLL NORTH (? –1900)	1871	191 Canal St.
	1874	190 Canal St.
	1879–92	188–190 Canal St.
SAMUEL ANDERSON ROBB	1876–88	195 Canal St.
(1851–1928)	1888–1903	114 Centre St.
	1903–04	10 West 13th St.
	1902–04	223 East 43rd St.
	1904–05	329 West 24th St.
	1908	11 Summit St., Brooklyn
	1910–21	516 West 156 St.
	1921–28	222 Seaman Ave.
CHARLES ROBB (1855–1904)	1877–88	195 Canal St.
	1888–1903	114 Centre St.
CLARENCE ROBB (1878–1956)	1902	214 East 46th St.
	1903	10 West 13th St.
	1904–05	329 West 24th St.
	1906	339 West 24th St.
	1908	345 West 49th St.
FREDERICK KAIFFER (DATES UNKNOWN)	1860–92	157 Wooster St.
HENRY F. METZLER (DATES UNKNOWN)	1857	191 Lewis
J. DENGLER (DATES UNKNOWN)	1870	21 Gay St.
WINTER LINDMARK (DATES UNKNOWN)	1863–70	241 South St.
JAMES A. BROOKS (1869–1937)	(*see* Chicago)	
	1897–1902	144 South 3rd St., Brooklyn
		Standard Show Figure Co.
	1903	144 South 3rd St., Brooklyn
	1910–37	Tampa, Florida (home)

Philadelphia, Pennsylvania

WILLIAM RUSH (1756–1833)	1800–33	172 North Front St.
SAMUEL H. SAILOR	1857	103 Harmony St.
(DATES UNKNOWN)	1885	128 South 2nd St.
JAMES BROWN (DATES UNKNOWN)	1883	717 Sansom St.
FRANCIS JACOB DEKER (? –1924)	1888	2332 Seybert St.
	1898	1435 North 29th St.

CHARLES J. HAMILTON (1832– ?)

(*see* Washington, D.C.)

1855	423 North 11th St.
1856	431 Ninth ab. Poplar
1857	783 Coates
1858	1214 Girard Ave.

Providence, Rhode Island

CHARLES DOWLER (1841–1931)

1869	84 Orange St.
1870	52 Pine St.
1871	56 Peck St.
1875	49 Peck St.
1875	581 Smith St. (home)
1896–1919	33 Eddy and
	47 Washington Sts.

Washington, D.C.

CHARLES J. HAMILTON (1832– ?)

(*see* Philadelphia)

1859	133 G St. North (home)
1859	East St. North about 13th St. West
1872	Charleston, South Carolina
1881	1536 I St. N.W.

PRICES PAID AT AUCTION

(The prices are the fair market value for the years indicated and do not reflect the current value)

PARKE-BERNET GALLERIES, INC., NEW YORK

The Haffenreffer Collection of Cigar-Store Indians and other American Trade Signs

Sale No. 1668, April 11, 1956   (Part One)

1.	Indian Squaw (32 inches on stand 4½ inches)	$ 300
2.	Indian Chief (41½ inches on stand 4½ inches)	300
3.	Negro Minstrel, cast metal (33½ inches)	500
4.	Indian Chief (47½ inches on stand 13 inches)	400
5.	Indian Squaw (34½ inches on stand 7¼ inches)	300
6.	Indian Squaw (34½ inches on stand 5 inches)	400
7.	Captain Jinks of the Horse Marines (42½ inches on stand 18½ inches)	1,150
8.	Indian Squaw (42½ inches on stand 6 inches)	325
9.	Punch (39 inches on stand 16 inches)	375
10.	Blackamoor (37 inches on stand 5 inches)	400
11.	Indian Squaw (42 inches on stand 4 inches)	425
12.	Indian Chieftain (42½ inches on stand 19½ inches)	325
13.	Indian Chief (59 inches on stand 8 inches)	1,025
14.	Indian Squaw (46 inches on stand 5½ inches)	375
15.	Indian Chief (46½ inches on stand 26½ inches)	450
16.	Indian Chief (48 inches on stand 18½ inches)	450
17.	Princess of the Ottawas (51 inches on stand 17 inches)	1,300
18.	Indian Squaw (49½ inches on stand 13¼ inches)	375
19.	Indian Brave (50 inches on stand 25½ inches)	400
20.	Belle of the Gay Nineties (49 inches on stand 12¾ inches)	600
21.	Race Track Tout (68 inches on stand 7½ inches)	800
22.	Indian Princess, Wm. Demuth/cast iron (52 inches)	400
23.	Indian Chief (52 inches on stand 15 inches)	450
24.	Indian Chief, cast iron (64 inches total height)	750
25.	Indian Squaw and Papoose, cast iron (66 inches total height)	1,200
26.	Indian Squaw (53 inches on stand 6 inches)	400
27.	Indian Chief (53½ inches on stand 9 inches)	350
28.	Indian Princess (56 inches on stand 6 inches)	350

29. Turk with Hookah (64½ inches on stand 8¾ inches) 600
30. Turkish Lady (66 inches on stand 4 inches) 350
31. Indian Chief (66 inches on stand 16½ inches) 425
32. Florentine Page, Wm. Demuth/cast metal (54 inches on stand 21½
    inches 725
33. Indian Chief (68 inches on stand 10 inches) 1,500
34. Indian Princess, Demuth/cast metal (69½ inches on stand 4 inches 1,100
35. Indian Chief (57 inches total height) 300
36. Turk (56 inches on stand 4 inches) 325
37. Indian Squaw (57 inches on base 24½ inches) 400
38. Rare Thin Indian Chief (66¼ inches on stand 6 inches) 2,050
39. Indian Squaw (58 inches total height) 350
40. Indian Squaw (58½ inches on stand 13½ inches) 350
41. Indian Chief (70 inches on stand 13½ inches) 1,400
42. Indian Princess (60 inches on stand 6½ inches) 450
43. Indian Warrior (61 inches on stand 7 inches) 425
44. Indian Chief Scouting (70½ inches on stand 8½ inches) 1,500
45. Indian Princess (72 inches on stand 7 inches) 900
46. Indian Chief (62 inches on stand 14½ inches) 300
47. Indian Princess (63 inches on stand 18½ inches) 500
48. Indian Brave (72 inches on stand 26 inches) 850
49. Indian Brave (62 inches on stand 26 inches) 475
50. Indian Princess (72 inches on stand 7½ inches) 1,900
51. Indian Chief (73 inches on stand 11 inches) 1,850
52. Indian Squaw and Papoose (68 inches on stand 2 inches) 700
53. Indian Chief (65 inches on stand 16½ inches) 650
54. Indian Chief (76 inches on stand 15 inches) 500
55. Punch (73 inches on stand 8½ inches) 350
56. Judy, Pantaloon or male clown (54 inches on stand 20 inches) . . 350
57. Indian Brave, Wm. Demuth/cast metal (75½ inches total height) . 1,050
58. Indian Princess (73 inches on stand 5 inches) 325
59. Indian Squaw (68 inches on stand 9 inches) 300
60. Indian Brave (70 inches on stand 13 inches) 475
61. Indian Chief (68 inches on stand 5 inches) 425
62. Indian Chief (66 inches on stand 14½ inches) 400
63. Indian Chief Scouting (63 inches on stand 5 inches) 425
64. Indian Brave (62½ inches on stand 6½ inches) 350
65. Black Joe (T. D. Rice as Jim Crow), (67 inches on stand 13 inches) . 1,100
66. Indian Chief (61 inches on stand 21½ inches) 400
67. Indian Brave, J. W. Fiske/cast metal (61 inches total height) . . 725
68. Indian Squaw (59 inches on stand 4½ inches) 275
69. Warrior with Spear (60 inches on stand 6 inches) 375
70. Indian Princess (65 inches on stand 12½ inches) 575
71. Indian Squaw (58 inches on stand 19 inches) 300
72. Indian Princess (57 inches on stand 21 inches) 450
73. Indian Chief (57 inches on stand 4 inches) 425
74. Aged Indian Chief, papier mâché (64½ inches on stand 6 inches) . 275
75. Indian Brave with Musket (67 inches on stand 7½ inches) . . . 1,300

76. Indian Squaw (57 inches on stand 4½ inches) 350
77. Indian Chief (56 inches on stand 4 inches) 275
78. Sultan (56 inches total height) 200
79. Indian Princess (63 inches on stand 9 inches) 425
80. Indian Scout (66 inches on stand 8¾ inches) 600
81. Indian Squaw (54 inches on stand 17¼ inches) 275
82. Indian Squaw (53 inches on stand 22 inches) 350
83. Jenny Lind (56 inches on stand 5 inches) 850
84. Gentleman of Fashion, Dundreary (61½ inches on stand 5½ inches) 1,900
85. Indian Chief, composition (53 inches on stand 11½ inches) . . . 300
86. Indian Chief (52½ inches on stand 5½ inches) 275
87. Indian Squaw (51½ inches on stand 5½ inches) 250
88. Sultan (54½ inches on stand 7¾ inches) 300
89. Indian Maiden, plaster (56 inches total height) 300
90. S. Florian (?) (49½ inches total height) 100
91. Indian Maiden (51 inches on stand 5 inches) 150
92. Indian Squaw (49 inches on stand 7 inches) 200
93. Blackamoor (48½ inches total height) 100
94. Nubian Warrior with Spear (54 inches total height) 425
95. Indian Squaw (45¾ inches total height) 250
96. Indian Chief (43½ inches on stand 4½ inches) 175
97. Blackamoor (39½ inches on stand 6½ inches) 225
98. Indian Squaw (34 inches on stand 5 inches) 225
99. Indian Chief (37½ inches on stand 6½ inches) 175
100. Indian Chief, plaster cast (29½ inches on stand 8½ inches) . . . 125

*The Haffenreffer Collection of Cigar-Store Indians
and other American Trade Signs*

Sale No. 1695, October 10, 1956   (Part Two)

1. Indian Squaw (29½ inches on stand 14½ inches) . . . . . . $ 90
2. Turkish Gentleman (29½ inches total height)   50
3. Nubian Page (39 inches total height)   80
4. Turk (39½ inches on stand 17½ inches)   130
5. Indian Princess (44 inches on stand 21½ inches)   130
6. Highland Chief (48 inches total height)   310
7. Merchant Captain (50½ inches total height)   400
8. Nubian Chief (44 inches total height)   170
9. Indian Princess (45 inches on stand 26½ inches)   350
10. Indian Princess (46 inches on stand 25½ inches)   285
11. Peace (57¼ inches total height)   225
12. Columbia, Goddess of Liberty (60 inches on stand 12 inches) . .   500
13. Indian Princess (45½ inches on stand 17½ inches)   285
14. Indian Squaw (46 inches on stand 21 inches)   150
15. Indian Princess (58 inches on stand 15 inches)   325
16. Indian Chief (61 inches on stand 13 inches)   350
17. Indian Squaw (49 inches total height)   420
18. Indian Chief (46 inches on stand 26½ inches)   160
19. Indian Chief (47½ inches on stand 12½ inches)   225
20. Jenny Lind (59 inches total height)   500
21. Negro Minstrel (61½ inches total height)   150
22. Demon Warrior with Spear (49 inches total height)   50
23. Turkish Gentleman (51½ inches on stand 13½ inches)   130
24. Indian Maiden (51 inches on stand 5½ inches)   150
25. Ringmaster (61 inches on stand 13½ inches) 2,000
26. Gypsy Maiden (64½ inches total height)   400
27. Indian Princess (55 inches on stand 15½ inches)   250
28. Indian Maiden (55½ inches on stand 9½ inches)   320
29. Indian Princess (55½ inches on stand 15 inches)   240
30. Aged Indian Chief with Bow, papier mâché (62½ inches total height)   310
31. Indian Warrior (54 inches on stand 7 inches)   375
32. Indian Princess (56½ inches on stand 14 inches)   225
33. Indian Chief (57 inches on stand 21½ inches)   200
34. Indian Princess (62 inches on stand 10½ inches)   250
35. Turkish Maiden, Moorish Queen painted plaster (63 inches total
   height)   125
36. Sultan (64 inches on stand 12 inches)   300
37. Indian Princess with Star Sceptre (57 inches on stand 23½ inches)   250
38. Indian Princess (57½ inches on stand 7 inches)   200
39. Indian Princess, Wm. Demuth/cast metal (59½ inches total height)   350
40. Clown (67 inches on stand 7 inches)   475

41. Indian Chief (69½ inches on stand 8½ inches) 600
42. Indian Princess (60 inches total height) 250
43. Indian Chief (60 inches on stand 10½ inches) 200
44. Indian Chief (61 inches total height) 250
45. Indian Princess (70 inches on stand 8 inches) 475
46. Indian Princess (61 inches on stand 20 inches) 250
47. Indian Chief Scouting (62 inches on stand 5 inches) 575
48. Indian Princess (62 inches on stand 16½ inches) 250
49. Turkish Woman (63 inches on stand 4 inches) 350
50. Indian Squaw and Papoose, Wm. Demuth/cast metal (71 inches on
    stand 6 inches) 550
51. Indian Chief Scouting (71 inches on stand 6 inches) 550
52. Indian Princess (63 inches total height) 275
53. Indian Maiden (65 inches on stand 11½ inches) 285
54. Indian Princess (68 inches on stand 4½ inches) 225
55. Indian Princess (74 inches total height) 500
56. Indian Scout (66 inches on stand 6 inches) 240
57. Indian Princess (66½ inches on stand 6½ inches) 200
58. Indian Princess (68 inches total height) 200
59. Indian Warrior (37½ inches total height) 120
60. Indian Scout, Wm. Demuth/ cast metal (78 inches total height) . . 325
61. Indian Group (36½ inches total height) 80
62. Two Indian Statuettes, painted plaster (25½ inches total height) . 60
63. Carved Pine Bust (20 inches on pedestal 25½ inches) 80
64. Two carved and Painted Totem Poles (25½ and 39½ inches) . . 80

*Early American Furniture & Folk Art—The Major Portion
of the Stock of Helena Penrose*

Sale No. 1948, February 5 and 6, 1960   (Part One)

Cigar-Store Indians, Ships' Figureheads and Carnival Figures

85.	Indian Chief (29 inches total height)	$ 160
86.	Angel Figurehead from the ship *Gloria* (47½ inches total height) .	250
87.	Minstrel (51 inches on stand 22½ inches)	525
88.	Flute Player: Circus Bandwagon Figure (67 inches on stand 9 inches)	650
89.	Indian Heads: Pair Insignia, Wild West Show, carved by Spanjer Bros., Newark, N.J. Now at the Shelburne Museum (38½ inches each)	ea. 225
90.	Indian Chief (56 inches on stand 17 inches)	375
90A.	Nymph (30 inches total height)	100
91.	Classical Maiden; Circus Bandwagon Figure (64 inches on stand 7 inches)	200
92.	Indian Warrior Chief (61 inches on stand 17 inches)	850
93.	Squaw with Papoose (67½ inches on stand 16½ inches)	1,100
94.	Indian Chief (75 inches on stand 8 inches)	850
95.	Indian Chief (72 inches on stand 21 inches)	1,000
(no 96.)		
97.	Indian Princess (69 inches on stand 23 inches)	400
98.	Liberty (89 inches on stand 7½ inches)	500
99.	Mrs. Godey, Girl of the Period (71 inches on stand 11 inches) . .	1,400
100.	Man of Fashion (72 inches on stand 10½ inches)	1,100
101.	Mephistopheles (63 inches total height)	500
102.	Indian Brave (75 inches on stand 10 inches)	250
103.	Indian Princess, Insigne (42 inches, 33 inches wide)	800
104.	Cuban Boy, Wm. Demuth & Co./cast metal (see Caffir Smoker) (30 inches total height)	275

Sale 1948

(Part Two)

284.	Indian Maiden cast metal (25¼ inches total height)	$ 275
285.	Indian Brave (33 inches total height)	100
286.	Mohawk Warrior, Ship's Figurehead (76 inches total height) . .	2,500
287.	Admiral Dewey, Ship's Figurehead (converted from tobacconist's figure) (56 inches on stand 20 inches)	3,300
288.	Indian Princess (56½ inches on stand 23 inches)	450
289.	Indian Warrior (67 inches on stand 9½ inches)	800
290.	Spread Eagle, Ship's Figurehead (52½ inches total height) . . .	225
291.	Negro Boy (42 inches total height)	200
292.	Indian Chief Scouting (61 inches on stand 22 inches)	650
293.	Punch (60 inches on stand 9½ inches)	1,000

293A. Indian Maiden, incised on base Robb. Carver, 114 Centre Street, N.Y.
    (57 inches on stand 21 inches)   350
294. Sir Walter Raleigh (67 inches on stand 20 inches)   700
295. Indian Princess (73 inches on stand 17 inches)   900
296. Henry Ward Beecher (62 inches on stand 8 inches)   425
297. Salem Girl, Ship's Figurehead (68 inches total height)   450
298. Indian Chief (69 inches on stand 11 inches)   400
299. Grenadier Guardsman (77 inches on stand 8½ inches) 1,000
300. Sultan (77 inches on stand 9½ inches)   800
300A. Captain Jinks of the Horse Marines (68 inches on stand 8 inches) . 1,100
301. Indian Chief (74 inches on stand 19 inches)   525
302. Indian Chief (71 inches on stand 8½ inches) 1,500

*Cigar-Store Indians, Property of the Estate
of the Late Edwin P. S. Newman,
Washington, D.C.*

Sale No. 2689, April 20, 1968

175.	Indian Scout (72 inches on stand 17 inches)	$3,400
176.	Squaw (39 inches on stand 6½ inches)	600
177.	Indian Chief (44 inches on stand 6 inches)	1,300
178.	Squaw (52 inches on stand 6 inches)	1,700
179.	Squaw (44 inches on stand 6 inches)	650
180.	Squaw (42 inches on stand 5½ inches)	1,100
181.	Itinerant Irishman (40 inches on stand 4 inches)	550
182.	Indian (50 inches on stand 6½ inches)	800
183.	Squaw (57 inches on stand 7 inches)	1,100
184.	Indian Hunter (53 inches on stand 4½ inches)	950
185.	Squaw (45 inches on stand 18 inches)	700
186.	Indian Chief (58 inches on stand 5 inches)	1,600
187.	Indian Maiden (78 inches on stand 8 inches)	1,300
188.	Pair of Indians, European (35 and 36 inches each)	pr. 700
189.	Indian Chief (62 inches on stand 10 inches)	4,100
190.	Squaw (57½ inches on stand 19 inches)	1,400
191.	Squaw (65 inches on stand 9½ inches)	800
192.	Squaw (76 inches on stand 2½ inches)	1,400
193.	Eastern Star (59½ inches on stand 7½ inches)	600
194.	Indian (73 inches on stand 4½ inches)	1,100
195.	Theatrical Figure (56½ inches on stand 4½ inches)	650
196.	Indian (30 inches on stand 1 inch)	750
197.	Squaw (62 inches on stand 13 inches)	850
198.	Squaw (62 inches on stand 18 inches)	900
199.	Indian Hunter (75 inches on stand 7 inches)	1,200
200.	Indian Hunter (60 inches on stand 11 inches)	1,500
201.	Indian Chief (50 inches on stand 4½ inches)	1,100
202.	Indian Chief (60 inches on stand 18 inches)	1,050
203.	Indian Chief (69 inches on stand 4 inches)	800
204.	Squaw (63 inches on stand 10½ inches)	1,100
205.	Indian Hunter (52 inches on stand 8 inches)	900
206.	Squaw (70½ inches on stand 11½ inches)	1,400
207.	Squaw, Wm. Demuth/ cast metal (62 inches on stand 1 inch)	1,300
208.	Indian Hunter (46 inches on stand 22 inches)	600
209.	Squaw (55 inches on stand 19 inches)	650
210.	Indian Warrior (30½ inches on stand 20½ inches)	700
211.	Indian Warrior (45 inches on stand 4½ inches)	1,600
212.	Squaw (34 inches on stand 4 inches)	500
213.	Indian (52 inches on stand 4½ inches)	850
214.	Indian Hunter (54 inches on stand 4½ inches)	1,500

COLLECTIONS OF
SHOW FIGURES

The Abby Aldrich Rockefeller Folk Art Collection. Williamsburg, Virginia.
The Albany Institute of History and Art. Albany, New York.
Chicago Historical Society. Chicago, Illinois.
Edison Institute. Dearborn, Michigan.
Everhart Museum. Scranton, Pennsylvania.
Henry Ford Museum and Greenfield Village. Dearborn, Michigan.
Henry Francis du Pont Winterthur Museum. Winterthur, Delaware.
Historical Society of Berks County. Reading, Pennsylvania.
Long Island Historical Society. Brooklyn, New York.
Maryland Historical Society. Baltimore, Maryland.
Mercer Museum and Bucks County Historical Society. Doylestown, Pennsylvania.
Merritt's Museum of Early Americana. Douglasville, R. 2, Pennsylvania.
Musée du Quebéc. Quebec, P.Q. Canada.
Museum of American Folk Art. New York, New York.
Museum of the City of New York. New York, New York.
Newark Museum. Newark, New Jersey.
New York Historical Association. Cooperstown, New York.
New-York Historical Society. New York, New York.
Rhode Island Historical Society. Providence, Rhode Island.
Shelburne Museum. Shelburne, Vermont.
Staten Island Historical Society. Staten Island, New York.
The Van Alstyne Folk Art Collection. Smithsonian Institution. Washington, D.C.
Virginia Museum of Fine Arts. Richmond, Virginia.
Western Reserve Historical Society. Cleveland, Ohio.

BIBLIOGRAPHY

Books

Albion, Robert G.	*The Rise of New York Port*. New York: Scribners' Sons Ltd., 1939
Anonymous	*Detroit Today: The City of the Strait*. Detroit: Phoenix Publishing Company, 1893.
————	*Picturesque Chicago and Guide to the World's Fair*. Hartford: D. S. Mosely, 1893.
————	*Sculpture Traditionelle du Quebec*. Quebec: Musée du Quebéc, 1967.
————	*Tobacco Trade Directory, 1872–73*.
Apperson, G. L.	*The Social History of Smoking*. New York: Putnam, 1916.
Armstrong, Perry A.	*The Sauks and the Black Hawk War*. Springfield: H. W. Bokker, 1887.
Bain, John Jr.	*Tobacco in Song and Story*. New York: H. M. Caldwell Co., 1896.
Baker, Sir Richard	*A Chronicle of the Kings of England*. London: Daniel Frere, 1643.
Barbeau, Marius	*Louis Jobin, Statuaire*. Montreal: Libraire Beauchemin, 1968.
Barbour, J. E.	*The Jim Crow Song Book*, 1847. (Library of Congress, Music Division.)
Besant, Sir Edward	*London, North of the Thames*. London: A & C Black, 1911.
Blunt	*Strangers' Guide to the City of New York*. New York: J. Seymour Printer, 1817.
Bolton, Theodore, and Cortelyou, Irwin F.	*Ezra Ames of Albany*. New York: New-York Historical Society, 1955.
Boyd, W. H.	*New York City Tax Book, 1856–57*. New York: Boyd, 1857.
Brathwait, Richard	*Smoking Age or The Life and Death of Tobacco*. London: E. Griffin, 1617.

Brewington, M. V.   *Shipcarvers of North America*. Barre, Massachusetts: Barre Publishing Co., 1962.

Brown, Henry Collins   *Valentine's Manual of Old New York, 1927*. New York: Brown, 1916–1928.

Chambers, John W.   *A Condensed History of the American Institute of the City of New York and Its Exhibition*. New York: 1892 (pamphlet).

Chapman, Dennis   *Economic History Review*. Glasgow: 1940.

Christensen, Erwin O.   *Early American Wood Carving*. Cleveland: World Publishing Co., 1952.

Clark, Arthur H.   *The Clipper Ship Era*. New York: Putnam's Sons, 1910.

Conover, Richard E.   *The Affairs of James A. Bailey*. Xenia: R. E. Conover, 1957.

————   *The Telescoping Tableaus*. Xenia: R. E. Conover, 1956.

————   *The Great Forepaugh Show*. Xenia: R. E. Conover, 1959.

————   *The Fielding Bandchariots*. Xenia: R. E. Conover, 1969.

DeLeeuw, R. M.   *Both Sides of Broadway*. New York: DeLeeuw-Riehl Publishing Co., 1910.

Dickens, Charles   *Dombey & Son*. New York: Crowell & Co., 1928.

Dodge, Robert   *Tristam Dodge and his Descendents in America*. New York: J. J. Little & Co., 1886.

Dunlap, William   *History of the Arts of Design in the United States*. Boston: E. E. Goodspeed & Co., 1918.

Dunshee, Kenneth H.   *As You Pass By*. New York: Hastings House, 1952.

Durant, John and Alice   *A Pictorial History of the American Circus*. New York: A. S. Barnes & Co., 1957.

Earle, Alice Morse   *Stage-Coach and Tavern Days*. New York: The Macmillan Company, 1900.

Gleichen, Edward   *London's Open Air Statuary*. London: Longman, Green and Co., Ltd., 1928.

Gottesman, Rita Susswein *The Arts and Crafts in New York*. New York: The New-York Historical Society. Vol. 1 (1726–1776), 1936; Vol. 2 (1777–1799), 1948; Vol. 3 (1800–1804), 1949.

Greenwood, Isaac J.   *The Circus: Its Origin and Growth Prior to 1835*. New York: Dunlap Society, 1898.

Griffiths, John W.   *Treatise on Marine and Naval Architecture*. London: G. Philip & Son, 1860.

Hall, Edward Hagaman   *The Hudson-Fulton Celebration 1909: Fourth Annual Report of the Hudson-Fulton Celebration Commission*. Albany: J. B. Lyon Company, 1910.

Hammerstein, Oscar (comp.)   Cigar & Tobacco Manufacturing Directory, 1882–1883.

Haswell, Charles H.   *Reminiscences of An Octogenarian of the City of New York (1816–1860)*. New York: Harper & Brothers, 1897.

Hayward, Victoria	*Romantic Canada*. Toronto: The Macmillan Company, 1922.
Hermann, Robert K.	*Tobacco and Americans*. New York: McGraw-Hill Book Company Inc., 1960.
Hutchins, J. G. B.	*The American Maritime Industries and Public Policy*. Cambridge: Harvard University Press, 1936.
Hutton, Lawrence	*Curiosities of the American Stage*. "Negroes on the Stage." New York: Harpers & Bros., 1891.
Kouwenhoven, John A.	*Columbia Historical Portrait of New York*. New York: Doubleday & Company, 1953.
Larwood, Jacob and Hotten, John Camden	*The History of Signboards*. London: Chatto and Windus, Ltd., 1884.
Lewis-Hind, Henriette	*Gari Melchers, Painter*. New York: W. E. Rudge, 1928.
Lipman, Jean	*American Folk Art in Wood, Metal and Stone*. Meriden, Conn.: Pantheon, 1948.
Magnen, Johann Chrysostone	*Exercitations De Tobaco*. Pavia: Giovanni Andrea Magri, 1648.
Marceau, Henri	*William Rush*. Philadelphia: Pennsylvania Museum, 1937.
Marvin, Winthrop L.	*American Merchant Marine, 1620–1902*. New York: 1902.
Maury, John	*Handbook of the Prince Consort National Memorial*. London: 1882.
McCabe, James D.	*The Illustrated History of the Centennial Exhibition*. Philadelphia: National Publishing Co., 1876.
McKechnie, Samuel	*Popular Entertainment Through the Ages*. London: Sampson Low, Marston & Co., Ltd.
Morley, Henry	*Memoirs of Bartholomew Fair*. London: Chapman & Hall, Ltd., 1859.
Morrison, John H.	*History of New York Shipyards*. New York: Wm. F. Sametz & Co., 1909.
Murphy, Hon. John McLeod	*American Ships and Ship Builders*. New York: Chas. W. Baker, 1860.
Pendergast, A. W. and Ware, W. Porter	*Cigar Store Figures in American Folk Art*. Chicago: Lightner, 1953.
Pinckney, Pauline A.	*American Figureheads and Their Carvers*. New York: Norton, 1940.
Pope, Alexander	*An Essay on Man*. Portland: William Hude, 1843.
Pougin, Arthur	*Dictionnnaire du Théâtre*. Paris: Librairie de Firmin-Didot et Cie, 1885.
Reynolds, Harry	*Minstrel Memories*. London: Alston Rivers Ltd., 1928.
Rice, Edward Leroy	*Monarchs of American Minstrelsy*. New York: Kenny Publishing Co., 1911.
Ritter, Abraham	*Philadelphia and Her Merchants*. Philadelphia: Ritter, 1860.

Ross, Peter	*A History of Long Island*. New York: Lewis Publishing Company, 1902.
Ruggles, Edward W.	*A Picture of New York in 1846*. New York: C. S. Francis & Company, 1846.
Sanborn, Kate	*Hunting Indians in a Taxi-Cab*. Boston: Gorham Press, 1911.
Sand, Maurice	*The History of Harlequinade*. London: Martin Secker, 1915.
Smith, Matthew Hale	*Sunshine and Shadow in New York*. Hartford: J. D. Brown & Co., 1869.
Stiles, Henry R.	*History of Kings County*. New York: W. W. Munsell & Co., 1884.
Stokes, I. N. Phelps	*Iconography of Manhattan Island*. New York: R. H. Dodd, 1915–1928.
Tuckerman, Bayard	*The Diary of Philip Hone*. New York: Dodd, Mead & Company, 1889.
Ulmann, Albert	*A Landmark History of New York*. New York: D. Appleton-Century Company, 1939.
Watson, J. F.	*Annals of Philadelphia and Pennsylvania in the Olden Times*. Philadelphia: E. L. Carey and A. Hart, 1850.
Wingate, General Geo. W.	*History of the Twenty-Second Regiment National Guard*. New York: E. W. Dayton, 1896.
Wietek, Dr. Gerd	*Galionsfiguren*. Hamburg-Altona: Th. Dingwort & Sohn, 1961.
Woodward, T. R.	*Dodge Genealogy*. Chicago: Lanward Publishing Co., 1904.

Magazines

American Collector Magazine
Eberlein, Harold Donaldson, and Hubbard, Cortlandt Van Dyke. "The Cigar Store Indian and His Competitors." February 1938.

Antiques
Howe, Florence T. "Carved Wood Circus Wagon Figures." August 1947.
Jessup, L. F. "The Tabocconists' Tribe of Treen." September 1930.
Shaw, Charles G. "Black Boys and Their Playfellows." March 1934.
———. "Speaking of Wooden Indians." September 1939.
Swan, Mabel M. "Boston Carvers and Joiners." March 1948.

Illustrations: Vols. 18, 223–235; 20, 221; 23, 42; 25, 101–103, 114; 27, 239; September 1947, 166; December 1951, 528.

Auction
Fried, Frederick. "American Cigar Store Indians." June 1968.

Bandwagon
Conover, Richard E. "The Allegorical Pony-Drawn Parade Floats." September–October 1960.
———. "The European Influence on the American Circus Parade." July–August 1961.

Canadian Cigar & Tobacco Journal. Toronto, Canada. January 1903.

Canadian Magazine
   Hayward, Victoria. "Jobin, The Wood-Carver." December 1922.

Canadian Review
   Barbeau, Marius. "An Old Carver of Saints on the Beaupré Coast."

Canadian Review of Music and Art
   Barbeau, Marius. "Louis Jobin." January 1946.

Epoch, The
   "Highways and Byways." September 5, 1890.

Grit
   "Flat Wooden Indian Made of Carved Pine." February 2, 1969.

Harper's New Monthly Magazine
   Sheldon, G. W. "The Old Ship-Builders of New York." Vol. 65 (July 1882).
   "The Old Packet and Clipper Service." Vol. 68 (January 1884).

Harper's Weekly
   "Cartoon of Indian and Policeman." December 22, 1883.
   "Italian Image Makers of New York." February 27, 1869.
   "Wood-Carving." January 6, 1883.
   "The Montreal Ice Carnival." February 3, 1883.

Hobbies Magazine
   Allen, Mabel. "The Forgotten Man." January 1939.

House & Garden
   Shaw, C. G. "My Little Indians." May 1948.

Independent Woman
   Helm, F. "She Put Wooden Indians Back to Work." April 1949.

International Studio
   "Early American Wood Sculpture." October 1927.

Le Canada Français
   Barbeau, Marius. "Côté, sculpteur." October 1942.

Le Soleil
   Barbeau, Marius. "Louis Jobin, Statuaire." June 10, 1945.

Lippincott's
   Gilliams, E. Leslie. "A Philadelphia Sculptor." August 1893.

Magazine of Art
   Weitenkampf, Frank W. "Wooden Indians." December 1948.

Nation, The
   "Modern Women and What is Said of Them." October 22, 1868.

News From Home
   Dunshee, Kenneth H. "Happy Hunting Ground." Winter 1957.

Photo Magazine
   ". . . Bit The Dust." December 1937.

Realm of Marvel
   Barnum & Bailey, Ltd., "Superb Pageantry." March 1904.

Saturday Review
   Redfield, J. R. "Girl of the Period." October 22, 1868.

Science News Letter
    Davis, E. C. "Wooden Indians." November 13, 1937.

Scribner's Magazine
    Morrison, J. L. "The Passing of the Wooden Indian." October 1928.
    ———. "Poor Lo Still Active" (Letters). January 1929.

Scribner's Monthly
    King, Edward. "The Liverpool of America." March 1875.
    Farnum, Charles H. "A Day on the Docks." May 1879.
    Mayer, Frank B. "Signs & Symbols." September 1879.

Tobacco
    "Designed By Whittling Yankees." May 14, 1886.
    "Manufacture of Dummy Indians." November 12, 1886.
    "The Tobacconist's Sign." April 8, 1887.
    "Death of Edward Hen." May 6, 1887.
    "Jersey Jim Campbell." January 11, 1888.
    "Lo Takes a Spring Suit." April 12, 1889.
    "A Stogie Display At Newark." November 27, 1896.

Tobacco Leaf
    "Demuth's Exhibit of Figures at Centennial." July 1876.

United States Tobacco Journal
    Clements, George. "Olney." May 2, 1936.
    "Death of Leopold Demuth Brings To Close Brilliant Chapter in Pipe Industry History." April 24, 1943.

Newspaper Articles

L'Action Catholique (Canada)
    "Nouvelles toiles au Musée." August 9, 1949.
    "Pour le Musée de la Province." March 15, 1948.

Albany-Gazette (New York)
    Caldwell & Solomons advertisement. January 13, 1820.

Baltimore *Evening Sun*
    "Chief Six Cigars is Given New Coat of War Paint." March 15, 1927.
    "Cigar Store Indian Becomes a Museum Relic." May 14, 1926.
    "Historical Society Gets Two Wooden Indians." February 5, 1953.
    "I Remember the Heydey of the Wooden Indian." December 4, 1966.
    "Lo, Wooden Indian Goes to Historical Tepee." October 29, 1952.
    "Lo's Creator." n.d.
    "Lo's Missing Arm, Cigars and Tomahawk Recovered." February 22, 1927.
    "100 Cigar Store Indians Bring $54,700 at New York Auction." April 12, 1956.
    "Watcha Looking at Mister." December 6, 1932.
    "Wooden Indian Here Sees Others Do Scalping Now." March 29, 1923.
    "Wooden Indian Keeps Lonely Vigil Down in Little Italy." November 16, 1926.
    "Wooden Indians of Baltimore." October 25, 1943.

Baltimore *Morning Sun*
    "Eight Hundred Wooden Indians—And Then There Were Eight." February 17, 1947.
    "Goes Alien Indian One Better with Statue Carved in New York." May 18, 1926.
    "Traditional Cigar Store Wooden Indian Not Extinct in Baltimore." December 19, 1921.
    "Wouldn't It Be Nice to Have a Wooden Indian." November 30, 1958.

Le Canada Français (?) (Quebec)
   Barbeau, Marius. "Côté, Sculpteur." Vol. 30, No. 2 (October 1942).

Detroit *Free Press*
   January 15, 1876.
   September 28, 1871.

Detroit *News-Tribune*
   Greusel, John Hubert. "Art's Sake! Sculptor Julius Melchers on Sacrifices."
   August 22, 1897.
   Junkin, J. H. "The Wooden Indian is Passing Away." July 23, 1899.

Detroit *News*
   "Apoplexy Takes Julius Melchers." January 15, 1908.
   Catlin, George B. "Old Detroit Artists Found Trade Dull but Market for
      Wooden Indians Brisk." January 4, 1925.
   "Julius Melchers Suffers a Stroke." May 30, 1907.
   "Lo the Indian is Pretty Low." April 10, 1934.

The Evening Citizen (Ottowa, Canada)
   "What Has Become of Old Store Signs?" April 14, 1934.

Fremont *News-Messenger* (Ohio)
   "Tecumseh, the Wooden Indian." October 24, 1956.

Gazette de Quebec (Canada)
   "Neptune Inn." May 11, 1809.
   "William Arrowsmith." December 21, 1809.

Mon Clocher (Canada)
   "Louis Jobin." September 1, 1968.

The New York Times
   Schwartz, Marvin D. "Lo, The High-Priced Indian." April 27, 1968.
   Weitenkampf, Frank W. "Lo, the Wooden Indian; The Art of Making Cigar-
      shop Signs." August 3, 1890.
   ———. "Some Signs and Others—Sign Painters and Sign Painting Artists."
      July 3, 1892.
   "Queries for Times Readers. The Tobacco Shop Indian." March 12, 1916.
   "First Wooden Indian." May 2, 1926.
   April 9, 1916.
   May 4, 1926.

Philadelphia *Bulletin*
   "Resolution to Purchase Figure of Washington from William Rush." Septem-
      ber 9, 1831

Philadelphia *Evening Telegraph*
   "An Appreciation" (by a shipcarver). n.d.

Philadelphia *Inquirer*
   Brady, Francis X. "Legend Bites Dust." January 11, 1962.
   Cole, Ann Kilborn. "When Indians Sold Cigars." November 15, 1964.
   "Questions and Answers." June 6, 1966.

Philadelphia *Ledger*
   "Miss Rush Visits in the City." June 6, 1915.

Philadelphia *Public Ledger*
   "Art News of the Week." n.d.

Philadelphia *Times*
   Gilliams, E. Leslie. "A Pioneer Sculptor." June 26, 1892.
   ———. "Cigar Store Indians." December 18, 1892. Illustrated.

Providence *Evening Bulletin* (Rhode Island)
    "Charles Dowler, Sculptor, Dead." January 25, 1931.
    "Smith Street Couple Married 60 Years." n.d.

Le Semanier Paroissial (Canada)
    "Louis Jobin." September 1, 1968.

Le Soleil (Canada)
    Barbeau, Marius. "Louis Jobin, Statuaire." June 10, 1945.

Tacoma *News-Tribune* (Washington)
    Anderson, Lenny. "Seattle Pays Big Heap Wampum to Lure Chief Tacoman
        for 58 years." October 9, 1946.
    Hunt, Herman. "Legendary Pioneer Owner of Tacoma Cigar Store Passes at
        90; Sold his Famous 'Indian' Last Year." November 10, 1947.
    James, Dave. "He's No. 1 Indian Chief." February 13, 1937.

Tacoma *News-Tribune and Sunday Ledger*
    "The Chief is Missing." August 25, 1968.

Tacoma *Times*
    "Chief Skookum." February 11, 1937.

Washington *Star* (Seattle)
    "Cigar Store Indian Becomes a Valuable Relic." August 21, 1932.

Manuscripts and Files

Circus World Museum. Baraboo, Wisconsin.
    Files and Records

Cooper Union. New York City
    Annual Reports of the Trustees
    Attendance Records

Department of Health. New York City
    Death Certificates

Department of the Navy. Washington, D.C.
    Miscellaneous Letters, Proposals, etc.
    Naval Records

Les Pères Redemptoristes. Ste. Anne de Beaupré
    Files
    Les Livres des Comtes et Deliberations

Library of Congress. Washington, D.C.
    U.S. Patent Office Records

Marriage License Bureau, Municipal Building. New York City.
    Marriage Certificates

National Academy of Design. New York City.
    Student Records

National Gallery of Art. Washington, D.C.
    Index of American Design

New-York Historical Society. New York City
    Annual Reports, Board of Trustees
    Bella H. Landau Collections

New York Historical Association. Cooperstown, New York.

Peabody Museum. Salem, Massachusetts
Fernald & Pettigrew Papers

Princeton University Library. Princeton, New Jersey
McCaddon Collection

Shelburne Museum. Shelburne, Vermont.
Acquisition Lists

Smithsonian Institution. Washington, D.C.
Division of Cultural History Files
Growth of the United States Files

Surrogates Court (formerly Hall of Records). New York City
Finance and Taxation
Judgments
Probate
Real Estate

Miscellaneous Private Files

Braecklein Papers
Frank J. Deker Letter
Demuth Papers
Dowler Files
Fiske Records
S. M. Frank & Co. Records
L. C. Hegarty Papers
Mrs. Wilbur L. Martin Papers
Edwin P. S. Newman Records
Robb Papers
Teubner Records
John Philip Yaeger Files

CITY DIRECTORIES

Ashland, Wisconsin.
Baltimore, Maryland.
Boston, Massachusetts.
Brooklyn, New York.
Charleston, South Carolina.
Chicago, Illinois.
Detroit, Michigan.
Gloucester, Massachusetts.
Lancaster, Pennsylvania.
Montreal, Canada.
Newark, New Jersey.
New York, New York.
Philadelphia, Pennsylvania.
Providence, Rhode Island.
Quebec, Canada.
Ste. Anne de Beaupré, Quebec, Canada.
Tampa, Florida.
Tiffin, Ohio.
Washington, D.C.

INDEX

Page numbers in *italics* refer to illustrations. *"Col."* refers to color section.

Adam and Eve, 82, 154, 211
Adams, 119
Admiral Vernon Tavern, 14
Africa (show figure), 46
Africa (tableau), 103, *105,* 218, 219, *220,* 222
Aidala, V., Tobacco Store, 156
Albany, 15, 16, 173
Albany *Gazette & Daily Advertiser,* 15, *17*
Ali Baba and the Forty Thieves, 100
Allard, Pite, 157
Aloha, 236
America (tableau), 103, *104,* 218, *220, 221*
American Institute, 33, 34, 40, 63, 194
American Revolution, The (spectacle), 100
American Tobacco Company, 59
Ames, Ezra, 16, 17
Amsterdam, 137, 231
    Turk (show figure), 12
Anderson, Jacob & Co., 241
Anderson, Jacob S., 175, 193, 194, 241, 242
    David Crockett (figurehead), 241
Anderson, John W., 241–42
    Great Admiral (figurehead), 242
    show figures, 242
Apollonicon, 89
Armamaxa (circus wagon), 87
Art Establishment (foundry), 62
Ashland (Wisconsin), 153–54
Asia Tableau, 103, 218 219, *221*
Auction of figures, 270–77
Auger, Elzéar, 166
Automatodeon, 89
Averbeck, Ferdinand, 150
Aztec, 105

Bacchus, 45, 71
Bailey, James A., 93, 100, 101, 113, 217
Balduc, Edmond, 160
Baltimore (Maryland), 7, 18, 81, 83, 119, 125–34
    Indian, 20, *21*
    shipcarvers of, 4
    signs, 125
Bandwagon No. 1, 93
Bangetor, Mary, 139
Baraboo (Wisconsin), *97, 98,* 99, 106, 112, *113,* 204
Barbeau, Marius, 163, 164, 239

Barnum, Bailey and Hutchinson, 93, 94
    carvings
        1883, *207*
        Robb's shop, 204, 205
Barnum, P. T., 93, 99, 100, 211
Barnum & Bailey, 94, 97, 100, 105, 107, 108, 217
    wagons, *98a,* 109, 222
Barnum & Bailey, Ltd., 100, 101, 217, 218, 219
Barnum & London, 93, 97, 203, 206
    carvings, T. J. White, 182
    Robb's corner figures, 50
Barth, Charles, 183
Bartholdi, 210
"Bartholomew Fair," 12, 86
Baseball Hall of Fame, 212, *213*
Baseball player, 78, 79, *197,* 210, 212, 226, 227, *col.*
Baxter, 148
Beauport, 165
Beauty and the Beast, 100
Beecher, Laban S., 174, 178
Bell, J., 102
Bell, R. and E., 125
Belinguet, Bonhomme, 157
Berlinguet, François-Xavier, 157, 158, 165
Berlinguet, Thomas, 157
Bertrand, Narcisse, 157
Bids, Mr., 119
Black Ball Line, 4, 5
Black Bear, The, 125
Black Boys (*also* Virginians), 10, 11, 12, 13, 166, 170
Blackhawk, 125, 139, 147
Bluebeard, 97, *98,* 99, 211
Bolton, John. *See* Boulton, William
Bon Pasteur, Le, 158
Boston, 4, 7, 18, 25, 59, 181, 198
Bostonian Society, 14, *15*
Boulton, William, 158, 238–39
Bowery Amphitheatre, 87
Bowery Girls (show figures), 78, *235*
Brathwait, Richard, 12, *13*
Brebeuf, Le Père de, 159
Bridgeport (Connecticut), 106, 107, 108, 206, 222
Brintzlinghofer, W. A., 82
Brooklyn (New York), 49, 63, 78, 173, 238
Brooklyn Bridge, *2,* 178, 185, 239

Brooks, Thomas V., 23, 81, 82, 87, 93, 178, 181, 182–93, 194, 202, 243
  circus carvings, 87, *90*, 93
  New York–Chicago Carving Co., *186*
  show figures
    at auction, 238
    Baseball Player, *213*
    Indian, *184, 190, 233*
    Jack Tar, *187*
    leaners, 23, 67, *183*, 185
    Negro, 184
    New York policeman, 193
    Osceola, 82
    Scout, *187*
    Squaw, *186*
    "Skookum," *191*
Brother Jonathan (show figure), 123, *124*, 139, *col.*
Brown, Charles, 231, 243–46
Brown, Henry Collins, 210
Brown, James, 122
Brown, John, 119, 125
Brown, William H., 5
Brown & Williamson Tobacco Corporation, 44
Browning King & Co., 100
Buberl, Casper, 56, 64
Buchanan, Fred, 107
Buckley and Wicks Circus, 86
Buffalo Bill, 55, 123, 154
Buffalo Bill Wild West Shows, 100, 154
Bush & Trexler, 124

Cadet (show figure), 227
Caffir Smoker (show figure), 55
Caldwell & Solomons, 15, 17
California, 4, 5, 6, *235*
Callanan, Richard, 134
Campbell, James, 134
Canada, 82, 105, 107, 157–70
Canvas Back, 125
Cape May (New Jersey), 231, *236*
Captain Jack (show figure), 50, 78, 145, 146, 188, 190
Captain Jinks (show figure), 44, 193, 198, *199*
Captain Jinks of the Horse Marines, 198, 200, 201
Captain Smith's Rescue (tableau), 100, *110*
Carpeaux, Jean Baptiste, 137
Carrier Dove, 125
Castle Garden, 34, 63, 158
Catlin, George, 80, 147, 148
Cavalier (show figure), *44*
Center Square Water Works, 119
Charles H. Marshall, 6
"Charleston Square," 137
Chesapeake, 117
Chestnut Street Theatre, 117, *118*
Chichester, James M., 29, 30, 32, 87, 177, 178, 183
Chinaman (show figure), 49, 65, 66

Chinese, 34, 35, 162, *163*
Chinese Woman (show figure), 70, *229*
Christoval, Don, 38
Christy, George, 106
Cinderella, 97, *98*, 99, 211, *col.*
Circus, 89, 90, 91, 93, 100, 107, 112, 113, 204, 206
  bandwagons, 80, 87, 90, 91, 110, 112, 179
  Bridgeport winter quarters, 106, 107, 108, 206, 222
  carvers. *See* Brooks; Cromwell; Robb; Spanjer Brothers; White
  dens, 94
  destruction of, 99, 108
  museums
    Circus Hall of Fame, *107*, 108
    Circus World Museum, *94, 97, 98*, 99, 106, 112, *113*, 204
    Ringling Circus Museum, *93*
    Shelburne Museum, *207*
  private collections, 206, *208, 209*
  publication, 108
  tableaux, 50, 87, *88*, 91, *92*, 93, 96, 100, 108, *109*, 110, 204, *205*, 211, 218, 219, 222
  wagon builders. *See* Fielding Brothers; Sebastian; Stephenson
Circus Maximus, *86*
City of Glasgow, 6
Civil War, 7, 32, 41, 53, 63, 127, 139, 140, 154, 183
Cole Brothers Circus, 99
Collins, Harry, 243
Collins, Nicholas E., 185, 242–43
Collins & Brown, 243, 244
Collins line, 6
Collyer Monument, 156
Colossal Car of the Muses, 89
Columbia (show figure), 54, *59*, 93, 105, 154
Columbian Exposition, 59, 193
Columbian Hose Company, 198, 199
Columbus, Christopher, 9, 10, 110, 193
Comedy and Tragedy (show figures), 117
Comical Bust (show figure), 53
Congress, 117
Constellation, 117, 125
Constitution, 80, 174
Cooper, James E., 93
Cooper & Bailey, 100
Cooper Union, 34, 195
Cooperstown (New York), 20, 145, 185, 212
Côté, Claude, 166, 167, *169*
Côté, Jean-Baptiste, 165–69
Côté, Laure, 166, 167
Cotton Exposition, 59
Cromwell, John L., 23, 178–81, 183, 243
  carvings
    at auction, 238
    circus, 87, *88*, 179, 180

ship, 5, 179
  signed, 198
  show figures, *180*, 181
Crongeyer, Theodore, 150–51
Crongeyer & Averbeck, 150
Crowninshield, Jacob, 86
Crusoe, Robinson, 35, 99
Crystal Palace, 63, 137
Currier & Ives, 42
Cutbush, Edward, 116

Darkey, 66
David Crockett, 241
Davie, Howard, 100
Deker, Francis Jacob, 124
Demuth, Christopher, 14
Demuth, William, 28, 32–61, 62 ,63, 75, 123,
    181, 183, 193, 194, 197, 212
  cast-metal figures, 33, 61, 65, 70, 73, 188,
    204
  pipe sign, 60
  show-figure catalogue, *39–57*, 64
Demuth Tobacco Shop, 14
Detroit, 4, 81, 137–52
Dewey, Admiral George, 225
Dewey, Samuel W., 174
Dibblee, Henry, Iron Works, 75, 188, *190*
Dixey, George, 173
Dodge & Sharpe, 174
Dodge, Charles J., 5, 83, 173–77, 239, 241
  figurehead design, 80
  Jackson head for *Constitution*, 174
  Jim Crow, *8*, 26, 177
  portrait of father, 83, 175
  seated Indian, *176*
Dodge, Jeremiah, 5, 18, 83, 173, 174, 175
Donaldson, John M., 141
Dowler, Charles Parker, 154–56
Dressmaker's figure, *230*
Dreves, F., 134
Drowne, Shem, 14
Druggist's sign, *135*
Drum Major (show figure), 123, *124, 202*
Dude (show figure), 78, 79, 201, 227, *230,
    231*
Duffield, D. Bethune, 143
Dundreary (show figure), 57, 79, 124, 202,
    227, *231*
Dupont, Oscard, 162
Dutch Tobacco Shop, *12*
Dwight & Davis, 171

Eagles, 55, *244, col.*
Eakins, Thomas, 119
East River, 3, 4, 5, 182, 185, 208
Eckford, Henry, 173
Edel, Alfred, 100
Ehret, George, 96
Eldredge, Captain Herman, 179
Elliott, Jesse D., 174
Emma Giles, 134
Ericsson, 7

Europa and the Bull, 103, 114, 219
Europe (tableau), *102*, 114, 218, 219, *220*

Fairmount Park, *17*, 18
Fairmount Water Works, 119
Faith, Hope, and Charity, 119
Falcon, 5
Fall of Nineveh (tableau), 100
Farragut, Admiral David Glasgow, 242
Female busts, 57
Female Indian with spear, *56*
Fernald & Pettigrew, 175, 178, 179
Fielding & Schuchman, 95
Fielding Brothers, 90–95, 96
  1856–1867 circus wagons, 90, 91
  1867–1877 circus wagons, 91
  1877–1882 circus wagons, 93, 94
Fireman (show figure), 198, *199*, 216
Fiske, J. W., 64, 65, 73
  metal-show figures, 45, 62, 65, *66, 67, 68,
    69, 70, 71, 72*
Fitch, B., 216
Five Graces, 91
Flanagan, John, 83
Flat board (show figure), 18, 19, *20*
Fleckenstein, Max, 64
Flying Childers, 125
Foble, A. J., 18, *121*
Foley, J. H., 102
Forepaugh, Adam, 50, 91, 93, 96, 100, 182,
    202, 204, *205*, 211
Forepaugh Globe (tableau), *92*, 93, 96
Forrest, Edwin, 210
Forrest, Edwin, Home for Aged Actors, 117
Forty-Niner, show figure, 123
Foundries, 62–65, 73, 74, 75
Fowle, Isaac, 18, 178
Franconi, Antoine, 89
Freeman, Samuel T. & Company, 136
French, J. M. and Company Circus, 91
French Canadian Trapper (show figure),
    20
Frey, Joseph, 16
Friedman, Dan J., 53
Frontenac, le Compte de, 159
Fulton, Robert, 64, 231
Funny Folks (tableau), 108, 219

Gabriel, 160, 162, *163*
Galerie des Machines, 101
Gambrinus (show figure), 34, 45, 71, 193,
    216
Ganges, 116
Garnet, 7
Gaspari, Pierre G., 134
Geneva, 60
George III, 171
Georgia, 5
Girl of the Period (show figure), *42, 43*,
    44, 78, 139, *152*
Globe Chariot, *92*
Gloucester (Massachusetts), 156

Goddess of Liberty (show figure), 54, *59*, 63, *65*, 73, 75, 93, 139, 210, *col.* circus, *92*
Golden Age of Chivalry, 105, *106*, 219, *col.*
Gori, Octavini, 89
Gott, John, 16
Goulet, Pierre, 167
Grand Exhibition. *See* Thornton
Great Admiral, 242
Great European Circus, 91
Grecian bend, 43, 139
Greek Slave, 82, 182, 211
Greenman & Co., 241
Greenwich Street (New York City), 15, *16*
Grenadier (show figure), *202*
Grenadier Guards, 103
Grenier, Helene, 165
Guhle, Charles, 152
Gunshop figure, 231, *235*
Gutenburg, *168*, 169

Haar, Henry M., 96
Hadden, Elias W., 22, 135, 136
Haffenreffer, Carl W., 212
Haffenreffer, Rudolph, 160, 238
Hall, W. L., 64
Halpert, Edith Gregor, 19
Hames, Bill, 112
Hamilton, Charles J., 22, 23, 42, 80, 82, 135–37
Hamilton, James, 136
Hamilton, Tody, 108
Handy, Thomas J., 125
Hanner, G., 170
Hanswurst (Jack Sausage), 38
Hardcastle, Henry, 171
Harriot, Thomas, 11
Havre Line, 5
Hawkins, Sir John, 11
Hawthorne, Nathaniel, 14
Hayward, Victoria, 163
Hebenthal, Frank, 231, *236*
Hegerty, C. E., 75
Hen, August F. T. Edward, 30
Hen, Edward, 30–32, 183
Hercules, 80, 174
Hermes, 18
Herzberg, Professor Constantine, 195
Heyman, Doctor, 137
Hiawathas (show figures), 148
Highland Laddie (show figure), 12, *13*
Highlanders (show figures), 12, *202*, 203, 227
Hoffman, Jack, 183
Hoffman, William, 96
Holland's hatter shop, 14
Honsiger, C. S., 170
Howes, Seth B., 91, 99
Howes Globe (tableau), 91, 93
Howes Great London Circus, 93
Howes London Circus, 91
Hubbard, Bela, 140, 141

Hudson, Henry, 231
Hudson-Fulton Celebration, 231
Hupfel, Adolph, 96
Hutchinson, James L., 93
Hyde de Neuville, Baroness, 15, *16*

Imperial Chariot, 108, 218
Imperial Persian Chariot, 87, *88*
Index of American Design, *14*, *21*, *161*, *162*, *189*, *229*, *234*
Indian(s)
  Chief, 54, 68, 73, 75, 105, 160, 193, 212, *214, col.*
  Hunter and dog, 72
  seated, *176*
  show figures, 41, 49, 67, 68, 69, 158, 166, 185, *col.*
    Maiden, 46, 47, 150
    North American, *74, 75*
    warrior, 52
  Trader, 116
Inexhaustible Cow, 211, 212
Ireland, George, 173

Jack, Kapitan. *See* Captain Jack
Jack Sausage (Hanswurst), 38
Jack Tar (show figure), 67, 163, 185, *187*
Jackson, Andrew, 125, 174
Jackson, Robert E., 242
Jacobi, 33, 62
Jacques, Mr., 172
Jäger, John. *See* Yaeger, John Philip
James, Arthur Curtiss, 224, 226
James I, 11, *13*
Jane St. Presbyterian Church, 195, 201
Japanese (show figure), 70
Jim Crow, *8*, 23, 24, 25, *26, 27*, 177. *See also* Negro figures
Jobin, Louis, 81, 157–64, 198, 239
  ice and snow sculpture, 159, 160
  religious and secular carvings, *159, 160, 161, 162*, 163, *164*
  shipcarvings, 82
  show and tobacconists' figures, 82, *159, 160, 161, 162*
Jockey, 65, 66, 227
John Adams, 117, 172
John Bull. *See* Pickwick
Jonson, Ben, 12
Joshua, 12
Josiah, Captain, 116
Judy (Punch), 38
Junkin, J. H., 138

Kaffirs, 55
Kaiffer, Frederick W., 65
Kalchook Pond, 208
Karagheus, 38
Kate Hooper, 125
Kennedy, Elizabeth, 201
Kenny, John, 148
Keokuk, Chief, 82, 146, *147*, 148

Keppler, Joseph, 56
Kerner, J. F., 15
King Lager. *See* Gambrinus
Kinkel, Julius, 154
Kissinger, Marie, 209, 223
Klein, Joseph, 128, *129*
Knight Templar, 105
Kruschke, Herman, 153–54

La Africana (show figure), 46
LaCasse, Napolean, 157
Lacasse, Télésphore, 162
Lady Godiva, 193
Lady of Fashion, *col.*
Landing of Columbus (tableau), 110
Landing of the Pilgrims (tableau), 100
Lane, Walter, 11
Lapp, Ferdinand, 143
Larsen, Otto C., 188
LaSalle, 140
Latrobe, Benjamin H., 117
Le Vasseur, Jean, 157
Leaners (show figures), 23, 67, *183*, 185
Lee & Bennett's Circus, 90
Lefevre, Bishop, 138
Lent, Lewis B., 91
Lewin (Lewis), Isaac, 185, 193
Lewis, Isaac. *See* Lewin (Lewis), Isaac
Liberty (show figure), 117
Liliuokalani, Queen, 236
Lillie, Major Gordon W., 110, *113*
Lion and Mirror Bandwagon No. 1, 204, *205, col.*
Lion with mortar, 55
Lismer, Arthur, 164
Little Admiral, 14, *15*
Little Red Riding Hood. *See* Red Riding Hood
Livingston (Montana), 190, 191, *192*
Lloyd, H., 170
"Lo," 72, 128, *129*, 210
Lo, the poor Indian (Pope), 29
Long Branch (New Jersey), *235*
Longeau, 162
Lonnergan, P., 158
Lorillard, George, 195
Loudon, James, 201
Loudon, William, 201, 206, 207, 208, 209, 236
Low, M., 242

McAlpin, Charles, 23
McAlpin, David H., 23
McComb, John, 173
McCutcheon, James & Co., 224
McKune, 148
Maccus, 38
MacDowell, P., 102
Machyn's Diary, 12
MacNeil, Captain, 158
Male Busts (show figures), 53, 57, *58*, 61
Mancel's Cigar Store, 156

Mangin, Joseph, 173
Manley, Charles, 190, 191, *192*
Marcotte, Edouard, 160, *163*
Market Slip (New York City), 3, 175, 194
Market Street (Philadelphia), 18, 121, 122
Marquand, Fannie E., 175
Marquette, Father, 140, 141
Marsh, C. A., 42
Marshall, Charles H. & Co., 5
Mason, John W., 80
Masonic Hall (Chestnut Street, Philadelphia), 119
Matzen, H., 44
Mayer, Frank B., 201
Mazeppa Cigar Store, 170
Mechanic's Bell, 4
Medusa, 131
Melchers, Gari, 144
Melchers, Julius Theodore, 44, 63, 81, 82, 137–50, 198
Melchers & Siebert, 143
Melpomene, 63, 89
Merchant's Shot Tower, 127, *128*
Mercury, *10*, 18, 115, 121
Merrimac, 7
Metal Bust Figures, 53, 57, *58*
Metzler, Rothschild & Co., 188, *190*
Metzler & Co., 198
Meyerbeer, Giacomo, 46
Meyers, John, 148
Michigan, 5, 137–53
Mighty Haag Circus, 112
Millard, Thomas, Jr., 5, 29, 119, 177–78, 183
Miller, Dubrul & Peters Manufacturing Co., 73, 74
Miller, Isaac S., 138
Miller Bros., 101 Ranch, 112
Milliken & Co., 224
Milliner's figure, 230
Minsterman, 137
Mohawk (show figure), 180
Monitor, 7
Montgomery, 131
Moody, John B., 14
Moore, Henry, 83
Moorish Queen (show figure), 52, 64, *152*, 193
Morse, Samuel Finley Breese, 194
Mother Goose, 97, 99, 211
Mott, J. L., Iron Works, 59, 75
Mount, William S., 14
Mullen, James, 125
Mullins, W. H., 59
Murphy, John McLeod, 5

Negro figures. *See also* Black Boys
dialect, minstrel, 23
druggist's figure, 135
in Africa (tableau), 103
Jim Crow, 23–27, 250n, 251n
Jobin carving, 158

tobacconists' figures, 20, *24*, 60, *136, 184, 185, 232*
 woman (show figure), 36, 124
Negus, T. S. & J. D., 242
Neptune, 158, 159, 172
Neubert, Oscar, 64
Newman, Edwin P. S., 128, 134
New Theatre, 117, *118*
New York
 Seelig foundry, 62, 63, 64
 shipbuilding, 3, 4, 5, 6, 7
 show-figure carvers, 171–247
 woodcarvers in census report, 77
New York–Chicago Carving Co., 186
New York Journeymen Shipwrights' and Caulkers' Benevolent Society, 4
Nicklin and Griffeth, 116
Nicot, Jean, 10
Nicotiana, 10
Nixon, J. M. and Company Circus, 90
North, Justinus Stoll, 246, 247
North American Indian, *74*
Norton, Eliza, 154

O'Brien, John, 100
Ogden, Harry, 100, 106
Ohio (vessel), 5
Ohio, 174
Old Alms House, 194
Old Darby and Joan, 16
Old Santa Claus, *96,* 97
Old Woman That Lived In A Shoe, The, *97,* 99, 211
Oriental Girl (show figure), 75, 152
Osceola (show figure), 82
Osebold, Anthony, Jr., 152
Ouellet, 157
Our Country (tableau), 108, *109,* 219

Page (circus figure), *206, 207;* (show figure), 35, 36, 37, 50, 204
Palmer, N. B., 241
Paris Exposition, 59
Parke-Bernet auctions, 270–77
Parsons, Bob, 153, 154
Pattison, G. W. & Co., 148, 149
Pawnee Bill, 110, *113,* 223
Pawnee Bill Bandwagon, No. 80, *98a, 110,* 112
Peale, Charles Willson, 14, 117
Pearson, George, 16
Pelham, Emma Jane, 195, 196, 198, 238
Pelham, Thomas M., 195
Pelletier, Mr., 162
Pendergast, A. W., 46, 52, 75, 81, 131, 146, 238
Penn's Treaty (tableau), 100
Perron, Regis, 162
Pettigrew, Mr., 37
Philadelphia
 as a shipbuilding center, 115
 carvers of, 115–24

 early signs and sign painters, 14
 shipcarvers at work, 4
 show figures in the streets of, 123, 124
Philadelphia Theatre, 117
Phoenician Galley, *114,* 218, 219, 222
Pickwick (John Bull; show figure), 78, *244*
Pike Slip (New York), 181, 182, 183, 239, 242
Plaquette, *61, 151,* 253n
Pocahontas (show figure), 16, 110
Poillon, C. & R., 6
Policeman (show figure), 79, 191, 193, *226,* 227
Polichinelle, 38
Pompey (show figure), 122, 123, 124, 231
Pontiacs (show figures), 148
Pony-drawn parade floats, *96, 97, 98, 99*
Pope, Alexander, 29, 71
Popp, Eva Catherine, 126
Porter, Colonel Joseph, 198
Poss, Phillip, 183
Pratt, Matthew, 14
Pressler's Vienna Restaurant, 134
Prince Albert Memorial, 101
Prince Consort, 101, 102
Princess of the Ottawas (show figure), 148, *149*
Proctor, David R., 156
"Progress," 166
Providence, Rhode Island, 154–56
Puccio, d'Anielle, 38
Puck (show figure), 56, 64, 78, 79, 193, *col.*
Pudding, Jack, 38
Pulcinella, 38
Pulzinella, 38
Punch (show figure), 30, 38, *42,* 43, 78, 79, 123, 136, 182, *col.*
Punchinello, 38
Purdy & Welch, 86

Queen of Burlesque, 42
Queen of Hearts, 100
Quick, C. C. & Co., 89
Quider, John, 14

Racetrack Tout, *155,* 156, *230, col.*
Raleigh, Sir Walter, 9, 10, 11
 show figure, 44, 79, 182, 196, 197, *226,* 227
Randolph, James, 125
Rattler, 125
Realm of Marvels, 108
Red Riding Hood, 97, *98,* 99, 211
Reeber, J. & Co., 231
Rice, "Daddy," 25
Rice, Thomas Dartmouth, *8,* 23, 24, 25, 26, 27, 177
Richard, August, 157
Richard, Father Gabriel, 140
Ridder, Herman, 231
Riggs & Brother, 122

Ringling Brothers Barnum & Bailey Circus, 100, 107, 113, 204, 206
Ringling Circus Museum, 93
Rip Van Winkle (show figure), 227
Rising Star (show figure), 37, 48
Ritter, Abraham, 119
Robb, Samuel Anderson, 34, 35, 78, 79, 80, 81, 82, 93, 100, 177, 181, 182, 183, 185, 191, 193–238, 244, 246, 247
   circus carvings
      Canal Street, 50, 93, 94, 97, 98, 99, 204, 205, 206
         Sebastian Wagon Company, 101, 114, 217, 218, 219, 220, 221, 222
   figure carvings, 43, 44, 53, 60, 79, 190
   shipcarvings, 60, 236
   signed and accredited works, 48, 99, 109, 110, 198, 199, 211, 212, 213, 214
   small figures, 231
   techniques of, 78, 79, 80, 81, 82, 209
Robbins Brothers Circus, 99, 107
Robinson, Alexander, 91
Roman Circus, 86
Roosevelt, Teddy (show figure), 227
Rosa, Narcisse, 165
Ross, John, 116
Rough Riders, 227
Rowland, A. J., 7
Royal Palace, 62
Rubicon, 9
Ruby, 7
Rumney, W. H., 181
Ruppert, Jacob, 96
Rush, William, 81, 82, 83, 115–22, 172, 179
   designs for shipcarvings, 80
   figureheads, 116, 117, 125
   show, tobacconists' and other figures, 16, 17, 18, 19, 21, 117, 118, 119

Saal, Louis. See Saul (Saal), Louis
Sailor (show figure). See Jack Tar
Sailor, Samuel H., 122, 238
Ste. Anne de Beaupré, 159, 160, 162
St. George and the Dragon, 50, 93, 96, 159, 204, 205, 206, 211
Saint Jean, 163, 164, 166
St. Roch, 157, 165, 166
Sally, 116
Samoset, 179
Samuel Elam, 173
Sanger's Royal British Menagerie, 93
Santa Claus (show figure), 203, 237
Sarasota, 93, 107, 108
Sauks and Fox, 139, 146, 147
Saul (Saal), Louis, 95
Schaeffer, The F. & M. Brewing Company, 96
Schawler, Catherine, 126
Schmitz, Henry, 150
Schmitz & Crongeyer, 150
Schneider, P. & Sons, 195

Schott Brothers, 145, 146
Schuchman, George, 95
Schwartz's Antique Shop, 134
Scott, Gilbert, 101
Scotten, Daniel, 148
Scotsmen (show figures), 30, 78, 79, 182
Scottish Highlander (show figure), 12
Scribe, The (circus figure), 220
Sea Pigeon, 246
Seaman's Bride, 125
Sebastian, Jacob, 95, 96, 237
Sebastian Manufacturing Company, 96, 100
   carvings by Robb, 99
   pony-drawn floats, 97
   St. George and Dragon (tableau), 96
Sebastian Wagon Company, 95, 96, 100, 101, 109, 110, 111, 112, 113, 114
   designs of tableau wagons, 101, 102, 103, 105, 107, 108
   list of wagons, 218, 219
   Robb's carving shop, frontispiece, 107, 110, 114, 220, 221, 222, 223
Seelig, Moritz J., 61, 62–64
Seelig, Morris, 33, 52, 61, 63
Seiders, Charles, 124
Sells Brothers, 100
Seminole, 82
Semper, Professor, 62
Sharpe, Cornelius N., 174
Show Figure exhibitions, 33, 34, 251n, 252n
Show figures
   Africa, 46
   Amsterdam, Turk, 12
   at auction, 238
   Baseball Player, 213
   Bowery Girls, 78, 235
   Brother Jonathan, 123, 124, 139
   Cadet, 227
   Caffir Smoker, 55
   Captain Jack, 50, 78, 145, 146, 188, 190
   Captain Jinks, 44, 193, 198, 199
   Cavalier, 44
   Chinaman, 49, 65, 66
   Chinese Woman, 70, 229
   Columbia, 54, 59, 93, 105, 154
   Comedy and Tragedy, 117
   Comical Bust, 53
   Drum Major, 123, 124, 202
   Dude, 78, 79, 201, 227, 230, 231
   Dundreary, 57, 79, 124, 202, 227, 231
   Fireman, 198, 199, 216
   Flat board, 18, 19, 20
   Forty-Niner, 123
   French Canadian Trapper, 20
   Gambrinus, 34, 45, 71, 193, 216
   Girl of the Period, 42, 43, 44, 78, 139, 152
   Goddess of Liberty, 54, 59, 63, 65, 73, 75, 93, 139, 210
   Grenadier, 202
   Hiawathas, 148

Highland Laddie, 12, *13*
Highlanders, 12, *202*, 203, 227
Indians, 41, 46, 47, 49, 52, 54, 56, *58*, 67, 68, 69, *74*, 75, 105, 150, *156*, 158, 166, *184*, 185, *190*, 212, *214*, *233*
Jack Tar, *187*
Japanese, 70
La Africana, 46
Leaners, 23, 67, *183*, 185
Liberty, 117
Male Busts, 53, 57, *58*, *61*
Metal, 45, 62, 65, *66*, *67*, *68*, *69*, *70*, *71*, *72*. *See also* Foundries
Mohawk, 180
Moorish Queen, 52, 64, *152*, 193
Negro, *184*
Oriental Girl, 75, 152
Osceola, 82
Pickwick (John Bull), 78, *244*
Pocahontas, 16, 110
Policeman, 79, 191, 193, *226*, 227
Pompey, 122, 123, 124, 231
Pontiacs, 148
Princess of the Ottawas, 148, *149*
Puck, 56, *61*, 64, 78, 79, *82b*, 193
Punch, 30, 38, *42*, 43, 78, 79, 123, 136, 182
Raleigh, Sir Walter, 44, 79, 182, 196, 197, *226*, 227
Rip Van Winkle, 227
Rising Star, 37, 48
Roosevelt, Teddy, 227
Santa Claus, 203, *237*
Scotsmen, 30, 78, 79, 182
Scout, *187*
Squaw, 47, 48, 51, 69, 81, 136, 185, *186*, 190, 197
Sullivan, John L., 210
Sultana, 30, 42, 79, 135, 182, 227, *232*
Theatrical Figure, *44*, 79
Turk, *12*, *30*, 35, *42*, 68, 70, 79, 135, 182, 227, *232*
Uncle Sam, 139, 182
Wooden, *28*, *190*
Show-window figures, 53, 232
Siebert, Henry A., 143
Signing of Declaration (tableau), 100
Signs
  Albany, *17*
  Baltimore, 125, 128
  Canada, 170
  Chicago, 188, 189
  Detroit, 152
  England, *10*, *13*, 55
  exhibitions, 251n, 252n
  New York, 215, 216
  Philadelphia, 123, 124
  Providence, *155*
  San Jose, 231, *235*
  Wisconsin, 154
Simonson, Jeremiah, 6
Sinbad the Sailor, 97, 99, 211

Sioux, 147, 154
Sitting Bull, *153*, 154, *190*
Sitting Indian (show figure), 56, *58*, 156
Skillin, Samuel, 173, 178
Skillin, Simeon, 173, 174
Skookum, 191
Sleeping Beauty, 99, 100
Smith, Dr. Dennis, 83
Smith, John, 110
Smith & Dimon, 5
Smoking Age, 12, *13*
South Carolina, 137
South Street (New York)
  shipbuilders of, 3, 4, 5, 7
  shipcarvers of, 3, 29, *76*, 93, 171, 178, 182, 183, 185, 192, 239, 242, 243, *244*
  street of ships, *2*, 3
Spanjer Brothers, 107
Sparks, John (monument), 156
Spaulding & Rogers Circus, 89
Spirit of the Time, 125
Spring House, *17*, 18
Squaw (show figure), 47, 51, 69, *col. 81*, 136, 185, *190*, 197
  with Pappoose, 48, 51
Stadler, Charles A., 96, 114, 218, 219, 238
Standard Show Figure Company, 193
Stanley, General David S., 139
Steenbach, Anthony, 173
Stephenson, J. & Co., 87, 88, 89, 91
Stephenson, John, 87, 179, 180
Stephenson, Nellie, 246
Stratton, Mary, 242
Strauss, Bertha, 239
Strauss, Joseph, 241
Strauss, Minnie May, 241
Strauss, Simon, 158, 239–41
Strauss, Solomon Hirsch, 241
Stremenski, G., 170
Stuart, Gilbert, 83
Sullivan, John L. (show figure), 210
Sullivan, William, 172
Sultan. *See* Turk
Sultana (show figure), 30, 42, 79, 135, 182, 227, *232*

Tableaux. *See* Circus
Tamanend, 18
Tarquin, Lucius, 85
Tea Shop Figure, *49*, 68, 69, 70, *229*
Teubner, Charles W., 134
Teubner, Gordon E., 134
Teubner, William, *133*, 134
Teubner, William, Jr., 133–34
Thayer & Noyes, 91
Theatrical Figure (show figure), *44*, 79, *col.*
Theed, W., 102
Theobold, Fred H., 172
Thompson, Lydia, 42
Thompson, Smith and Howes Circus, 91

Thornton, Bennell, Signboard Exhibition, 251n, 252n
Throne Tableau Car, 108, *109*, 218, 222
Tobacco, 9, 10, 34, 46
Toneelgek, 38
Toothpick, 125
Towson, Mary Catherine, 134
Toys & Games (parade wagon), 100
Train, Daniel N., 119, 172
Triumphal Car, Van Amburgh's, 91
Triumphal Car of Balkis, 108, 218
Tryon, Elijah, 243, 246
Tucker, Richard H., 179
Turk (show figure), *12*, 30, 35, *42*, 68, 70, 79, 135, 182, 227, *232, col.*
Two Hemispheres Bandwagon, 106, 107, 108, 218

Uncle Sam (show figure), 139, 182

Valentine's Manual, 210
Van Amburgh, Isaac A., 87, 91
Van Amburgh's Golden Chariot, *90*, 91
Van Amburgh's Triumphal Car, 87, 179
Varden, Dolly, 182
Virginians. *See* Black Boys

Wagener, Captain Philip, 116
Wagner, Bertha, 31
Wagner, Jacob A., 108
Wagner, John, 31
Wallabout, 4, 172
Warburton, George, 171
Ward, John Q. A., 72
Warren, William L., 206, *208*, *209*
Warrior, Indian (show figure), 52
Washington (D.C.), 22, 35, 43, 130, 134, 135
Washington, General George, 82, 89, 116, 172, 216, 227
Washington's Inauguration (tableau), 100

Water Nymph and the Bittern, 117, 118
Watson, Edith, 163
Watson, J. F., 116
Wayne, General, 89, 125
Webb, Isaac, 4
Webb, William H., 4, 5, 6, 194
Webb & Bell, 6
Weber, Henry, 138
Weinman, Adolph Alexander, 145
Weitenkampf, Frank W., 99, 177, 182, 210, 215
Welch, Delevan & Nathan's National Circus, 87, *88*, 180
West, Benjamin, 14
Westervelt & Mackay, 5, 194
Wheelington, Captain, 198
White, Stanford, 172
White, Thomas J., 181–82, *183*, 197, 198, 206, 209, 215
  circus carvings, 21, 82, 93, 211
Whitlock, Inc., 106
Wildfire, Madge, 43
William Penn, 116
Williams, William, 14, *15*
Wills, Lt. Colonel, 116
Wilmarth, E., 194, 195
Wolfe, General, 158
Woman, Chinese (show figure), 70, *229*
Wood, Joe, *231*
Wooden figures, *41, 42, 44*
Wooden Indian Shop, 30
Wright, Joseph, 120

Yaeger, John Philip, 80, 81, 126–32, 133
  carved figures, 128, *129*, 132
Yankee Doodle, 123
Youngman, J., 183

Zimmerman, Gene, 106
Zinngrabe's tobacco shop, 188
Zorach, William, 83